Go Noles!

Stan Marshall

Praise for *The Tumultuous Sixties*

This is an important and astonishing book. There was a time in the 1960's when Florida and the nation faced hurricane-force winds of change even more cataclysmic than Ivan or Katrina. They say if you can't remember that remarkable decade then you weren't there. Stan Marshall was there. And he remembers. He is an educator in the truest sense. By reporting fairly and dispassionately from the eye of the storm he captures the feel of a profoundly tumultuous time that shaped a nation and rocked a generation. Whenever I try to explain to friends what it was like to attend the Berkley-of-the-South, that unlikely radical hot spot in Tallahassee, they find it hard to believe. All I have to do now is hand them this book!

--Doug Marlette, Author of The Bridge and Magic Time, Flambeau editorial cartoonist, 1970-1971

If you are an FSU grad or fan, you'll love this book. You will find out what really happened during Stan Marshall's time. And by the way, tell Dr. Marshall thanks for getting it right the second time. (Read the accounts in Chapter Nine to understand what I mean.)

--Bobby Bowden, Florida State University Head Football Coach

An interesting and informative account with supporting data of conflict and tension at Florida State University during the late sixties and early seventies. Amid strong differing opinions on how to proceed, Stanley Marshall courageously and effectively led the university through those very difficult times. We are indebted to Dr. Marshall for the time and effort he put into this work. The quotes from the former head football coach Bill Peterson are a delightful bonus to a good book.

--Reubin Askew, Governor of Florida, 1966-1974

Vivid and dramatic. So many of Stan Marshall's recollections land squarely in the center of my own memories and experiences of life at Florida State University in the late 1960's. Often I found myself reliving an event through Marshall's eyes, since after all, I was there. No matter what your politics may have been, or on which side of the picket lines you found yourself, for anyone whose formative years were shaped by the unrest that rolled across this country in the late 1960's, Stan Marshall's memoir of this time is a well-told chronicle and an essential read.

--Jeff Shaara, author, Gods and Generals and other books

Stan Marshall was the right man at the right time. As the new President of FSU, he was thrown into the fray. He proved he could "talk the talk and walk the walk" between various factions of students, faculty, politicians and the media. His leadership saved FSU from becoming "the Berkeley of the South."

--Larry Campbell, Sherrif, Leon County, Florida

Dr. Marshall's historical memoir compellingly recalls the turbulent times at Florida State University and, by extension, at college campuses throughout the country. He recounts, at times in riveting manner, "the heat of the controversies" and how he used his leadership skills to deal with those controversies. Dr. Marshall's book is a timely, insightful must-read for those who believe that history is the great teacher.

--George Waas, editor of The Flambeau, 1968-1969

Stan Marshall was a university president in exceptional circumstances, faced with the challenges that society served up in the late 1960's and 1970's. Luckily for the university, he was an extraordinary president and this account of those turbulent times reavels a man who cares about the university and about those with whom he is engaged in conflict. This account resonates with me because I lived through this period and knew many of the people who figure in this drama. Stan Marshall responded to crisis with principle and passion and most of all, with humanity and respect for others.

--Talbot "Sandy" D'Alemberte, Florida State University President Emeritus

The book is essential reading for anyone who wants to understand the conflict that rocked FSU in the upheavals of the late sixties.

--Jack Lieberman, "Radical Jack," 1968-1971

THE TUMULTUOUS SIXTIES

Campus Unrest and Student Life at a Southern University

THE TUMULTUOUS SIXTIES

Campus Unrest and Student Life at a Southern University

by

J. Stanley Marshall

Designer: Karen Towson Wells
Dust Jacket Design:Robert S. Davis
Printer and binder: Rose Printing

Library of Congress Number: 2005939177

ISBN: 1-889574-25-2

Sentry Press
424 East Call Street
Tallahassee, Florida 32301

Dedication

To Shirley
Who never missed a beat

TABLE OF CONTENTS

ACKNOWLEDGEMENTS

In the summer of 2004, this book was nothing more than poorly defined conjecture; that's when the thought of producing a written record of my years as FSU President took shape. I mentioned it to President T.K. Wetherell and Provost Larry Abele, and they were encouraging. T.K. very kindly provided an office and the services of a research assistant. The Pepper Center has been an ideal location for my research and writing, Associate Vice President Steve McNamara has been a congenial and generous landlord, and I've been aided in many ways by other Pepper Center personnel, including Monica Laughlin, Robert Ryals, Brandon Wilson, and Christopher Schmitt.

Bob Sanchez, my colleague at The James Madison Institute, is the best wordsmith I've ever worked with, and his editorial help has been invaluable. Administrative Assistant at the Institute Keri Gordon has been helpful in many ways. Jack Levine's interest and his good counsel and have also been valuable.

My research assistant Christie Revis is a master's degree student in the History Department. She has been an invaluable aide in the research, in mastering the computer and all of the related tasks that entails, and in more other ways than I can count. A student of her ability and resourcefulness speaks well for FSU's History Department. Tallahassee friends who have read and provided valuable comments on parts of the manuscript include Pam Forrester, Anna Johnson, Ruth Akers, and the late Phil Fordyce.

Not least, the good people in the Special Collections Section of the Strozier Library have extended privileges and given special help. They include Lucy Patrick along with Garnett Avant, Alice Motes and Michael Matos.

Members of the Florida State family have helped in countless ways. They include Vice President Kirby Kemper and his very able secretary Lezlee Brand. Then there's Dean of the Faculties Ann Rowe, former Dean Steve Edwards, Professors Jan Wells and Billie Jones, former Governor Reubin Askew, the late Paul Piccard, Mydia Diefenbach, Bob Bickel, Ruth Wester, Pat Hogan, Bill Tanner, Canter Brown, Chuck Sherman, Jeff Savlov, Sam Miller, Jack Lieberman and Doug Marlette. From the Department of Athletics, important help came from Mike Martin and Rob Wilson.

My publisher, Sentry Press, is headed by my friend of many years, Bill Rogers who, along with his designer, Karen Wells, have been helpful in many ways.

I must also mention the dozens of friends who somehow got word that a book was in the works and offered encouragement. Their excited interest was wonderful stimulus that usually came at just the right time.

My own five children and their spouses have read parts of the manuscript, but more importantly, they've always encouraged and inspired me in most of the challenging tasks I've taken on. What I owe them, they'll never collect.

And speaking of indebtedness, my innumerable debts to Shirley Marshall, my wife, are beyond calculation.

As acknowledgers usually do, I will say up front that any errors in the book should be attributed to the author and no one else.

INTRODUCTION
Why This Book Now?

The late 1960s and early 1970s were a time of tumult in American higher education. Florida State University was part of the national movement by college and university students to bring about change, often with dire consequences for the institutions involved. FSU escaped the educational disruption, the destruction of property, and the violence that had occurred at some other universities, but not by much. What happened on the campus, in the legislature, and in the state of Florida to forestall such problems is the story that I attempt to tell in this book.

The story will be told from the vantage point of the man who became president of the university on one tumultuous day in February 1969, and whose tenure extended through the student protests and demonstrations that continued for the next several years.

The most compelling reason for the book is my belief that the events at Florida State University during this period should not go unrecorded. Those of us who were members of the university community during the period would surely think of those events as important by any definition. Faculty members, staff, and students would say that unusual and often disturbing events were going on all around them. Judged by public interest, the number of news stories and editorials in Florida's newspapers, and the intensity of the interest on the part of state legislators, the campus activities deserve a place in Florida's recorded history, most especially the history of higher education. There may be still another reason for my wish to report on the protests of that period, and that is a personal urge to tell a story that was for me intensely interesting.

Of special interest to me has been a doctoral dissertation in the University's History Department by Stephen Eugene Parr, which covers mostly the same period. Parr earned his bachelor's degree in sociology at FSU in 1970, a master's in economics in 1974, and he returned in 1989 to pursue doctoral studies in history. From 1991 to 1995 he served as a graduate and teaching assistant in the History Department, where he completed his dissertation in 2000.

Dr. Parr's research resulted in a voluminous publication, thoroughly researched and skillfully written. I have used it extensively in my own research and have found the bibliography especially helpful; it has saved me considerable time and has enabled me to locate sources that I might otherwise have missed. Readers will see references throughout this publication to the findings of his research and his perceptions and opinions. I am, however, obliged to take note of our juxtaposition of views, which deserves mention here. Steve Parr, as an FSU student in the earlier period, seems to have often been in sympathy with some of the protesters. He reveals this in many passages. He was opposed to some of my actions as president, and he attributes motives to me that are uncomplimentary. At the same time, his research is solid by accepted academic standards, and his opinions, easily identifiable as such, are for the most part understandable by me today. Many of his opinions were not different from those I might have held if I had been an FSU student then, who got most of my information from news reports in the campus newspaper, *The Flambeau*, and especially from its editorials, and from a few faculty members who were in sympathy with the protesting students.

This caveat must extend to my belief that Steve Parr, in his student days, seems not to have been well informed about some of the most important campus issues. He charges the president with yielding to pressures from legislators, regents, and prominent businessmen in important decisions and cracking down on the demonstrators to assuage angry legislators. This position might have seemed valid based on the information available to him then; that information was, however, often incomplete and inaccurate. I attempt to provide more complete and more accurate information in this report and can only wish that Steve Parr and others had been so informed then.

When I discovered Parr's dissertation in the first few weeks of my research, I got in touch with Dr. Parr and told him of my appreciation for his work and added that I hoped to meet and talk with him in the next few months. He replied that he would look forward to doing so, but added that he was seriously ill and staying with family in Brooklyn. Word reached me in December 2004 that Steve Parr had died, which caused me to regret the missed opportunity for the interview, but more so sadness in the loss of a person who I believed would have become a friend.

In the research for this book, I have found a surprisingly large number of information sources. When I left the president's office in 1976, the members of my staff presented me with "my papers"—a large collection of documents carefully packed in six large cartons. Those boxes remained in my home, undisturbed, until I began my research for this book in September 2004. Their contents include copies of communications to and from the president, speeches, inter- and intra-office memoranda, copies of newspaper articles of note, photographs, and hundreds of copies of *The Flambeau*. Examination of these documents has enabled me to report in detail on events about which I've retained distinct but sometimes generalized memories and to capture the campus atmosphere, confident that my descriptions of events and people are accurate and reliable. In the text, I make frequent references to my examination of those documents and offer my thoughts and interpretations now from the vantage point of 30 years or more.

There are occasional accounts that reflect unfavorably on

some of the actors. I have written candidly and critically on some of those, knowing that some of them would very likely read my words. In nearly every instance, my personal relations with those people—both FSU faculty members and former students—have been cordial down through the years. I take that to mean that all of us acknowledge that we might not always have acted prudently and that personal friendships and respect now trump whatever tensions we felt at the time. Nonetheless, I have not avoided reporting those moments of tension because they were an important part of the story, and because history is history, and it deserves our respect.

If the case I make in this book is to be taken at face value, readers may want to know who I am and how I came to be the University's president in this tumultuous period. So a brief biographical sketch may be useful.

Acting President Marshall—Who is he?

I attended the public schools in suburban Pittsburgh, where my family lived, and then enrolled at Slippery Rock State Teachers College in Pennsylvania in 1940. World War II interrupted my education—I served in the U.S. Army from 1943 to 1946; I spent about a year in the European theater as a medic—an enlisted man—in a U.S. Army field hospital. I returned to graduate with a B.S. in Education in December 1946. My first teaching job was as a high school science teacher (I taught mostly physics, my first love) and athletic coach at a public high school in Seneca Falls, New York, where I stayed for six years. I began taking graduate studies at nearby Syracuse University, where I earned my M.S. and Ph.D. degrees, both in Science Education. I taught undergraduate courses in physics at the State University of New York College of Education at Cortland for five years, and from there, I came to FSU in 1958 to establish a new Department of Science Education. What appealed to me about FSU then was the determination of the University, especially the Dean of the College of Education, to train science teachers (along with teachers of math, English and social studies) who would be well grounded in the subject matter to teach in the secondary schools, teachers who would also be well prepared for teaching by taking practical, down-to-earth courses in professional education. I was also given a courtesy appointment in the Physics Department, and I caught the spirit of a young, vibrant institution that I was certain was soon to become a nationally distinguished and respected university, and I wanted to be part of it.

In 1965, I became Associate Dean of the School of Education and Dean in 1967 upon the retirement of the venerated Dean Mode Stone. In February 1969, I was appointed by the Board of Regents to be the University's first Executive Vice President, to take office at the start of the new fiscal year, on July 1. The account of my becoming Acting President (today, we call it Interim President), a week later upon the unexpected resignation of President John Champion is told in appropriate detail in the first chapter of the book.

A further word about my teaching experiences before FSU: While I loved (yes, that's the word) teaching in my previous positions, my experience as a high school teacher and athletic coach was, for me, a mountain-top experience that had a profound influence on my professional life and my career. Mynderse Academy, where I taught science and coached athletics in Seneca Falls, was one of upstate New York's best public high schools, and I was incredibly lucky to have landed there for my first job. The town was small, and the student body was ethnically diverse (as a result of an in-migration of Italians in the teens and twenties); the community was deeply committed to supporting its schools, and school administrators and teachers were well qualified and committed to preserving the quality of their schools. The Mynderse teachers were as competent and dedicated a high school faculty as I have ever seen; the townspeople knew that they had good schools, and they treated the teachers accordingly. The unspoken message for me as a new teacher with no teaching experience was: We think we're good at what we do; yes, we're open to new ideas; come join the team, and if you can convince us that you have a better way, that'll be fine, but until then, you'll be expected to just be a good team player. I learned a lot about what makes a good teacher, about respect for tradition, and I quickly learned that the welfare and educational progress of students is what it's all about. There was also a message that good teaching and learning are not likely to take place in the absence of good order throughout the institution, and personal styles and ambitions must often give way to the larger concern for institutional mission.

I've worked with some great teachers at the college level too, especially at FSU, but there's an important difference in attitude between high school and college, and it's largely a matter of accountability. High school teachers in good schools are judged by their productivity, meaning mostly the job they do in the classroom. They report to a department head who reports to the principal, and everyone in the chain respects the system. Does the system always work? Certainly not, and that's one of the things that differentiates good schools from the others. Accountability tends to be defined differently in higher education, where tenure comes into play—and in some cases faculty unions—and faculty members' loyalties are more diffuse, extending to one's discipline, to the professional associations and sometimes to the organizations that provide outside support, especially research dollars. Those differences came into play at Florida State University as I attempted to set a new standard for administrative authority during the early days of my presidency.

The Marshall Imprint

Readers are asked to view the early weeks of my presidency in the context of the way my appointment came about. On the morning of February 16, 1969, I had no notion about my role as a university administrator except to start thinking about what I would do when I became Executive Vice President on July 1. By 6:00 PM on that day, John Champion had told me he was stepping aside, and by eight o'clock, the Chancellor of the State University System had informed me that I was Acting President (to be confirmed the next day by the Board of Regents). I was well acquainted with the campus turmoil that had prompted Champion's decision and had been following closely the troubles on at least a dozen other campuses. When I met with the leaders of Students for a Democratic Society (SDS)* on my second full day in office, I was told of their intentions to hold a rally in the University Union whether or not they were given permission to use the building (they were an unregistered organization, and thus prohibited by standing regulations from using the University's facilities). My charge seemed clear: Keep the University open and operating in a close-to-normal manner, maintain order on the campus and assure the SDS members and all others that there would be no needless display of administrative authority, and that the First Amendment rights of all would be scrupulously respected. I was mindful of the disorder that had caused destruction of property, the loss of life, and the breakdown of educational services at other universities, and I saw nothing in the picture at FSU to convince me that it could not happen here. I reminded students—and yes, faculty members too—that there were rules, and they would be enforced. Indeed, I interpreted the signals from the SDS—some who were students, and some who were not—to mean that disruption would happen here if they had their way. In the recent experience with President Champion, I had seen that firmness was needed; I was sure there would come a time for conciliation, but I be-

*Students for a Democratic Society (SDS) was a far-left organization that came to life on the University of Michigan campus in1962. SDS soon became a catch-all acronym that excited and motivated students throughout the country. It is discussed in detail in Chapter Four.

lieved that immediate, resolute leadership was positively essential if FSU was not to become another victim of serious disruptions such as those at Berkeley, Columbia, and Cornell. I decided during that first week as president to stake the future of my administration and in a very real sense the integrity of the University on that proposition.

Campus Protests Today

Now some thoughts about the future. I am often asked whether the increased student activism of the past few years portends campus dissent of the kind we experienced 35 years ago. The answer, I believe, is no. The conditions that fostered the intense feelings by students at that time simply do not exist today. Young people in the 1960s wrestled with an array of societal problems including tensions in race relations, the birth of the New Left movement and of black power, campus tensions created by Berkeley's Free Speech Movement, *in loco parentis** as an operating system for the regulation of student life on campus, and not least, the military draft that presented many young men with the choice of going to Canada or to war in Vietnam. Those were some of the reasons why many college students expressed their dissatisfaction with and often contempt for the existing order and their determination to change it. Readers may judge for themselves as the account of those events is told in the chapters to follow what the future might hold for our country in this regard.

College and university presidents were part of the problems on the campuses. None had been faced with issues of this kind before, and most were by temperament and training quite unprepared to provide the leadership the times required. The evidence for this is abundant and none so compelling as the large number of resignations and firings of presidents that

---

*The Latin, *in loco parentis,* translated to English means "in place of the parent". In practice it meant that universities were to exert parental control over their students who resented the rules and regulations even more than did the administrators who had to enforce them.

occurred on the troubled campuses. I took note of two important consequences of the disturbances at other universities;
first, those universities suffered serious damages internally and
to their reputations beyond the campus, and second, many of
the presidents ended up being dismissed. Neither of those developments had any appeal for me.

This is not to say that social and political issues do not
trouble today's young people. At this writing, no one can pre-
dict the outcome of the war in Iraq or the effects that war may
have on our nation's psyche. Poverty remains an issue, as does
the enormous cost of health care and the impending crisis in
Social Security. It will be surprising—and disappointing to
some—if young people do not express themselves on such
matters, perhaps in ways that will garner public notice and
which may well differ from the conventional. But today's university administrators have learned something from the fail-
ures of their predecessors and would surely not stand idly by,
as before, if protests should threaten to become violent.

Plan for the Book

When I first discussed the idea of writing a book on the
period of my service as president of the University, I discussed
it with a number of people in the administration, including
President T.K. Wetherell. All of those people provided very
substantial encouragement. I thought of the project originally
as a memoir in which I would relate the history of the period
as seen through the eyes of the person most directly involved:
the University President. However, as I got further into the
project, it seemed to me to be more of a history of the time
than an account of my own participation. So I decided to do
what I had seen in a number of other history books—write the
history in the first person. In so doing, I would describe at
length my own participation, but the primary focus would be
on the events that transpired.

In the early stages of the project, I considered making the

story a chronological record of the events—one in which I would report on things that happened strictly in sequence, starting with President John Champion's resignation in the spring of 1968 and following through my own service as president, which ended in 1976. I abandoned that pattern because there were some parts of the story that did not lend themselves to a straight-line chronology. The account would have more appeal and be more fully understood if I could, for example, describe the activities of the SDS, or anti-war protestors, or black students as they were related to other campus events and activities that were ongoing for most of my seven-and-a-half years as president.

I have not attempted to be totally inclusive, that is to describe every event that occurred during this period, or even all of the important ones. Doing so would simply have made the book too long. So I have included things that I thought were representative of the period to try to give readers a good feel for campus events and the prevailing atmosphere.

The book has been written primarily for a specific group of readers—members of the FSU family then and now. It's an attempt to describe what happened on one American university campus during this turbulent period, as seen through the eyes of the person who presided over the University at that time. If the book serves a broader purpose and attracts the interest of a wider audience, that would be fine.

I have done my best to be impartial and objective throughout the book, but I feel certain there are those who participated in the events I have described who might in some cases have different interpretations. Those who might disagree with my representation of the record should feel free to publish their own views if they believe that doing so would help to right the record.

My report includes descriptions of some events that relate indirectly to my service as University President—my visit to the White House and my attendance at the Florida Governor's baseball dinner. Those events would not have occurred had I not been University President, and therefore, I decided to include them.

Readers will see more than occasional references to Shirley, my wife. She was not an inconsiderable influence on my thoughts and actions during the period of my presidency, as well as before and since. Shirley and our children were often participants in the events in those days, and they shared in both the turmoil and the joy. I hope the story I tell here reveals that there was far more joy than turmoil for all of the Marshall family.

Living in Interesting Times

One of the major events of the decade of the 1970s was the takeover of the American embassy in Tehran and the ouster of the Shah of Iran. I had more than a passing interest in those events as I had made friends in Iran during my work in international science education in the Middle East in the sixties. A few months before the Shah's government fell in 1979, I had a visit from an Iranian friend, 75-year-old Dr. Amman Birjandi, who was a senior education officer in the Shah's government. His assignment had been to improve the literacy of the men and boys serving in Iran's military—in plain words, to teach them to read. He was a respected educational innovator, a world-class mountain climber, and a fascinating man of infectious enthusiasm. What an interesting man he was! He told me that he had been born 150 kilometers north of Tehran in a village that had no schools. His father understood the importance of schooling and placed his son on a camel caravan headed for Tehran, where the boy managed to support himself and go to school. When he returned home after what would have been the equivalent of our elementary school, he found five new brothers and sisters. Dr. Birjandi had come to Tallahassee to renew our acquaintance and to tell me first hand about events in Iran. He was also in this country to visit his two grown children, both situated in attractive professional positions, and they encouraged him to remain in the U.S. When I incredulously asked him why he would not stay, his voice rose in excitement as he said, "Oh, it's going to be a very interesting time in my country, and I want to be there!"

So after the first few weeks as president of Florida State University in the spring of 1969, I knew the times were interesting and were likely to be even more so in the future, and I wanted to be there. Whether we'll ever again see student insurrections, or whether young people will find more useful, peaceful and productive ways of bringing about change, I really don't know. But for a few more years at least, I want to be there.

PART I

The first seven chapters of this book describe in considerable detail events that occurred on the Florida State University campus during the time I was privileged to serve as the University's President. Those events are described against a backdrop of disturbances on hundreds of college and university campuses across the nation.

I have had the good fortune to discuss those events and the campus climate in which they occurred with many people who were at Florida State then, both students and faculty members. Most of them acknowledge that those years were some of the most interesting times of their lives. I certainly found the sixties to be that.

Part I of the book is my attempt to provide enough information to give readers— both those who are part of the extended FSU family and others who have maintained interest in the period known as "The Sixties"—an understanding of those events and their meaning in terms of the evolution of our country's culture, its political dynamics, and its values. If I've succeeded in painting a reasonably clear picture of that period, my efforts in the research and writing will have been well rewarded.

CHAPTER 1
Night of the Bayonets

Terry Anderson, describing those years in his definitive book published in 1995, writes that The Sixties rivals "the Progressive years, the Great Depression and World War II as one of the four most important periods of the twentieth century." He adds:

> And when one considers the history of the Republic, it would be difficult to find more significant issues than those the activists raised and confronted: equality or inequality, war or peace, national interests versus individual rights, personal behavior versus community standards. Indeed, the protesters questioned the very nature and meaning of America.[1]

Part I of this book is about the turbulent sixties and seventies at Florida State University. Much has been written about the protests at countless American colleges and universities, leaving no doubt that the country was caught up in a relentless pageant of political and cultural protest. The most widely recognized opening event was the sit-in at Greensboro, North Carolina, on February 1, 1960; this was followed by two marches at Selma, Alabama. These marches served to engage college students who were trying to bring racial inequality to the forefront of public concern in America. There were other issues of concern to young people, especially college students, who came to embrace ideas that would move them to repudiate the morals and values of their elders.

The part FSU students played in the national movement and the methods they employed to aid the movement will be a subject of interest in this book and will be examined in some

3

detail. Did we really earn the sobriquet "Berkeley of the South" (or East)? Did the protests and demonstrations at FSU contribute to the strength of the movement nationally? How did the people of Florida regard the behavior of protesters during this period? And were there changes made on the campus or in Florida government that made a difference in the policies and practices that were followed in our state in subsequent years? The accounts of events presented in this book will, I hope, lead readers to answers to some of those questions.

Some say that Florida State University was lucky to have avoided the destruction and violence that befell other American colleges and universities during the student activism of the 1960s and early 1970s. While I concur that we were indeed fortunate, a historical review of those times reveals that it was more than luck that enabled our University to avoid the mayhem, the internal student and faculty tumult, and the bloodshed that marked the protests on other campuses.

In his unpublished doctoral dissertation, Dr. Stephen Parr describes the situation in American higher education in that period aptly. The opening statement in his first chapter captures the atmosphere and describes the events at FSU on the evening of March 4, 1969.

> In the parking lot behind the University Union, an angry, hostile and growing crowd of 350 students thundered 'Pigs off campus!' and 'Police State!' while a few students beat on the two paddy wagons with their fists. They were enraged by the sight of fifty-eight students being led down the back steps of the union by Leon County police officers, away from a room illegally occupied under the terms of a court injunction obtained by University President J. Stanley Marshall. Among those arrested was Fred Gordon, recently elected Education Secretary of the national Students for a Democratic Society, who had come to speak on the importance of

the South in student rebellions. Separating the main
body of students from the building and wagons was a
menacing line of 35 volunteer sheriff's riot police,
armed with clubs, M-1 rifles, loaded and fixed with
bayonets. Standing amid the pandemonium of the
crowd, local SDS leader Phil Sanford shouted for bail
money and screamed 'You see?…We told you they
were like this!…. You see what kind of justice we get
from them?….' Police then waded into the crowd and
nabbed Sanford for arrest. As they did so, across Tennessee Street, the main highway next to the university, a
group of students from the Kappa Alpha fraternity
came running to the scene. Unknown to the sheriff's
deputies, the K.A.s were unfriendly to the radicals.
Some of the relatively untrained volunteers, thinking
they were under attack, fell back and readied their rifles,
but did not fire. Thus on the evening of March 4, 1969,
known as the 'Night of the Bayonets,' Florida State
University, sometimes called the 'Berkeley of the
South,' nearly became the 'Kent State of the South.'

This was the most dramatic event at Florida State
University (FSU) during the turbulent period of the
sixties. It occurred at a university in the Deep South, an
area contemporary historians usually consider a back-
water of New Left activity. The issue that sparked the
confrontation concerned the attempts by FSU's Students for a Democratic Society to obtain from the University administration recognition as a regular campus
organization, with the right to use campus facilities for
its activities. When the University denied recognition,
SDS used the facilities anyway, claiming a 'natural'
democratic right to free assembly that the administration had no right to deny.[2]

The near-violence that occurred on March 4 had been
building for months, well before President John Champion's

retreat from the presidency in February 1969. Having failed to achieve the status of a recognized and registered student organization, the SDS was not entitled to use University facilities or equipment. When the SDS announced its intention to move forward with its plans to bring Fred Gordon, the National Education Secretary for SDS to the campus, and to hold their rally in the University Union, the new president, after consultation with the University's legal advisors, obtained a temporary injunction barring the SDS from occupying the Union. As the injunction was read at the start of the SDS rally by Chief Bill Tanner of the FSU Police Department, many in the crowd voluntarily left the Union. Tanner advised those in the room that if they did not comply with the injunction, they would be subject to arrest. Some students decided to remain, forcing the administration's hand. Leon County Sheriff Raymond Hamlin then ordered his deputies to arrest those who refused to leave, and they were loaded in paddy wagons parked nearby and taken to the Leon County Jail. Thus Parr's comment placing FSU in the company of the troubled, violent campus at UC-Berkeley might have seemed fully justified.*

This event, described in *The Flambeau* the next morning as the "Night of the Bayonets," marked the culmination of intense activity on the campus that had begun with John Champion's abrupt resignation two weeks earlier. In the tumult and confusion that followed, I had good reason to believe the SDS would attempt to occupy the University Union, and based on what I had learned about disruptions with similar origins on other campuses across the country, I would have

---

*At this point, I wish to define a few key terms. The first—"radicals"—has been applied too widely in describing the whole of the participants in the FSU protests. At least two other kinds of students were involved: those who sincerely wanted change—much of it constructive—on campus and in the broader society, and a second group of students who were looking for nothing more than a little excitement. The second term, "student demonstration", is somewhat misleading. While most of the demonstrators were students, some were not; they were professional agitators from well beyond the campus and their purpose was to confront and, if possible, defeat and displace authority.

been foolish to assume that violence would not happen here. I could only assume that if violence would serve their purpose, the SDS leaders would not hesitate to resort to violence.

In the days following my meeting with SDS representatives on my second day as Acting President (February 18), I spent a substantial part of my time meeting with those whose views I felt I needed. They included faculty and student leaders, Chancellor Bob Mautz, members of the Board of Regents, Chief of University Police Bill Tanner, as well as my administrative team. The question I posed to all of those was simply put: How can we permit the protesters—both students and outsiders—to demonstrate without interference from the University administration while at the same time maintaining the University's regular functions? The protesters' First Amendment rights, I emphasized, must be guaranteed, but we must absolutely prevent any disruption of the University's normal operations. This was the question that stood at the top of the administration's agenda and occupied the minds of many throughout the FSU community in one form or another.

There were, of course, other concerns competing for my time and attention. Two of our three vice presidencies were vacant, and the third was soon to be. There was my own recently vacated deanship of the College of Education that needed to be filled. Although I don't recall any real crises elsewhere in the University at that time, a feeling of unrest and uncertainty, going back to President John Champion's aborted attempt to resign nine months earlier, pervaded the campus.

The Campus Atmosphere Following March 4

If a roving reporter had toured the campus in the spring of 1969, he would have had many unusual items to report. Let us now review some of the most important.

Making the Injunction Permanent

In April 1969, the University filed a motion in the Leon County Circuit Court to make permanent the injunction denying the SDS the use of University facilities. The case came before Judge Ben Willis in January 1970. The University's lawyers cited a number of incidents during the 1968-69 academic year to support their claims: the occupation of President Champion's office on February 7; the SDS disruption of a rally sponsored by the Young Liberals on Landis Green on February 21 at which I was to speak; the attempted takeover of the University Union on March 4; the disruption of a meeting of the American Association of University Professors (AAUP) by the SDS on April 16; and finally, the threats and intimations of violence directed against the President throughout this period as well as reports from police of weapons being purchased by the protesters.

ACLU attorney Richard Wilson of Gainesville represented the SDS. He claimed that it was the University that caused the confrontation and it was President Marshall and the police who committed or threatened violence. Rick Johnson, a prominent SDS leader throughout this period, testified that he knew of no violent incidents committed by SDS members. The display of bayonets by police was seen as provoking violence. Wilson argued that the University and its facilities were public, not private property, and SDS members were merely exercising their First Amendment rights. An SDS handout distributed to the AAUP at its April meeting stated: "It is a basic principle that at a certain point an oppressive government should be overthrown by the majority of the people," and "…it may be necessary to employ apparently undemocratic means so that genuine free speech can emerge."

The Circuit Court ruled to make the injunction permanent. Attorney Wilson, however, appealed to the Florida Supreme Court, arguing again that the University had violated students' rights to free speech. Attorney Wilfred Varn, representing the University, countered that the real issue was the right of a university to control its own facilities; it was not a matter of free speech, he said, stressing that the University's refusal to grant the SDS recognition was based on the organization's record of violent actions throughout the country.

The Role of the Faculty Senate

From the beginning, some of my most severe critics on the SDS matter were found in the Faculty Senate, which met on March 5 to hear my comments on the crisis of the night before. The meeting was attended by some 1,500 students who, *The Flambeau* reported, repeatedly interrupted the meeting with "laughter, applause and hissing." The Senate passed a resolution condemning the use of rifles and bayonets, which the Senate asserted was "beyond the pale of propriety." In January 1970, by a vote of 23 to 22, the senate passed a resolution condemning the effort to make the injunction permanent.[4] It should be noted that the faculty had come under attack by the Florida Legislature's Select Committee on Campus Unrest and Drug Abuse. The Committee's report stated "in nearly every instance of campus unrest…the leaders were for the most part being counseled, guided, and occasionally directed by faculty members."[5] Many legislators let me know that they were aware of the attitude of the FSU Faculty Senate. The legislators' displeasure, in return, added to the tension that had been building for at least two years between faculty members and legislators. Persuading the legislators that the faculty who supported the protesters were a very small group became a major challenge for me during the early post-Champion period, for I did not believe that the faculty in general played a major role in the protests. Nonetheless, keeping the two sides apart and convincing legislators that no new legislation was needed to maintain order on the campus became a significant part of my job as president.

The events on the evening of March 4 set in motion a

wave of dissent that I probably should have expected. The Faculty Senate Steering Committee became a vigorous critic of the administration, and its criticisms focused, as might be expected, on the Acting President. That did not surprise or alarm me as members of the Steering Committee had often been critical of John Champion for most of the past year, and my actions in the non-recognition of the SDS were seen as an extension of the earlier policies. But those events also brought out a segment of the University which, to my considerable satisfaction, expressed its disapproval of the tactics of the SDS and whose members let me know that they approved of my actions the night of March 4.

The situation at FSU was much like what I had observed on other troubled campuses: A highly vocal group of the faculty, usually a small minority, joined protesting students and received the media attention that they sought.*

The Faculty Senate, and the Steering Committee in particular, became the vanguard for the small but active group of the faculty who would challenge the Acting President on many occasions.

The Role of *The Flambeau*

I did not believe that *The Flambeau* had a decisive role in the formation of student opinion on the matters before us, but the paper was out there every day, and I was obliged to pay it heed. Most students, I felt, knew that *The Flambeau* editors came and went, and its news reports often expressed the biases of the reporters in the stories they wrote.

Nonetheless, the part *The Flambeau* played in the events of 1968-1972, and to a considerable degree beyond, is an impor-

---

*One of my favorite lines in speeches to the alumni given around the state at this time went like this: "You've read about 100 students demonstrating on the campus one night last week. At that very moment there were 300 members of the Marching Chiefs practicing their routines, about 800 students studying in the library, fifty or so at religious services, and some 300 participating in intramural sports…The media didn't seem to notice all of those."

tant part of the story. From my vantage point, *The Flambeau's* news stories were to be viewed much as I quickly learned to regard news stories about campus events in the state's newspapers: Reporters must find something to write about, they have deadlines to meet, and bad news sells more papers than good. I don't mean that I dismissed reports in *The Flambeau* out of hand. I did not; I found things that I needed to know in its pages many days. As for the paper's editorials and opinion columns, they varied on the one hand from vigorous opposition to nearly everything that came out of my office, to editorials that appealed to students' sense of fair play and even their respect for authority. Editors of both kinds come to mind; George Waas, who served as editor in the 1968-1969 school year (until February 1969 when he resigned to accept appointment as attorney general for student government), wrote often of the obligation he believed students had to afford the administration the same freedom of speech that they espoused for the protesters. Waas was often a voice for reason and moderation. *The Flambeau* is discussed in greater detail in Chapter Three.

The Florida State University story in 1968 and early 1969 was largely the story of John Champion, of his actions, of the unusual activities of his vice presidents, and of the campus perturbations that followed in his wake. Chapter Two tells more of that story.

CHAPTER 2
A President Leaves

Growing Tension in Tallahassee

The resignation of John Champion as University President and my appointment as his successor is surely one of the more unusual chapters in the University's history. It is doubtful that any earlier transition was so contentious.

John Elmer Champion had been a much respected professor of accounting in the School of Business. He came to FSU in 1956 and soon established a reputation as an excellent teacher and a valuable member of the School's faculty. He and a colleague, Homer Black, co-authored a highly popular accounting textbook used nationwide.

His appointment in 1960 by President Gordon Blackwell as Vice President for Administration surprised no one. John was the epitome of a Southern gentleman. His wife Mary was beautiful and charming—they seemed cut out for leadership in a Southern university, and where better than FSU?

When President Blackwell resigned in 1965 to assume the presidency of his alma mater, Furman University, the Board of Regents moved quickly to confirm John's appointment to succeed him. The University was undergoing rapid growth in student enrollment, the new law school was about to open, and we were moving into the group of elite research universities toward which we had expended much effort for at least 15 years. They were, in important ways, the best of times.

But it was also a time of growing tension on many college campuses. In the mid-1960s, the baby-boomers were entering college. They saw the Vietnam War and the civil rights protests as reflecting badly on the ideals of freedom, democracy and equality of opportunity that they believed all Americans should embrace. They also felt that most universities and their administrators were too bureaucratic and authoritarian; as students, they felt oppressed and restricted by the molds into which they had to fit. Tallahassee's early involvement in the civil rights movement was separate from other protests, but it probably encouraged the rise of the New Left* at Florida State. By the end of the decade, Tallahassee had been the scene of boycotts and nonviolent resistance fostered by Tallahassee minister Charles K. Steele, who had been a close associate of Martin Luther King Jr. Tallahassee had also been the scene of the South's second major bus boycott in 1956, which was followed by efforts to desegregate lunch counters, movie theaters and public swimming pools.

Reports from troubled campuses across the country made the front pages of most of the nation's newspapers. These reports certainly got my attention and were the focal point of many of our discussions in the Westcott administration building. While we did not really believe the disturbances at Berkeley, Columbia, and the other troubled universities were the vanguard of a movement that would sweep the country, I nonetheless urged my staff to be vigilant. The SDS is very active at Florida State, I reminded them, the organization's members had threatened violence here, and we would do well to follow closely events on other campuses to prepare for whatever might come. But we must do so, I said, without creating a climate of fear or repression, and we must not make the campus look like an armed camp.

THE TROUBLED CAMPUSES

UC-Berkeley

Starting in 1964, the University of California-Berkeley (UC-

---

* New Left grew from the perceived shortcomings of older left-wing political organizations that had focused on economic disparities. In contrast, a younger generation of leftists starting in the 1960s began looking at broader concerns of social justice and cultural issues, though they were still critics of capitalist inequality.

Berkeley) became the national model for student protest. Sparked by the University's announcement that it would enforce the ban on distribution of political materials on campus, a broad coalition of Berkeley students united to form the Free Speech Movement (FSM). When a graduate student was arrested in October for distributing political materials, hundreds of Berkeley students swarmed a police car, trapping two officers. As the crowd swelled, Mario Savio and other FSM leaders used the roof of the car as a lecture podium, crushing its roof under their weight.

President Clark Kerr opposed using force on the students for ideological reasons as well as practical ones, but he did use police in an attempt to regain control of the campus. While Kerr did not have the support of the majority of the faculty, particularly those in the liberal arts and sciences in his efforts to quiet the demonstrations, several respected faculty members condemned the demonstrators. Sociologist Lewis Feuer called the FSM "a magnet for the morally corrupt,"[1] and Seymour Martin Lipsett regarded them as totalitarians. Feuer noted their advocacy of drug abuse, group sex and nihilism. Both Feuer and Lipsett were highly respected figures on the national academic scene.

Tensions at Berkeley began to subside after a few years, but protesters across the country looked to Berkeley for some time. Based on the success of the 1964 uprising, Berkeley remained the model for campus political action. The California Board of Regents summarily dismissed President Clark Kerr in January 1967, an action that college and university faculty and administrators across the country noted with more than passing interest.

University of Michigan

Though the University of Michigan had been a politically active campus for some time, it became known across the country for the creation of Students for a Democratic Society (SDS).

The Port Huron Statement, the founding document of the SDS, was drafted at a meeting in Port Huron, Michigan, in 1962, and it would become a blueprint for the politics of the New Left.

In Ann Arbor, a sit-in was staged in 1967 to protest the policies of the Selective Service. After a demonstration at the Ann Arbor draft board, some three dozen participants had their deferments reviewed and were reclassified as 1-A, ready to be inducted into the Army. As peace vigils, draft card burnings, and sit-ins continued, tensions on both sides grew on the Michigan campus until some 200 counter-protesters charged and ripped apart an anti-war float in a parade. The SDS faithful believed that violence must be used to increase the cost of Vietnam to Americans on the home front. During the winter of 1970, in an effort to drive military recruiters off campus, the SDS staged daily sit-ins in front of offices being used by military recruiters. During on-campus recruiting by General Electric, the SDS stormed the engineering building, attacking students and breaking down doors to classrooms and offices to flush out the corporate representatives. In February 1970, some 5,000 students marched on the Ann Arbor city hall, vandalizing buildings and destroying a police car.[2]

University of Wisconsin

Michigan was not alone among Midwestern universities to feel the wrath of the SDS. In the spring of 1967, in an effort to expel recruiters from Dow Chemical and the Central Intelligence Agency (CIA) from the Madison campus of the University of Wisconsin, students staged regular sit-ins. Some of the protesters were arrested, and Chancellor Robben Fleming provided the bail money to secure the students' release from jail. This act seemed only to radicalize members of the SDS, who responded by firebombing the offices of the associate dean of academic affairs. The campus police, not wanting to give the protesters a pretext for a riot, voluntarily disarmed, which left them defenseless to the radicals and unable to come to the aid of students who were under attack. When city police arrived, protesters pelted them with bricks, and a battle between the police and protesters ensued. One-hundred-seventy-five SDS members were injured and many more arrested. SDS members then publicly vowed to "destroy" the University of Wisconsin. In an effort to quell the violence, the administration barred Dow Chemical and the CIA from recruiting on campus.

In August 1970, protesters attempted to destroy the Army Math Building with a massive explosion, but the adjacent physics building absorbed most of the blast. A post-doctoral student in the physics building was killed, and an employee was seriously injured. The graduate student left a wife and three children.

Columbia University

The uprising at Columbia in April 1968 was based largely on two factors: The University's relationship with the Institute for Defense Analysis (IDA), a federal government-sponsored research project, and the perception of racism in the University. Students targeted the IDA, which was seen as a symbol of the military-industrial complex, and thus an indication of Columbia's support of the government's policy in Vietnam. The Columbia campus borders the largely black and Hispanic community of Morningside Heights in Harlem, and as the University began to expand, it did so by acquiring and then demolishing nearby buildings, which infuriated black students.

The protesting students barricaded themselves in Hamilton Hall on April 23. Though this was initially a collaborative effort between the SDS and the Students' Afro-American Society, the black students asked the SDS to leave Hamilton so as not to overshadow their grievances with the University. The African-American students then changed Hamilton's name to Malcolm X Hall. Over the next two days, two more buildings were "liberated" by student radicals, including the office of the president. The school year was shortened with no final exams being given, and most professors simply gave students pass or fail grades. President Grayson Kirk decided to take early retirement before the opening of the 1968 fall term. The media attention on Columbia served to harden the positions on many campuses and with the public. Columbia became a watchword to people on both sides.

Cornell University

One of the most dangerous campus protests occurred at Cornell. On April 19, 1969, Willard Straight Hall was taken over by 50 black students wielding rifles and shotguns. During the occupation, the students overturned tables and wrecked furniture, broke billiard cues for use as clubs and demanded the building's master keys from the University's employees. Elsewhere on campus, they turned over bookshelves in the library and physically threatened faculty and students, especially any black students who refused to join them. Some of the Cornell faculty members moved their families to hotels in Ithaca.

The administration responded by trying to deal with the black students' demands and by setting up various committees and panels to defuse the crisis and restore order on the campus. The President's efforts seemed mostly to alienate a large segment of the faculty, to confuse the students, and to leave the University's trustees in a state of wonder. On May 31, President James Perkins asked the trustees to begin the search for his successor.[3]

San Francisco State

Unrest at San Francisco State University in 1968-1969 reflects the more militant position that many black students were beginning to take on campuses across the country. During a march on the administration building in October 1968, several hundred black students chanted, "Revolution has come.

Off the pig! Time to pick up the gun!"[4] The University trustees demanded that order be restored. Unable to regain control of his campus, President Robert Smith resigned. The trustees then appointed S. I. Hayakawa, a conservative professor who had been very outspoken in opposition to campus demonstrations following the uprising at Berkley in 1964. Hayakawa banned amplified speeches, and he threatened to fire any faculty member who supported the student strikes and to expel any student who had been arrested on campus. The California legislature, prompted by letters from angry citizens, passed laws to control university students and faculty and to impose harsh punishments on anyone who attempted to disrupt normal university functions.[5]

At the time, President Hayakawa was widely condemned by faculty members at Florida State and other universities who believed no university president should ever meet force with force. He remained in office for several years, and his actions were later acknowledged by many to have helped curtail disruptions on other campuses.

Meanwhile, on the Campus in Tallahassee...

The origins of the change in leadership at Florida State University go back at least two years before John Champion resigned. FSU students were caught up in the discontent over issues that troubled young people, especially college students, throughout the country. The Vietnam War was the plausible culprit for some of the discontent. The civil rights movement troubled many, again especially the young, who responded to the urgings of Martin Luther King Jr. to demand equality for all Americans. U.S. Senator Daniel Patrick Moynihan spoke truth when he said that the grand ambitions of the post-World War II years often left behind regret and bitterness. "I believe this danger," Moynihan wrote, "has been compounded by the increasing introduction into politics and government of ideas originating in the social sciences which promised to bring social change through the manipulation of what might be termed the hidden processes of society."[6]

Many of America's youth felt the impact of President Kennedy's assassination and the growing distance between the power centers of the country and the spirit of the people. The decline of the institutions their parents had taught them to trust—family, church, community leaders—troubled many young people, and they were moved to seek change as no other generation in this century had done.

Florida State University had been racially integrated in 1962, but there were tensions. Authorities in Tallahassee and Leon County, along with FSU administrators, worked together to control demonstrations. FSU's Dean of Students Ross Oglesby issued a statement enjoining students from participating in demonstrations and unauthorized parades or other acts of incitement. Students from Florida A&M University* and FSU were not allowed to visit each other's campuses, except with official permission by university authorities, and even then only if they could make a valid claim that the visit was for an educational purpose.

Editorial writers for *The Flambeau* during this time generally took a moderate stance on the issue of race and racial integration of the campus, pointing with pride to the peaceful way in which the University had accepted its first black students. They noted that the civil rights battles in Tallahassee in the early '60s demonstrated that FSU students were eager to support the struggles of black people. They strengthened the sentiments of the New Left, whose supporters later became involved in such issues as the Vietnam War and Women's Liberation. Before about 1967, liberal inclinations of students

---

*Florida A&M University, one of the country's historic black universities, is located just across town from Florida State University. The two institutions have always enjoyed cordial relations, and both sets of students and faculty members participate in many activities jointly.

and other young people often found expression in long hair, bare feet, and a certain infatuation with drugs, sex, and rock 'n roll. By 1968, the counterculture had arrived at FSU in force, and the campus was rather quickly transformed. *In loco parentis* was fast becoming a relic of the grand old days of Florida State College for Women, when college girls were much too gentle to challenge authority.

With this background, the events that overtook Florida State University in May 1968 might have seemed to be the next step in the evolution of student radicalism on the South's most active campus. And so they were.

A Campus in Controversy

In May of that year, the campus was rent by a controversy over a story authored by a student for publication in *The Legend,* a student literary magazine. "The Pig Knife" contained several four-letter words considered by most people then to be unsuitable for a campus publication. No question, the words were shocking to a large segment of the university community, but not to the Board of Student Publications (BOSP), whose approval was all that was needed.

But not so fast. The administration, upon their review of the story, notified the Board that the story would be banned, this despite the approval of several professors from the English Department, who pointed out that such language often appeared in contemporary American and English literature. Champion replied that as President, he was officially the publisher of all University publications, and he believed that such language was simply not appropriate. The University's Faculty Senate weighed in, recommending that the story be published over the President's objections, and students began a peaceful 24-hour vigil outside of the Westcott Building to protest Champion's decision. The vigil grew in size from about 50 students to several hundred over its week-long life. The Student Grassroots Movement was organized to preserve and strengthen the protests.[7]

The College of Arts and Sciences faculty held a special meeting in Moore Auditorium on Tuesday afternoon, May 14 to consider the President's actions in refusing to permit the publication of "The Pig Knife." Champion spoke at the meeting and told the faculty members that his decision was unchangeable, and any appeal should be made to the Board of Regents. He was criticized by faculty at the meeting for his refusal to consider the views of his fellow academic administrators in the censorship matter, meaning one or more of his vice presidents, people the faculty senate believed to be uncomfortable with his stand. This was seen by some as an attempt to drive a wedge between the President and his fellow administrators.[8] The Arts and Sciences faculty adopted a resolution calling for him to reverse his stated position and to refer the matter to a faculty committee. The A & S faculty then considered a second resolution that called for the censure of the president for "his actions concerning the censorship" but made it clear that the vote of no confidence should not be extended to "other administrators," meaning the vice presidents. The resolution called for the President's resignation if he could not meet the faculty's demands. A motion to table the resolution passed by a vote of 175 to 165, so the resolution to censure was itself never debated.[9]

I observed the Arts and Sciences faculty meeting, and it was an experience that left a strong impression with me for a long time. I happened to be walking across campus past Moore Auditorium, returning from some business in Westcott to my office in the Education Building, when I was hailed by Jim Tait, a law student and family friend. (Jim was the son of friends and faculty members—his father at FSU and his mother in the public schools of Leon County.) He seemed to be in a state of some excitement as he rushed over to tell me about the A & S faculty meeting going on "right now" just inside the auditorium. His excitement led me to believe that there was something special taking place, and I was very curious as I entered the building. The meeting was obviously under way, and I stood quietly in the back of the auditorium.

My first view was of John Champion standing alone at the microphone before the assembled faculty. He was clearly in distress. As I listened to the questions and comments addressed to him, I understood why. He was being censured for his role in the censorship of "The Pig Knife," and some of the faculty members seemed to be moving in for the kill. John was a shaken man, standing alone, and my eyes searched the room for his staff. His executive assistant Juanita Gibson was seated in the front row beside the empty seat that I assumed had been occupied by the President before he was called to the front. Where, I wondered, was Larry Chalmers who was senior among the vice presidents and Champion's closest lieutenant in the administration? And then I saw him. Chalmers was seated eight or ten rows back, about midway between the right and left aisles, and he was slouched low in his seat, elbows on the arms and chin resting on his folded hands. While I couldn't see his face from the rear of the room, I didn't need to. The message he was sending could not have been missed by anyone in the room: You're on your own, Mr. President; you're facing a faculty in revolt, and I want it known that I have had no part in bringing about the censorship problem you're facing. The impression this scene left on me was to come back many times in the next year, for it said a good deal to me about the depth of Champion's problem and the identity of the anti-Champion forces. I concluded that day that John Champion's tenure as President was uncertain if the leaders of the Arts and Sciences faculty and Vice President Chalmers had their way.

The Arts and Sciences faculty had made it clear that the President was to reverse his decision or resign. Afterwards, Champion in the company of Gibson walked back across campus to his office in Westcott from the meeting in Moore Auditorium. From there, he called Chancellor Robert Mautz and submitted his resignation, stating that he believed he had lost the confidence of a large segment of the faculty. Mautz notified the Board of Regents immediately, and the reaction from the Board and much of Florida was profound shock and anger.

The next day, May 15, the Board of Regents and the Chancellor were deluged with calls and telegrams urging that Champion reconsider his decision. A group of students—3,000 according to news reports—rallied on the campus in support of Champion. State School Superintendent Floyd Christian called an emergency meeting of the State Board of Education to ask for a moratorium on any action until the controversy could be carefully studied.

Champion had submitted his resignation in good faith, thinking it would solve the problem of faculty dissent.[10] But the spirit of the campus he left was a mixture of opposition and support for the resigned president, and there were strong feelings on both sides. Protesting students set up information tables on the campus to keep the University informed of events as they occurred and to distribute anti-censorship armbands, all in an attempt to keep up the momentum of the protests.[11]

Students and faculty members in support of Champion also found ways to express themselves. Student body President Lyman Fletcher announced that Champion's resignation had not been the students' goal, and the full Faculty Senate passed a resolution asking Champion to withdraw his resignation. Fletcher called for reason and restraint, while also calling on the Board of Regents to change its policy on student publications. He stated that the system was wrong, but Champion's resignation was not what the students wanted, and he personally regretted it.[12]

In a letter to the editor of *The Flambeau*, student René Holt wrote, "If we do not learn to solve problems in a rational manner, we could let a very, very small minority of students turn FSU into another Columbia University of last week."[13]

On May 15, the same day Champion's resignation became public, a group of students under the leadership of Larry González, former student body president and an outspoken supporter of President Champion, gathered on Landis Green with attendance estimated to be in excess of 1,000. The President of the Tallahassee Chamber of Commerce, James Joanos, a prominent FSU alumnus, also spoke at the rally, reporting on a resolution passed unanimously by the Chamber asking Champion to rescind his resignation. Football star Kim Hammond also spoke on Champion's behalf.[14]

Champion's resignation ignited a wave of criticism throughout the state. Comments by the press and members of the legislature revealed the intense, widespread public anger directed at the rebellious students who attended one of their state universities at taxpayers' expense. Many saw the FSU matter as a conflict between responsible university administrators and unruly students who simply wanted to use dirty words. Senator Mallory Horne of Tallahassee characterized the unrest as "a handful of students and senseless academicians who chose to dictate university policy by rallying behind stupid filth." Florida State Attorney General Earl Faircloth called the protests "open rebellion abroad in the land against authority" and he called for a full investigation.[15] Statewide, chambers of commerce, service clubs, and banks organized petition drives urging Champion to return. FSU's Alumni Association advocated that any faculty member or administrator who did not respect and accept Champion's censorship decision should be fired.

The *Orlando Sentinel,* the most stridently anti-protest newspaper in the state, called the students "immature children, who simply want to read obscenities supported by their degree-laden professors." The editor mentioned the "moral rot" at FSU.[16] The *Miami Herald* was somewhat more moderate, calling for Champion to return and to use "the wellspring of support" that he had received from the people of Florida to resolve the issue without further damage.[17] The *Orlando Sentinel* ran a petition on the front page of the newspaper on May 15, providing readers an opportunity to indicate whether they wanted Champion to return and face the radicals, or to leave his post. The editor reported receiving 37,000 responses urging Champion to return and virtually none supporting his resignation.

With such a massive demonstration of support, Champion withdrew his resignation on May 18 and resumed his duties, but on less than a full-time basis. Upon his return to office, he stated that he would solicit faculty and student participation in resolving the crisis, and that he would support the findings of the blue ribbon committee on student publications that had been set up in his absence by Vice President Chalmers.

This was no doubt a stressful period for the President. As a result, he suffered an episode on May 22, experiencing "extreme acute physical exhaustion." His personal physician, Dr. I. B. Harrison, ordered a rigidly enforced period of rest. The President was hospitalized and was away from his office until June 10. During his absence, Vice President Chalmers handled routine presidential duties, but the Board of Regents had made it clear that Champion remained the final authority.

Upon Champion's return to his office, the President exhibited a more compliant attitude toward students, and indicated his support for the recommendations of the blue ribbon committee. Champion announced that he would accept the committee's report, except that he would still not agree to the publication of "The Pig Knife." He agreed to set up regular meetings with student leaders. In July, the highly controversial faculty adviser of student publications (he had supported censoring "The Pig Knife")left the University while the BOSP sought to redefine the role of the publications technical adviser. The feeling among students was generally that they hoped the censorship controversy was over and a new spirit of conciliation was in place.[18]

However, students were still determined to publish *The*

Legend and "The Pig Knife" story it contained, and they found another way. They obtained private financial support for the magazine, and it was published in the first week of June with the stipulation from the administration that the seal, copyright and endorsement of the University could not be used.

But ultimately, the President's illness did little to calm the campus. Kathy Urban, editor-in-chief of *The Flambeau*, published an editorial on the day Champion was hospitalized. She wrote that "the issue is no longer the publication of 'The Pig Knife,' but the very essence of the university—what or who should determine its policies." What began as a simple protest had snowballed into a dramatic issue that threatened "to wreck the university."[19]

A New Beginning?

What followed the dramatic events of May 1968 was neither the end of the beginning nor the beginning of the end, though to some partisans it probably seemed to be one or the other. During the fall, there were those on the campus and throughout much of Florida who might have hoped that the campus climate would resemble the peace and harmony of an earlier time. There were periods when that seemed to be the case. Both student government President Lyman Fletcher and *Flambeau* editor George Waas were responsible student leaders whose moderate approach to their offices must have seemed to John Champion to be a harbinger of good things to come. The positive spirit of orderly and progressive change, if only fleeting, was surely a comfort to Champion and to many students and faculty.

Events and activities during the fall months may not have been much different from those that characterize normal student behavior, but to a President who had just weathered a fierce, unexpected storm, they could have brought no more than a small measure of relief. In any case, the resignations of three vice presidents soon to come presented clear evidence that all was not well within Champion's immediate team of administrators. Other stressful problems arose, often seeming to descend on the beleaguered President without warning. He must have looked forward to the Christmas break, to the end of fall quarter and on to 1969.

Enter 1969 and the Forces of Change

John Champion could not have foreseen the events that lay ahead when the new year dawned, nor could he have judged the extent to which his University would be subject to the forces shaping higher education across the land; but if he had, he could not have been heartened by the developing picture. Perhaps the President did have certain premonitions based on his observations and perceptions over the past year. He may have felt in his gut that there would be challenges of a kind he had never faced as a University President, and that some of the issues would threaten his position as head of the University. The campus over which he presided was torn by strong feelings and antagonisms such as those described below; but if he had any inkling of the insurrection within his own team of administrators, those around him saw no such indication. These were the signs:

- The SDS nationally had clearly established its position that force and other unlawful means were condoned in order to achieve its desired ends. SDS at FSU in the early days insisted that the local chapter, even though a part of the national organization, had the ability to formulate its own programs and establish its own policies. At FSU, the SDS seemed willing at times to distance itself from the national organization, but it was still the SDS.
- At an SDS rally to show "solidarity with San Francisco State," which entirely ignored the turmoil on

that campus, the group released a series of demands before a crowd of some 200 students. Their
demands included: "opening all secret records held
by the administration and campus police concerning
students including correspondence with the Defense Department, and documents concerning the
University's expansion into Frenchtown; disarming
the campus police...and banning all 'narcotic and
political spies' from campus; and establishing a program of studies in Afro-American culture and imperialism and exploitation in the Third World."[22]

- At a speech by Ambassador Arthur Goldberg on
January 15, two protesting students were stopped at
the door of the auditorium in Westcott to prevent
them from carrying signs into the auditorium.
(Goldberg had served on the U.S. Supreme Court
and as U.S. Ambassador to the United Nations.)
Vice President John Arnold met them and pointed
out that having signs inside buildings was in violation of university regulations. One of the students
fell back, and cries of "Assault!" and "Pigs!" rang
out from the group of protesters. Student Frank
Schrama was one of those arrested in the exchange
with Arnold. Student body President Lyman
Fletcher later issued a statement condemning the
demonstrations.

- A controversial Board of Regents policy on the
recognition of student organizations had been
referred to Florida Attorney General Earl
Faircloth, who ruled in favor of the BOR policy
stating: "from recognition flow rights and privileges that should be extended only to those organizations which subscribe to the fundamental
purposes, goals, and methods of the University."
The response of the SDS was to hold a rally on
the steps of Westcott with an invitation to Vice

President Arnold to speak. When he did so, *The Flambeau* reported that he was greeted by "harassment and open displays of disgust."[21] A *Flambeau* editorial the next day expressed regret that Arnold was denied his freedom of speech and urged the SDS to remember that student responsibility must be exercised before student power could result.[22]

The troublesome first weeks of 1969 were followed by new conflicts that John Champion's best efforts to control proved of no avail.

FSU Gets an Office of Executive Vice-President

On February 12, the President announced my appointment as the University's Executive Vice President, a newly established position at FSU and also the first such office in the State University System. (The office had been established but not yet filled at the University of Florida.) Champion's statement stressed that I would work with him "in the development and implementation of university-wide policies" and would help address "the increasingly greater number and variety of complex problems associated with University administration." My term of office was to be begin with the University's new fiscal year on July 1.[23]

I received numerous congratulatory messages and had no reason to believe that my appointment was not well received throughout the University. As things unfolded, I came to believe that I would not have been the choice of some of the faculty in the College of Arts and Sciences and surely not the leaders of the Faculty Senate. Larry Chalmers, who had just resigned as Vice President for Academic Affairs, the chief academic officer and senior among the three vice presidents, would not have applauded my appointment, and others among the A & S leaders would have followed his lead.

Chalmers had announced his resignation only the day before, on February 11, to become Chancellor of the University of Kansas. It had been a poorly kept secret for some time that Chalmers had hoped to succeed Champion as President, and my appointment might have made that seem less likely. At this point, along with many others on the faculty, I would have regarded Chalmers as Champion's logical successor in the event that John would step down, Larry's odd behavior at the A & S faculty meeting the previous May notwithstanding. Chalmers was a natural leader. He was very bright, and a skilled political operative among his faculty colleagues.[24]

I do not now recall any strong personal reactions on my part to my appointment as Executive Vice President. The effective date was several months off, I was busy being Dean of the School of Education, and I had plenty of time to get ready to assume my new office. But my tranquility was not to last. On Monday, February 17, *The Flambeau* reported a statement by student body President Canter Brown, who was sometimes given to intemperate statements, calling President Champion a frightened man. Brown accused the President of being "frightened of students and faculty;" He charged that Champion avoided consulting with faculty, adding that Champion did not relate well to either students or faculty. Brown went on to praise Chalmers's performance as the administrator in charge during Champion's illness last spring, saying that now "the University had lost its most successful and respected administrator." To me, and I believe to others among the faculty, Brown appeared to have strong personal ties to Chalmers. In the same statement, he was critical of my appointment as Vice President and the manner by which it was made, expressing his regret that it had been done without consultation with students and faculty.[25]

John Champion Resigns

The same issue of *The Flambeau* reported that Champion

would address the University community at four o'clock the next day, February 18. He would discuss the recent administrative changes including my appointment and that of Vice President Jack Arnold and the just announced resignation of Odell Waldby as Vice President for Administration. The unfolding of events caused that address to be cancelled.

During the latter part of the previous week, there was word around campus that several faculty members from A & S had once again raised questions about Champion's ability to lead the University, and doubts were expressed about whether he would—or should—remain in office. I was informed that a group of professors, along with some in the central administration, had met on Saturday to consider this question. A report on this meeting was conveyed to me by some of the A & S faculty because, I suppose, as the executive vice president-in-waiting, I would surely be a Champion loyalist, and maybe I should know. Those who came to me, I assumed, were not totally in sympathy with those who had organized the meeting, or its purposes.

My response was to call a meeting on Sunday afternoon of a group of faculty members from across the University. I told the gathering that I sensed an effort on the part of the Saturday group to question Champion's leadership, and they had seemed to suggest once again that it might be time for a change at the top. I believed this to be an unjustified insurrection—a sort of academic *palace coup*—and I wanted to assess the level of faculty support for Champion. I learned that his support was strong, and those in attendance were eager to step forward and let the President know that he had a solid base, a group of veteran faculty members who regarded him as the University's legitimate leader, and they stood ready to support and if necessary to defend him vigorously.

John and Mary Champion were out of town on a speaking tour that weekend and were scheduled to return late Sunday afternoon. I met them at the President's home at about five o'clock and related what I had learned about the Saturday meeting and also described the Sunday meeting. I emphasized that the President could count on the support of a clear majority of the faculty. His reaction took me completely by surprise.

I cannot remain as President, he told me, going on to say that he would call Chancellor Mautz and resign at once. I sensed in John's decision that he was not surprised by my report of the Saturday meeting, that he had an intuitive feeling that forces were at work to force his resignation and he wished to extend the fight no longer. I spoke emphatically about his support among the faculty who, I said, were in the majority and awaited only his leadership to defend his record and to support him vigorously. With his wife Mary by his side, Champion announced sadly that it was no use, that he no longer wanted to serve as President, and he asked that we discuss the matter no further.

John then put in a call to Chancellor Bob Mautz, who evidently recognized that John's decision was non-negotiable. Mautz then called me to ask me to become the Acting President. He told me that the Council of State University Presidents was scheduled to meet in Tampa the next morning (Monday), and he asked that I accompany him and John to the meeting so that the three of us might meet with Burke Kibler, chairman of the Board of Regents, in order to gain his approval and to release the news to the media on Tuesday morning.

John sat through the Council of Presidents meeting impassively. I sat in a chair back from the table around which the presidents were assembled and did not participate in their deliberations. They might have wondered what I was doing there, but no one raised the question, which led me to believe that they had somehow received word on developments at FSU.

The depth of John Champion's problems with a group of the faculty was not understood by most of the university community. Hard news on the subject was difficult to come by, and probing by reporters from the state's newspapers provided updates that were followed closely by those of us at the University as well as the general public. The *Orlando Sentinel* reported in a front page story in the days following Champion's resignation that "a significant segment of the faculty met Sunday night and agreed to submit their own resignations if Champion did not submit his by Thursday."[26] The story was written by David Lawrence, a veteran reporter who covered happenings at FSU during this period and for whom I had great respect.

The Champion resignation made headlines in the *St. Petersburg Times*, the *Orlando Sentinel*, the *Florida Times-Union*, the *Pensacola Journal* and of course, the *Tallahassee Democrat*. Most papers noted that this was Champion's second resignation in less than a year, and they gave credence to his statement that he believed the University would be better served by new leadership.

At the conclusion of the presidents' Monday meeting in Tampa, BOR Chairman Kibler, Chancellor Mautz, and I drove to Kibler's office in Lakeland. During the trip we discussed the transition at FSU, and Kibler gave me his and the Board's enthusiastic endorsement. I was to address the problems on the campus and exert a measure of control that had been lacking.

Taking the Reins

Back in Tallahassee, Champion announced that he would make a statement to the faculty, explaining his decision and asking for their support of the new president. He and I appeared together at a well-attended meeting in the Westcott auditorium on Tuesday afternoon, February 18, and Champion told the faculty that the president must work for the entire University, and that "...ultimate authority for decisions must be firmly fixed in the office of the president." Professor Homer Black, John's longtime friend in the School of Business, presented the departing president with a resolution of appreciation from the Faculty Professional Relations Committee. John then wished me well, and I closed the meeting by telling the faculty that we must maintain control of the University. There may be those who believe they can run the University better than we can, I said, and we must prove them wrong. The specter of legislative interference threatened our treasured independence, and it concerned me even at this early point in my administration.[27]

Meanwhile, the Florida legislature was moved to try to control what the lawmakers saw happening at FSU, events that caused them great concern and over which they had no control, and they resented that. Those protesting students were attending a state university supported with tax dollars; they were engaging in activities that most legislators found abhorrent, and the legislators wanted to do something about it. That something was to pass laws that would strengthen the hands of the university presidents and impose penalties on students who went too far.

One of the issues at the University of Florida at the time was the controversy over a dissident professor who had encouraged students "to shut down the University." Dr. Kenneth Megill, a professor in the Philosophy Department who had advocated for radical student organizations, had been a thorn in President Steve O'Connell's side for a year or more, and Senator Tom Slade of Jacksonville—a UF alumnus—knew just what to do: President O'Connell should simply fire the guy and solve the problem. There were tempting reasons for O'Connell to do just that, but as the President said, there was also the First Amendment to the U.S. Constitution to take into account. O'Connell refused to follow the urgings of Slade and other legislators, saying he lacked sufficient grounds to fire Megill.[28]

If O'Connell down in Gainesville had troubles with well-meaning legislators, he must have been thankful not to be in Tallahassee. Here, the legislators saw the protests up-close;

they heard the dirty words, they watched the demonstrators in their bare feet and long hair, and they faced the most active of the protesters on the Capitol steps. The result was just what was expected: lots of grandstanding by legislators in the introduction of legislation that Steve O'Connell and I neither wanted nor needed. In fairness to the legislators, I must state that not all of those who objected to the students were exploiting the situation. These were citizens who had never before witnessed such behavior by the children of their friends and neighbors in Florida, and they had no experience in dealing with such matters. Should not an elected representative of the people, especially one right there in Tallahassee, be expected to do something about it? Of course he should, and that meant passing laws—that's what legislators do, they pass laws—and on all that's sacred, they were going to pass some.

But they were also intelligent and, for the most part, reasonable men (no women that I remember), and I found them eager to talk to me about events at FSU, and usually to listen. My argument was the place of the First Amendment guarantees—the obligation I had as head of the University to assure our students—all of our students—that there would be no abridgment of the freedom of speech. I gave that assurance to groups of concerned students more times than I can count. You may call me names or you may say anything you wish about me; you can rail against my administration and my policies; you may demonstrate and parade and carry signs – all with the assurance that you will not be molested. You may not, however, do anything to disrupt the University or to interfere with the orderly processes of education that take place here. And if you get any ideas about using force or occupying buildings, remember what I told you just after I took office: Do not take any buildings you do not intend to hold!

On Tuesday, my first day in office, I moved into the President's office, which Champion had vacated early that morning. I knew his longtime secretary, Alice Chambers, his

Executive Assistant, Juanita Gibson, and Pat Hogan, long-time aide to several presidents, and others around the president; I was pleased at the prospect of working with them, and the feeling seemed to be mutual. I asked Odell Waldby to remain at his post as Vice President for Administration for a few months, but he declined to do so, telling me of his long-standing wish to return to teaching. I met briefly with Vice President Chalmers, who candidly expressed to me less than his full support of my administration and some doubt about whether we could work together through the rest of the academic year before his departure for Kansas. My response, a performance that I do not now recall with particular pride, was that my voice rose and I told Chalmers that I expected—no, demanded—his cooperation, and if he failed to carry out his responsibilities in a professional manner, I thought the Board of Regents at the University of Kansas should learn of his questionable professionalism. Chalmers remained at FSU until he took his new post at Kansas, and while our relationship was not exactly cordial, I recall no instance in which he did not perform satisfactorily.

By the end of my first week there was no doubt that John's resignation and my appointment were the cause of deep feelings on the campus and throughout the state. The majority of the faculty members were people I knew; they were friends who, I believed, thought well of me and were ready to accept me as President. They were as shocked and saddened as I was over the circumstances that had overtaken our friend John Champion. They knew that I had not sought the job and there was no buzz around campus about Marshall as a candidate for the presidency. I was there to do a job that needed doing, and most—though not all—of the University community seemed to see it that way.

The response around the state was nothing like it had been following Champion's aborted resignation nine months earlier. People seemed to understand that he really wanted—perhaps needed—to vacate the office, and they were satisfied to leave it at that. John was welcomed back to the School of Business and to his old job as professor of accounting, and he seemed to me to make the adjustment comfortably.

If I believed there would be no faculty exception taken to my appointment as Acting President, I was soon to be denied that illusion. There were some among the students and faculty, especially the Arts and Sciences faculty, who expressed their feelings openly, and it seemed clear that those who appeared to have fostered Champion's resignation would not be pleased to have his successor come from any school or college in the University other than A & S.

During the remaining school year, Florida State University was the scene of more institutional high drama than at any other time in its history. Some of the participants are no longer with us, as I said earlier, and those of us who have distinct—and we hope, clear—memories must not let pass the opportunity to record the history of that remarkable period. Chapter Three will reveal just how remarkable those next few months were.

CHAPTER 3
A New President Takes Office

The Marshall Years Begin

If John Champion on January 1, 1969, possessed no clair-voyance about the events that lay ahead at the opening of the new year, the same was true of my view of the future on the morning of February 16 of that eventful year. What had claimed the full attention of the University community* was the turnover in the presidency. While that did not incite the people of Florida as had the events of the previous spring, it was nonetheless big news on the campus and beyond. The requests I had for press interviews and invitations to speak to alumni and service clubs throughout the state left no doubt that events at FSU were decidedly newsworthy.

The most pressing issue as I began my acting presidency was the question of recognition of the SDS, which had caught the attention of the Board of Regents, the legislature, and many other Floridians in light of the stories about the organization's activities on other campuses.

The General Faculty Meeting of February 27

I had promised to study the SDS matter carefully during my first weeks as president and to give my answer on the SDS recognition question as soon as I could. A general faculty meeting seemed to be the right setting for my statement, and I called the meeting for February 27, ten days after I had assumed the

---

*The term "university community" needs defining in this context. Included are the students, faculty and staff, as well as alumni and a variety of the University's friends and supporters such as the athletic boosters. But also included are business people and civic leaders, mostly from Tallahassee, who might have attended other universities but who had developed strong ties to FSU. Many of our strongest supporters in Tallahassee—and I mean dollar donors—were passionate Gators who were also staunch friends of FSU and supporters of our athletic teams "in every game but one."

office. I knew that most faculty members and many students had been waiting eagerly for my answer on SDS, but I felt that they also wanted to know more about the person who had just assumed the presidency of their University, what kind of leadership he would provide, and what sort of vision he had for FSU.

I began my speech with some lighthearted comments about the rumors I had heard and read about myself: No, I was not of Lebanese descent, although some understanding of Middle Eastern culture might be a useful attribute, I said; nor was it true that Governor Claude Kirk might resign to be named vice president of the University. I told the faculty that I hoped they would hang loose and let me make some mistakes before we had at each other.

Turning more serious, I said that if there were unlawful elements of the community prepared to capture University facilities or otherwise disrupt the orderly process of education, they had escaped my notice. I conceded that there was dissatisfaction among some members of the University community, some of it serious, but most of it constructive. Adding that I had received "strong and nearly universal support" from the students and faculty, I reminded the faculty that "while there are some problems remaining, a strong, vibrant, healthy university can solve problems—indeed it becomes stronger in doing so."

I explained to the faculty that I would speak to three major points: First, to express my thoughts on what I think a university should be; then to present my analysis of several major problem areas that had surfaced at that point in the University's recent history along with how I proposed to deal with them; and finally, to say some things about the day-to-day mechanics of operation of the University in the weeks ahead.

I then focused initially on the need for improved communication among all segments of the University, and assured the faculty members that I would set aside time on a regular basis for conferences with students and faculty throughout the University. I told them that I had felt a sharp twinge of pain recently when a student told me that in three years at FSU he had never once seen the president. I assured the faculty that that would not be the case as long as I was president, and I described methods for improved communication.

It seemed important to explain my view of one role of the president—a requirement that I serve as an effective two-way agent of communication between the University community and the larger world beyond campus. The President, I said, must take special pains to reflect the views of the faculty to those outside. At the same time, he must protect and defend the faculty from attack by those whose efforts would be to weaken the University, and occasionally in doing so the president must take action or say things about internal University matters that might not be well understood by those in the University community.

I wanted to add a special word about the need for temperance in expressing one's views, especially on sensitive matters. "Members of the academic community should have all the freedoms that other citizens have," I said, "and no one should attempt to deny them those freedoms, but there's nothing in this that prevents a faculty member from expressing himself in tactful language if it conveys his thoughts adequately, or selecting a time and place for remarks to reduce the trauma among the audience...freedom is not strengthened by flaunting it," I said, "and while it is useful to test our freedoms, I doubt that it is necessary to push them to the limit every few days." I reminded faculty members that because we live in the Capital city, we have a history of interesting relations with the legislature, and that there are sometimes people from both groups who seem to operate on a policy of intemperance. "Just as some faculty people see an oppressive reactionary in every seat in the legislature, some legislators see a Marxist behind every desk in the University," and I added that temperance in one group might be returned in kind by the other.

At some risk of stretching my relations with faculty too far, I reminded them that faculty members are obliged to be as objective as they can be when expressing their personal opinions to students, that their authority in the classroom is a function of their expertise in their areas of specialization. "A faculty member does not have the right to use his classroom as a platform to inform or persuade his students in any area, save that of his own expertise," I reminded them.[1]

I added a brief comment about a relationship being developed between FSU and Florida A&M University, in which the two institutions would undertake efforts to enrich and extend opportunities for both groups of students. Plans were underway to arrange for the exchange of professors between the universities on a regular basis, and in addition, to undertake special projects in the areas of research and service in which the two institutions would cooperate.

But on to the issue of recognition of SDS.

I identified several reasons that seemed to me to favor recognition, and I spelled out several such reasons. They included the fact that Florida is one of the few states—perhaps the only one—in which a public university would arbitrarily deny recognition to SDS; my belief that a respectable segment of the university community believed SDS should be officially recognized; that my failure to give SDS official recognition would provide them a convenient cause for the headlines they seek; and whether or not we take official cognizance of it, SDS does in fact exist here and non-recognition does not lessen its presence. Finally, "FSU is a strong and viable democratic institution which has no need to fear dissent in whatever form it occurs—the orderly kind it welcomes, the disorderly kind it can control."[2]

In opposition to the recognition of SDS, I stated the following points: Despite the fact that the national and local SDS constitutions reflect no unlawful purposes, statements by national officers have repeatedly advocated violence; the national organization and its leaders who have been shown on many occasions to engage in destructive behavior would be strengthened by the establishment of a recognized chapter at FSU. It seems not to have been well understood that Vice President Arnold rejected the SDS application in January for good and acceptable reasons as he would have had to do for any organization. The sponsors were encouraged to appeal that decision, and their refusal to do so, following University procedures for this purpose, raises serious questions about their desire to participate constructively in the academic community; and SDS members have made threats in my presence to disobey the rules of the University with the strong implication, if not a promise, that violence would follow.

I explained that, during the past two weeks, I had looked for answers in the operating manual of the Board of Regents for instructions, and the answers I sought were not to be found. It was only in the last few days that I came to realize that in the fullest sense, those regulations were never intended as the sole guide for the administration of the University. It had become clear to me that I must go beyond the "four corners of the Regents' regulations" in the decisions I had to make, and that subjective judgments were required. I pointed out that in the end, there is no substitute for the exercise of human judgment by the person who must accept the final responsibility for the welfare of the University.

I then stated that on the basis of my analysis and evaluation I would deny recognition of the SDS. I added that it had been an anguished decision, and I was not sure if it was the right one, for I disliked the idea of seeing restrictions placed on any individuals or groups, whether they be in my own family or in the University.

I added that a major consideration for me all along had been the absolute necessity of avoiding the closing of the University. In my view, I said, the closing of the University was a real possibility—as it was elsewhere—over such issues as the one we face now. I told the faculty members that I believed some in the University did not fully comprehend the implications of the closing of a university. That would be a tragedy of enormous proportion to me, I said, and it must never happen here. "This is one university, which as long as I'm its Acting President, is going to remain open," I said, "open and free."

I closed my remarks by attempting to make clear precisely what the University's policy was with respect to violent action on the campus. I said that "the University's position with respect to any who attempt to interfere with the orderly processes of education will be to take whatever action is required to restore order immediately." I added that our security officers would be prepared to meet any emergency and that included enlisting the aid of other law enforcement agencies if they were needed. The following statement, which served as a policy guide for the next few years, is an excerpt from my speech:

"It must be understood by all members of the University community that stern action will be taken promptly against any who attempt to take over University facilities. On other campuses where such threats have been made, a period of deliberation has been allowed before an effort has been made by the university officials to dislodge occupation forces. At Florida State University, the period of deliberation must come before occupancy, not after. In other words, students should think carefully in advance of their actions about the consequences, and if they decide to occupy buildings or other facilities, they should be fully prepared for whatever counter action is taken against them. With all due respect and with malice toward none, I urge all members of the University community not to take any buildings with the expectation of holding them."

In closing, I reminded all faculty members of that great message that is attributed to Epicurus: "Only one principle will give you courage; that is the principle that no evil lasts forever; nor, indeed, for very long."

Facing the Realities

While the feeling about the change in the office of President seemed to be generally positive and events on the campus seemed pretty normal, there was an undercurrent of unrest that was hard to miss. News reports in *The Flambeau* and its editorials painted a picture of student dissent, and the reports of turmoil on other campuses could only leave me to wonder if the relative quiet of my first two weeks in the office of President was to last. I felt I had made my position on the SDS matter very clear, so when the SDS members challenged the authority of the University by holding their forbidden rally anyway, they knew as well as I exactly where I stood and what they could expect in the future.

Where I stood, literally, the night of March 4, was at my desk in the President's office in Westcott (yes, probably not sitting, but standing), where we had set up a command post in order to stay in touch with events in the Union. There was little doubt in the minds of FSU Police Chief Bill Tanner and me that a confrontation would occur—the SDS had made that clear. What we didn't know was whether it would be violent.

My request for a restraining order (the injunction) that afternoon might have been one of my best decisions during this highly volatile time. It placed the matter with the courts, where I concluded it properly belonged. And as I looked back on the problems at Berkeley and the other troubled institutions, I wondered why those presidents had not resorted to the courts as a way to avoid altercations with protesting students. We have since been able to find no instance of any university using this approach before FSU did in March 1969.

So our plan was to alert Leon County Sheriff Raymond Hamlin to what we had planned, and to suggest that there might be a need for crowd control and possibly arrests. Bill

Tanner, who knew Hamlin well, made the contact. (I had only recently met the Sheriff, but we became well acquainted and close friends in the months ahead.) Why had we contemplated such a need? Because we were determined to see that the lawful order was carried out, and that the demonstrators would learn at this first confrontation with the new president that the sincere outreach he had made to the SDS over the past two weeks must not be seen as reluctance to stand behind his decision denying them the right to use University facilities, even if doing so meant using force. The operative word in staff meetings in Westcott was "resolute," that we must not make any promises we did not intend to keep. I felt that it was important for the protesting students to understand that I would not hesitate to use the full authority of the office of the President.

Accordingly, Bill Tanner, accompanied by the Sheriff, went to the Union at the appointed hour, got the attention of the 300 or so people in the ballroom, and read the order. Sheriff Hamlin then informed the occupants that they must leave the building at once or face arrest. Their response was to leave by the doors facing Tennessee Street—all but 58, that is—and those 58 were arrested, placed in paddy wagons and taken to the Leon County Jail, where they were booked. The account of those events is told in appropriate detail by Steve Parr in his doctoral dissertation, which I have quoted in Chapter One.

The Next Day

I felt strongly that the Night of the Bayonets deserved to be addressed at once in a message to the faculty and students. I needed to let the University community and the public hear from me on what had happened: what had led to my seeking the injunction, what I had hoped it would accomplish, and how my administration planned to deal with the what-ifs.

I could think of no call on my time the next day, Wednesday March 5, more important than addressing the Faculty Senate. I felt that faculty senators had a hand in precipitating March

4 and the events that led up to it, so I decided to speak to the Senate at once, knowing that my words would be relayed to the University community without delay and indeed to the people of Florida. My speech was written during the long night on Tuesday and Wednesday morning.

The essence of that speech to the Senate on Wednesday afternoon follows.

I told the Senate that the confrontation between the SDS students and the law officers of the University and Leon County was one I earnestly sought to avoid. I explained that the rally scheduled for Landis Green that afternoon seemed to have been an attempt to bring about a confrontation as it violated several university regulations. *The Flambeau*, the day before, had reported that the rally scheduled for Landis Green on Tuesday afternoon and the meeting scheduled for the Student Union that evening were sponsored by SDS, and that the room for the meeting would not be checked out by another organization for SDS. Previously, other organizations had reserved rooms for use by the SDS, and I could accept that. The Young Liberals organization, which had reserved the room for the SDS meeting, canceled its reservation about noon on Tuesday.

I reminded the senators that I had asked for a clarification of the Regents' policy on student organizations. I had been moving toward a new policy on the matter, but I did not consider it appropriate for me to establish a new policy pending the clarification that I had requested from the BOR. I told senators that we would follow the Regents' policy for the time being, even though I wasn't really comfortable with it, and that I believed it would be clarified shortly, if not by the BOR, then by an internal review of our policy at FSU.

I explained to the senators that about mid-afternoon on Tuesday, it became clear that the SDS students would conduct Tuesday night's meeting under circumstances I could not accept. So after meeting with the state Attorney General, I made the decision to seek a court injunction, which I regarded as the most orderly and restrained way to proceed. Moreover, it brought into the controversy the laws of Florida and the United States. I told senators that I had hoped for some time that the SDS would have gone to court to make their case as a free speech issue. It was okay for SDS students to meet under the name of another organization, but as an unregistered organization, they could not reserve a room under their own name. That was clear from the Board of Regents policy. I explained that restraining orders are not simply issued upon request, and in this instance the Attorney General had weighed the merits of my request carefully and the judge of the Circuit Court listened carefully to my testimony before issuing the injunction. My actions, I thought, would give the SDS an appropriate legal basis to challenge my decision about their meeting. Doing this would have given SDS members a great deal of space in the newspapers—always one of their goals—and, at the same time, they would have shown respect for due process as the University had done.

My office let it be known during the late afternoon that we had obtained an injunction. I learned that this was widely discussed by the SDS students as they gathered in the Union for their meeting. I was informed that they had considered the matter and decided to deliberately violate the order of the court. And so I told senators my observation seemed irrefutable, that it was a confrontation the SDS wanted, and that freedom of speech, as they claimed, was not the issue.

I said that I doubted that anyone in the University regretted the display of weapons in the confrontation more than I. I pointed out that it was not my prerogative, however, to dictate the means by which the Sheriff carried out his duties, and the Sheriff, like most other law enforcement officers, believes that in crowd control, the display of weapons is a highly effective deterrent. At the same time, I added, the community must feel a sense of relief and gratitude for the professional performance of Sheriff Hamlin and his officers for the plain reason that we had no personal injuries and no property damage; for me, that was a very positive outcome of an unfortunate event. Unlike protests on other campuses, this event at FSU demonstrated that the appearance of outside law enforcement agencies would not always mean that violence must follow. I commended the restrained and responsible sheriff's deputies along with the University's own police officers.

I also commended the President and Vice President of Student Government, Canter Brown and Wayne Rubinas, for helping to distribute copies of the restraining order to those assembled in the Union, and for their attempts to call for restraint. These student leaders, I said, made a selfless and responsible contribution to due process and order on the campus. Before doing so, they had made it clear to me that their efforts should not be interpreted as approval of the actions I had taken regarding the non-recognition of SDS, and I made a special point of telling the senators that such was the case.

I also thought it would be useful to remind members of the Senate about several incidents that had occurred on the campus over the past few weeks as further evidence that the SDS, I believed, was an organization with seriously disruptive purposes. During the latter part of John Champion's tenure, several SDS students occupied a portion of the Love Building and remained there for several hours late one night. The University took no disciplinary action since the timing of their occupation did not interrupt classes. At about the same time, about 30 SDS students entered President Champion's office in response to his agreement to speak to a representative group of four of their members. When the larger group was requested to leave, they refused to do so. The students were warned twice by Vice President Arnold that they were subject to disciplinary action. They did leave, but not before making threats to President Champion against the University. And I added that, on at least two occasions, SDS students had made strong oral threats to me to take over university buildings and equipment if it served their purpose.

It seemed appropriate to mention to senators that while I had seen a statement in the newspapers in which a prominent public figure in Florida had referred to the SDS students as "bums," I indicated that I did not so regard them. While their behavior might have been inimical to the University's welfare and their lifestyles unsettling to some, this did not cause me to regard them as unworthy persons, nor to believe that the University should ever become a conformist agency of society in that sense. We must remember that they—or at least most of them—are our students.

In response to the oft-stated charge that I was responding to pressures from the public, the Board of Regents, or from any number of other people and organizations, I reminded senators that Chancellor Mautz had announced publicly that he had given me only one directive: to run the University as I saw fit, and that's what I was doing. I told senators once again that I intended to express myself to members of the Board of Regents on the question of recognition and registration of student organizations and to remind them that I thought there were points in favor of doing so with SDS.

In closing, I asked the members of the University community via the Faculty Senate to be temperate at a time when temperance might not come easily. I pledged to continue to execute my responsibilities of the office consistent with my own concepts of integrity, democracy, and justice, and I asked senators to do their best to do the same. None of us can do more, I said, and all of us should do no less.

How my speech to the Senate was received, I could not be certain. While I spent time in the next few days meeting with faculty members, including those in the Senate, there were other pressing matters that had to be addressed. Andres Segovia was scheduled to arrive for a concert in a few days, and I was expected to host a dinner for the Segovia party and participate in related events. I had agreed to write a column to appear in *The Flambeau* each week, this as a companion to one to be written by SGA President Canter Brown. There were vacancies left by the resignations of the three vice presidents, and I needed to make certain that their functions were being properly handled and to start the searches for their replacements.

The Resignations

One of my most serious problems was trying to operate with an administration gutted by resignations that had begun in the fall. John Carey's announcement on September 23, 1968, that he would step down from his administrative position on October 1 to resume full-time teaching in FSU's Department of Religion continued to reverberate throughout the University. Carey had become a member of the administration in May 1966, when he was appointed to the post of Dean of Students. He then became the University's first Vice President for Student Affairs when that office was created in 1967. Carey had been a member of the FSU faculty since his appointment to the Department of Religion in 1960, and he also served as University Chaplain.

On the day after Carey's resignation, SGA President Lyman Fletcher issued a lengthy statement characterizing the resignation as "one of the most unfortunate occurrences in the brief history of this University." Fletcher stated that there were behind-the-scenes pressures which forced Carey's resignation. He had made "four errors," Fletcher said, that brought upon him the displeasure of the alumni, the business community, the faculty, and in the end, the President of the University.[3]

Carey's first error, Fletcher said, was attempting to reorganize and modernize a Division of Student Affairs to better accommodate the needs of students. This change forced the retirement of Catharine Warren, who had been Dean of Women since FSCW days, and had "long stood as a symbol of old-line authoritarian control of women students' lives."

Carey's second error had to do with several of his key appointments of people who Fletcher believed did not relate well to the student body and the faculty, especially in the matter of student publications.

In Fletcher's list, Carey's third error was in establishing a Human Relations Committee to investigate complaints of racial discrimination. Fletcher cited one influential business person in Tallahassee, a ranking officer in the Alumni Association, who reportedly said that Carey's appointment of the committee was "proof that he had Communist sympathies."

The fourth error was related to Carey's disagreement with the President's decision on the censorship of "The Pig Knife." When President Champion decided not to take the advice of the special committee on publications, Carey said that he could no longer, in good conscience, represent the position of the administration. The Alumni Association then adopted a resolution stating that those faculty and administrators "who do not accept the views of Dr. John Champion in the exercise of his responsibility [should] seek other employment." Fletcher went on to say that Carey was systematically excluded from the decision-making process and policies and regulations related to student affairs. Fletcher also reported that at a meeting of the alumni, a statement was made that Vice President Chalmers would soon follow Carey in leaving the University, although to my knowledge, no other report of this kind has ever been found. Fletcher's report must be given credence because of his long-standing reputation as a person of integrity and independence. John Carey's public statement that he could no longer in good conscience represent the administration was widely noted on the campus, as he no doubt expected it to be. That statement could not have brought John Champion comfort as he thought about the challenges he had faced during the past year, and in which he was deeply mired in January 1969.

President Champion had not seen the end of resignations

from his administration, nor the fallout that would occur as those resignations were viewed by many in the University community. Vice President Odell Waldby's resignation on February 12 caused more shock waves. Waldby's decision to resign created an immediate problem for Champion in the sense that he did not need to lose another member of his administrative team. Waldby's resignation was troublesome also because of the timing: He wanted to leave at once, and he did so. It also created a problem for the person who was to become President in four more days, for surely a vacancy in another vice presidency was not the way I would have liked to start my administrative duties. In the first week of my tenure, I approached Waldby, hoping that he would remain in office a few more months, until I had the opportunity to get my arms around the job, but he declined to do so.

On February 12, Charles Wellborn, who had succeeded John Carey as Chaplain in 1966, also resigned to return to teaching. While Wellborn was not a member of the central administration, he was nonetheless seen to be part of the Champion team, and his leaving his position was widely viewed as another blow to the beleaguered President.

Everyone to the Stadium

As my fellow administrators and I looked forward to the opening of the fall quarter in 1969, we thought of a way to bring the entire University community together in a first-of-its-kind ceremony. I wanted to demonstrate yet again that this administration was open and available, and an open-air convocation in Campbell Stadium seemed like a good opportunity to meet in a setting in which we could all see and hear one another.

It featured the President's State-of-the-University address, which replaced the traditional fall faculty meeting. The convocation was the wrap-up of an entire day of special student activities including separate meetings with students and faculty members in the University's schools and departments. The convocation opened with a welcome by Professor Dorothy Hoffman, chairwoman of the Professional Relations Committee of the Senate and Distinguished Professor for 1963-64. Welcome was also extended by Student Body President Canter Brown and by Dr. Earl Frieden, Distinguished Professor (1969-70).

My speech summarized events of the past seven months covering the period since I had been appointed Acting President in February. I emphasized several of the University's major achievements during that time, especially the individual accomplishments of several of our faculty. I pointed out that the University had grown in student numbers dramatically in the past five years, and we were projected to grow even more rapidly in the years ahead. I said very little about the campus disturbances because I thought those events were not very significant as we took the long view of the University's growth and what I was sure would be a very bright future.

The convocation seemed to be well received by both students and faculty. Those of us in the administration, on reflection, felt it was a good way to start the new school year—my first as the University's President.

The Role of *The Flambeau*

As much as I might have liked to ignore *The Flambeau*—at least on some days—I could not do so. The paper, as I said earlier, often contained news that I might otherwise have missed. Its editorials sometimes expressed temperate sentiments that I found useful in a variety of ways, most notably in demonstrating to alumni and to legislators and others outside the University that sanity did prevail among most of our students. Letters to the editor were of great interest to me. They provided ways to learn more about the feelings of students with respect to actions by my administration and about the person in the presidency. I was pleased to read letters from students who said they were gratified that the administration had established conditions that enabled them to go to class and pursue the educational goals for which they came to Florida State. Student Will Bray Adams wrote, "As you calmly position yourself between the disruptive elements and the dedicated students, I feel a compelling urge to come join you...And so Dr. Marshall, you fight the battles and I'll fight the books. But if things at the front get too rough, you can count on me (and I hope many others) to pitch in beside you."[4]

One benefit of the letters feature was the emotional venting I believed it provided to some students. If they were among those who believed changes were needed in the way the University was run—or indeed the country—writing an angry letter to the editor might have released some of their fury. From my vantage point, that was better than facing another angry group on the campus. From the perspective of the University's acting president, who was attempting to maintain reasonable order on the campus while assuring everyone that there would be no abridgment of anyone's First Amendment rights, the paper sometimes seemed to surrender to the most extreme elements. There were, for example, editorials and major news stories in *The Flambeau* nearly every day during February and March; they wrote about the "administrative crises," or the "massive round of housecleaning," or the "shuffles and shakeups," or the "strange days" in Westcott or the "strange men" who run the University. There were other examples of the seeming lack of objectivity.

In early February 1970, *The Flambeau* carried an editorial condemning Champion for having appointed John Arnold as Vice President for Student Affairs shortly before he resigned without adequate advice from the students. "If Florida State is to become a great university," wrote *Flambeau* managing editor Gary Smith, "it is mandatory that administrators recognize students as mature adults." My response, if I had been asked, would have been to say that students' advice had been sought in all such appointments, but repeated demands by *The Flambeau* calling for the students to occupy the central role in the appointment of university officials was one I could not accept, and I knew would not be acceptable to the Board of Regents. Why not? Because those demands went beyond a role that would have been seriously considered by any university that I could imagine. Smith seemed to demand that students be given veto power over any and all appointments. He failed to take into account the fact that our students are here for a relatively brief period as the University's history goes; many undergraduates are here for fewer than four years; many come to FSU after completing two years of study at a community college. As for graduate students, most have educational and career goals that preclude heavy involvement in campus politics. On the same day that he demanded more authority for students in university affairs, Smith wrote that Chalmers was leaving "a University beset with political interference, a strong reaction against change and a budget insufficient to maintain the level of educational quality to become a great University." Editor Smith, it should be noted, had been in that position for only a few weeks. I did not question his motivation for making such statements, but I did feel he lacked the knowledge and the maturity of judgment needed to make such a pronouncement.

But *The Flambeau* had other editors and at times they took positions on campus issues that also deserve mention. During his tenure as editor, George Waas was often sympathetic to some of the student protests, and in particular he believed the SDS should be recognized as a student organization. Despite his support for their recognition, Waas was able to see that the SDS was using the issue as a ploy to gain attention for myriad other causes, and he said so. In a January 15 editorial he called for his fellow students to temper their penchant for protests. "At a time when student unrest has become the rationale for 'dissent by demonstration,'" Waas cautioned, "it is important

to consider a vital requirement for student power. It is STU-
DENT RESPONSIBILITY." The editorial went on to address
an incident that had occurred a few days prior, when Vice
President Arnold tried to make an address and was shouted
down by students. "Recognizing that one of the fundamental
rights of a democratic society is freedom of speech, is it not
the denial of that right when a speaker is subject to such
beratement?" Waas chastised. The editorial concludes, "Student responsibility must be exercised before student power
can result."[5]

The Flambeau published an editorial that reminded all of
us just how well intentioned and motivated many students
were, and what a positive role *The Flambeau* could play. Again
stressing the role of student responsibility in a respectful and
functional campus environment, Waas wrote the following
about the protests and arrests at the Arthur Goldberg speech:
"A few students dropped that mantle of responsibility and allowed their emotions to rule over their reason and logic." Waas
went on to observe, "There is no denying that we live in
troubled times in which the college student is calling into question many of the truths and values which have become an
integral part of our tradition—and which heretofore have been
accepted as rote without questioning. There is no denying that
peaceful dissent over inequitable rule of law is healthy in that
it promotes the exchange of many varied ideas as to ways of
resolving the difficulties affecting our daily lives." He concluded, "When violence rears its ugly head, dissent only serves
to antagonize, irritate and crystallize opposition when support
is needed. In short, violence serves no constructive purpose."[6]

I could not have agreed more with these sentiments. Peaceful dissent by citizens was a lesson I hoped they would learn
during their student days, one that would be a good rule to
follow throughout their lives.

CHAPTER 4
A Troubled Campus

The SDS issue was only one of many I would deal with in that first year of my presidency. The year 1969 was the high tide of student radicalism, and a great many campuses had been besieged by their own students, and their presidents had been backed into a corner over myriad issues. Florida State University did not exist in a vacuum; certainly, those upheavals greatly influenced public opinion about the unrest on our campus as they influenced the students both for and against the protesters.

In light of the general climate in higher education nationally, I felt compelled to act cautiously but firmly, resolving not to let FSU become part of the growing body of statistics of protest-related violence.

Spring and Fall 1969

Stephen Parr, in his FSU Department of History doctoral dissertation describes the first six months of 1969 as a "violent period for the SDS and the student Left in general, a fact that convinced many radicals that revolution was imminent." There were violent student uprisings at San Francisco State and again at UC-Berkeley. During the first half of the year there were 292 protests at 232 institutions, with 24 percent involving violence. There were 84 incidents involving bombing or arson, one at UC-Santa Barbara resulting in the death of a custodian.[1]

While the administration at FSU did not really believe violence of that kind would occur here—at least, we fervently hoped it wouldn't—I believed that we were obliged to view the threat seriously and to take reasonable precautions to prevent disruption and violence. It was widely understood that the FSU SDS group looked to universities on the west coast, especially UC-Berkeley, as models of protest, and it seemed reasonable to believe that they would like to see FSU become "Berkeley East."[2]

Meanwhile, the SDS at Florida State. . .

In April, I was invited to appear at an open rally in front of Westcott "to learn more about SDS." The SDS members reacted by booing and showering me with obscenities until I stepped aside. Phil Sanford led the chorus by shouting, "Marshall, get the hell away!" This performance by SDS brought criticism from *The Flambeau*, which accused SDS of hypocrisy and applying a double standard, demanding that SDS have freedom of speech, but denying it to the administration.[3]

Also in April the university sponsored a Symposium on Student Unrest attended by John Lawrence of CBS and Anson Mount of *Playboy* magazine. I decided to participate along with members of the faculty and student government. SDS, at the last minute, decided to boycott the event and seized the resulting publicity as an opportunity to distribute a statement that set forth the group's political positions and to criticize severely the media for being "controlled by a few corporate conglomerates." The media's function, the SDS said, was to "pacify and deaden social awareness of the American people by mesmerizing them with meaningless entertainment." The SDS statement also attempted to justify their disruptive tactics: "It is a basic principle that at a certain point an oppressive government should be overturned by the majority of the people. It follows that if the development of a subversive majority is blocked by organized repression and indoctrination, it may be necessary to employ apparently undemocratic means so that genuine free speech can emerge", in other words, armed revolt.[4]

One of the SDS's major demonstrations occurred later in April when some 40 members disrupted a meeting of the

AAUP* in the auditorium of the Education Building. I had advance information provided by disenchanted former SDS members that a disruption was planned. As I attempted to open the meeting, I was interrupted by students chanting "ROTC off campus!" and shouting that university officials were "fascist, racist and imperialist." As the disruption proceeded, I shouted for attention, and standing on a chair, I read a cease and desist order I had prepared for use if needed. I warned protesters that they were subject to immediate arrest and suspension from the University. They left the room and continued their protest out on the lawn. The meeting was attended, at my invitation, by Chancellor Mautz, Malcolm Johnson, editor of the *Tallahassee Democrat*, and several members of the Florida Legislature. I apologized to the group on behalf of the majority of FSU students who would not consider the protesters to represent them. The next day the Legislature voted into the general appropriations bill a proviso that would deny state funds to any student or university employee who advocated violent overthrow of the government or the university administration.[5]

The Flambeau again criticized the SDS stating that it had greatly damaged its case for recognition. Other students and faculty members also spoke critically of SDS; student Michael B. Frost wrote in *The Flambeau* that the SDS's version of democracy was "closer to that of the communists with their dictatorship of the elite with the sole possession of the truth."[6]

The SDS was but one agent of the radical campus activism; there were other groups that looked to the SDS as the pace car for protest. There was increased militancy by several segments of the student population as the late sixties gave way to the early seventies. At FSU, black students formed the Black Student Union (BSU)—the first in the State University

---

*The American Association of University Professors (AAUP) is a professional organization of college and university faculty members. Its primary mission is to represent the collective interests of the faculty on the campus of each member institution.

System—and began to press for black studies courses and other changes in academic programs. They objected to what they regarded as racist policies and demanded more black faculty and staff. These issues are more fully discussed in Chapter Five.

The Silent Majority

The San Francisco State strike, described by Parr as one of the longest and most violent student strikes in U.S. history wound down nearly four months after it began. Thanks to the strong stance of President S.I. Hayakawa, there seemed to be a change of attitude among college and university administrators and even some students. Hayakawa's determination to keep San Francisco State functioning and to restore order seemed to strengthen the resolve of administrators and students across the nation who were growing tired of the student Left's attempts to disrupt university operations.

At Florida State, a student organization known as the Silent Majority emerged to take up the growing support among students for a return to order. While FSU's Night of the Bayonets certainly was not the equal of San Francisco State's four-month-long student siege, the reaction on the two campuses was similar: a great many moderates and moderately liberal students grew weary of the New Left's antics.

In early May the Silent Majority also known as the "98 Percenters," was founded by two students—business majors Sid Raehn and John Gersheim—who described their goal as simply to show support for Acting President Marshall and his handling of the recent events involving the SDS. They mounted a petition campaign that they hoped would result in the BOR appointing Marshall as president. They also became strong opponents of campus disorder, stating that 98 percent of the student body agreed with them. The Silent Majority generated heated editorials and letters in *The Flambeau*, with some writers questioning their motives. While I appreciated their expression of support, I wanted to make it clear that I had no part in organizing or directing the group, so I asked that my name not be used in connection with their efforts. Football Coach Bill Peterson and various community leaders spoke up to offer support. Upon completing their stated goal of collecting petitions expressing support for the acting president, the Silent Majority voluntarily disbanded. The petition with some 6,000 signatures was submitted to the BOR as an endorsement of my actions.[7]

The Westcott Fire

Amidst the metaphorical fires that seemed occasionally to engulf the University, an honest-to-goodness fire broke out in one of the most sacred buildings at the University.

Students and faculty members of this period seem to have vivid memories of the burning of Westcott, which occurred on Sunday afternoon, April 27, 1969. I've been asked about it many times in the years since.

I've been asked: Was it arson? With all the radicals on campus and the talk about closing down the University, the fire must have been set—right? Well, I was reluctant to put down a rumor with such great promise for the news media, but a myth is a myth, and to the best of our knowledge, this was one. Our own investigation, along with that of the Tallahassee Fire Department, revealed no smoking match. The best guess—and it was not much more than that—was that the fire was electrical in origin, and it started in the rooms occupied by the Art Department on the fourth floor. That area was at the top of the building and really was sort of an attic, just under the roof. We found no evidence to suggest arson, and the character of the University's students really shone through in this crisis.

I was attending a swimming outing at the home of faculty member Phil Leamon when campus security found me. I jumped from my swimsuit into a pair of shorts—the only other garments I had with me—and headed for the campus. The fire trucks had just arrived and were hosing down the upper floors. Smoke was pouring out of the windows on several floors, and it seemed that the entire building would be consumed.

My attention turned immediately to the need to remove priceless equipment and documents from the building. Volunteers, mostly students, but some townspeople and I'm sure faculty members, were already carrying objects from the building. An area getting a good bit of water and smoke—it was directly under the fire—was the suite of offices occupied by the president and his staff, and I remembered that my desk contained some important and sensitive papers. I summoned the closest officer I saw, and the two of us raced up to the second floor offices where we found my desk, locked of course, but my keys were not in those Bermuda shorts. The officer with me was Deputy Larry Campbell (who was later elected sheriff of Leon County), and Deputy Campbell found a fireman's axe with which we quickly dismantled my desk; we then gathered up two armfuls of papers and made our way through the smoke and dripping water downstairs and out of the building. Sheriff Campbell and I have made lighthearted references to that adventure many times over the years past, each of us questioning the sanity of the other.

In *The Flambeau* the next morning, both SGA President Canter Brown and I issued statements on the fire. The essence of both was to express sadness on the loss of a historic University building and to express our admiration and thanks to those who had performed so heroically in salvaging valuable items, including one Rubens painting, the value of which was estimated at $30,000. Canter Brown's statement will be included in part here because it reveals in a new and different setting the complex attitude he and some other student leaders had about those stressful times. He wrote:

Yesterday at Westcott proved something about the

student body of Florida State. Charges from outraged citizens and State Legislators have flown back and forth for the past several months that today's students do not care for their school; that they only want to cause trouble. Politicians have used this as an excuse to appeal to voter sympathy by passing ridiculous repressive legislation under the guise of "law and order."

Hundreds of FSU students risked their lives to save art treasures, vital records, and expensive equipment. The state and university were saved considerable expense, and in some case irreplaceable loss, by their actions.

No one can say those students were acting for their own gain—only Florida State stood to gain. And Florida State did gain. The actions of her students were exemplary and an honor to her. They defy any politician to exploit them.[8]

While I appreciated much of what Brown had written, I regretted his using this unfortunate incident as an opportunity to take another swipe at our legislators. That did not help to restore the respect of each for the other that I had been trying to foster between the campus and the Legislature. Nor did Brown's remarks take into account a joint resolution of the House and Senate praising our students who risked personal injury to save priceless objects.

The damage to the building was such that the interior had to be substantially gutted. We took satisfaction in being able to preserve the exterior walls and the façade of this wonderful old building that contained so much history.

The administrative offices moved at once to new quarters in the University Health Center.* How the medical staff, their equipment and their patients could accommodate us I still

---

*The Health Center was later renamed the Thagard Health Center in honor of FSU graduate and astronaut, Norman Thagard.

don't know, but we operated out of that building and the Engineering Science Building for the next four years while Westcott was being restored.

The Anti-War Movement

The anti-war movement, the SDS protests, and student unrest are often used interchangeably in casual conversation about the period. While it is true that the ranks of the anti-war movement often attracted SDS organizers, and important changes in U.S. foreign policy were major objectives of SDS, getting America out of Vietnam had a broader appeal on most campuses than did the SDS's calls for revolution.

The loss of life by Americans in the Vietnam War—nearly 10,000 died during 1969—encouraged students on many campuses to engage actively in protests. The two major events of the fall were the Vietnam Moratorium Day in October and the National Mobilization to End the War (MOBE) a month later. At FSU, the Vietnam Moratorium was more successful than the MOBE rally. The Vietnam Moratorium Committee (VMC) was chaired by Student Government Vice President Wayne Rubinas, and the program was marked by a broad coalition of student support from moderate and liberal factions. Activities in 1969 got underway on Tuesday evening, October 14 with a march that originated on Landis Green at 8:00 p.m. and attracted some 3,000 people, of whom 200 students slept on Landis Green that night. The next day, October 15, Vietnam Moratorium Day was given over to several campus activities starting with a mass rally on Landis Green at 10:00 a.m., with speeches by student and faculty leaders. This was followed by a panel discussion moderated by Professor Tom Dye of the Department of Government, with participation by faculty members of the widest range of political persuasions. There followed an ecumenical religious service with Jewish, Catholic, and Protestant representatives taking part. An evening sing-in was held on Landis Green, featuring several well known, out-of-town musical groups. Throughout Tuesday night and Wednesday the names of those killed in the war were read aloud, with over 300 students taking part. I had received requests from various faculty and student groups asking that classes be cancelled for the day. I declined to take that action but left the decision about classes and what should be said about the Vietnam War to individual professors. Later, Sheriff Hamlin joined me in congratulating students for their peaceful, orderly demonstration.

A Tale of Two Revolutionaries

In 1969, the two most conspicuous radicals on campus were Jack Lieberman and Phil Sanford. These two were both widely recognized around campus, and they played a major role in SDS activities and in the anti-war movement generally. And while the two were often seen together and could often be found at student protests, their personalities were markedly different.

Jack Lieberman was, in most ways, an unlikely student to become the poster boy for the radicals. He came to FSU in September 1968 and enrolled in courses in our general studies program, appearing to be headed for a major in history. Jack's family had moved from Philadelphia to Miami Beach, where he graduated from Norland High. As it turned out, Jack's "major" at FSU was fomenting unrest; he specialized in challenging authority and tormenting whomever was in charge. I thought of him as the quintessential student protestor—one who believed the world was a cruel and dehumanizing place and that his job was to do something about it. His disruptive activities seemed to me to be essentially non-violent. I thought that he was often uncomfortable with the mantle of leadership that had been thrust upon him, mostly by the media. When I inquired along with others then and since as to how he came to be known as "Radical Jack," no one seemed to know, but the media picked it up (or maybe it was they who invented it) and early in the protests, he became, in the glare of the publicity the demonstrations attracted, the leading figure in the FSU protests. He was no doubt encouraged to be out front by those around him, principally the Phil Sanford group who used Jack to serve their purposes, which I believed were not always the same as his.

One campus meeting has remained vivid in my memory. I had left Westcott and was walking alone down Ivy Way when I saw Jack directly ahead of me, approaching from the other direction. We recognized each other at some distance and I remember seeing his familiar dimpled smile. I moved to extend my hand and began my "Hi, Jack" greeting and reached for Jack's extended right hand. I had noticed Phil Sanford walking with Jack to his right, and as we came to close range and I reached for his hand, Phil grabbed Jack's right arm at the elbow and pulled it back, preventing the greeting we both intended. That small incident revealed an important difference between Radical Jack and Phil Sanford.

By his second year here, Lieberman had gained notoriety as a major force within the SDS and the Committee for Immediate Action (CIA); indeed he missed few opportunities to join in whatever happened to be the protest *du jour*. The national SDS had even tapped Jack to be part of its peace delegation to travel to Vietnam.

Sanford, 28, was several years older than Lieberman and older than many of the students participating in the demonstrations. He came to the University from Australia as a philosophy graduate student. He was married and his wife, though not a student, was also a campus activist and, by her admission, a "Marxist-Leninist."

Sanford Goes Home

Lieberman and Sanford were arrested in mid-May 1969, along with other students, for harassing a military recruiter in the student union. Campus Police Chief Bill Tanner and I received word of the disturbance, and we both proceeded to the scene where we observed Sanford engaging in disruptive behavior. Sanford was at this time not registered as a student and therefore was regarded as a trespasser. After he ignored three warnings to cease and desist, he was arrested.[9] The University initially took action also to suspend Lieberman, but the student courts opposed the suspension and it was put on hold. Sanford's arrest helped to make the case for his later deportation. Sanford was arrested again a short time later at another disturbance.

Those arrests and suspensions served to further polarize students and probably some faculty into pro- and anti-Marshall forces. Following the announcement of the suspensions, several hundred students rallied on Landis Green and drew up lists of demands to present to the President; these included dropping all charges against those who had been arrested. After drawing up the list, the protesters moved to the lawn of the University Health Center, where my office was housed following the Westcott fire. They sent a delegation to present me with their demands and then held an all-night vigil on the lawn waiting for my reply. The next morning, I responded by recognizing their petition but acceding to none of their demands. A number of students then marched to the Health Center and attempted to check into the infirmary with the complaint that "I am sick to my stomach of Stanley Marshall."[10] I responded to these incidents with a written statement on May 19. In my statement I explained that the University must always take measures to protect and defend freedom to debate, to advocate and dissent on all manner of issues. It follows then that "the breaches of laws and regulations on the university campus...violate the very essence of the academic spirit;" thus such violations "must be met with the full application of academic discipline and, where necessary, the law."[11]

Phil Sanford had been convicted in Leon County court of disorderly conduct and interfering with police officers in the line of duty during the disturbance in the Union in March. During Sanford's trial, police officers testified that he enticed students to cross police lines and obstruct the arrests. A six-person jury found Sanford guilty and on June 3, Judge James Gwynn sentenced him to 12 months for interfering with police officers and six months for disorderly conduct. After the jury read the verdict, Sanford raised his fist in the courtroom and shouted "Power to the People."[12]

The United States Immigration and Naturalization Service had considered Sanford's case in a special hearing on May 28 to decide whether he should be deported back to Australia for violations of his exchange student visa. He was ordered deported. In the administration, we noted that Sanford had not registered for classes for the spring quarter of 1969—the time when he was most actively involved in disruption. His faculty adviser, David Gruender, head of the Department of Philosophy and also a member of the Faculty Senate Steering Committee, attracted the attention of the Registrar's office and my staff when Gruender testified that he had given Sanford permission to drop out of school for one quarter to make up work in courses that he had not completed; and Professor Gruender approved his readmission for the summer quarter. The INS attorney said that Sanford had dropped out of school because he was spending most of his time running a Maoist bookstore in Tallahassee, an activity surely not covered by his student visa. Sanford denied the allegation. To this charge, Gruender had no comment. I was asked by INS whether as University President I would make a special appeal to delay or cancel Sanford's deportation order. I'm sure it came as no surprise to many people in Florida that I declined to do so. Sanford spent seven days in the Leon County jail while his lawyer appealed to the INS in Washington, but he withdrew his appeal on June 9 and accepted deportation rather than serve the 18-month jail sentence.

On many occasions, Sanford had been described as a Communist. On June 11, before the Sanfords left the United States, Sanford's wife Isabel explained that she and her husband were "Marxist-Leninist." She said that they were not really Communists, claiming that they were instead part of an international movement to destroy the capitalist system. Back home in Australia, Sanford publicly stated, "They have this outside agitator myth in the South...and they can't stand any criticism of their racist, imperialist policies."[13]

The departure of Phil Sanford left a vacancy in SDS at FSU that was never really filled, though John Duffield, another student protester, was named as his successor. There were some others who called on the SDS name as they engaged in whatever protests suited their tastes. But after 1969, SDS at the national level was clearly in decline. The organization was torn by deep internal strife, and the competition for leadership was intense. The decline of SDS is told in Chapter Five.

The Office of University General Counsel

It will surely come as no surprise to perceptive readers that the office of the President had a desperate need for a lawyer. I had, of course, spent many hours with Tallahassee lawyers, sometimes in official meetings and sometimes in informal conversations, as I looked for reasonable ways to deal with problems that earlier presidents had never faced. I knew of no other university presidents who had full-time lawyers, so I had no precedents to guide me. Nonetheless, the need for a good lawyer to fill the general counsel role had to be taken seriously. The Board of Regents agreed, and I received permission to fill the position.

The FSU presidents before me rarely thought about using the services of an attorney in the day-to-day execution of their offices. It was a university they were administering, not a for-profit business or a government agency. Most of the decisions they made were academic in nature, and dealing with courts, injunctions, and litigation was not part of the job description. That changed abruptly and profoundly in the '60s.

The law came to define academic and student life in ways never before imagined. This change resulted both from events on the campuses and from a growing awareness among students and faculty of their freedoms as members of the university community and as citizens. The Civil Rights Act of 1964 had an immediate and enduring influence on higher education and special effects on universities in the South. Many university administrators in the region felt that students should curtail racial protests in deference to the university's *de facto* position which was to avoid trouble with local government authorities. The federal courts responded and changes in admissions policies for black students were soon adopted. The resistance to *Brown vs. Board of Education* was not a proud era for many Southern universities, and some would later regret their actions, or inactions, as the case may be.

Students at FSU were deeply involved in the national debate over war and civil rights. Those of us in the administration saw the need for a lawyer—a full-time University General Counsel—to address a vision of the University as a constitutional entity in a way that was shaping the future of higher education law.

Robert Bickel was my choice as the person to serve as our first general counsel, and it was an easy choice. He was the number one graduate in the FSU Law School's first class of graduates in 1968, and in 1972, he was on the legal staff of the Department of Justice in Washington. During the interview with Bickel, it became clear to me that he had the kind of tough, inquisitive mind that the times required.

The demands of groups beyond the campus were a task that occupied the general counsel and the president often. One of the most demanding groups was comprised of Florida legislators. Any state university must live with the ever-present attitude by state legislators that they have a right to help run the place. And in a sense they do if you accept the time-honored place of voters in a democracy. When legislators' constituents speak, they listen; and constituents very often have opinions about how the universities they help to pay for should be run. If that relationship holds true generally, it holds in spades for universities located in state capitals.

Were we approached by legislators who thought we should stop or at least strictly control the student protests? Of course, we were. Our job was to meet such political demands with the respect due the legislators, while at the same time providing a vigorous defense of free speech and academic freedom on the campus. Our stance at FSU was in a real sense futuristic, as the rulings of the Supreme Court had yet to emerge. When they did emerge, they vindicated our defense of the Constitution and sustained the university's image as a true marketplace of political thought and expression.

Senator Robert Haverfield, who chaired the Senate Higher Education Committee, led many of the get-tough-with-the-dissenters charges, but others would occasionally join in and introduce bills. Bill Young from St. Petersburg, who has been a distinguished U.S. Congressman since 1970, was then in the Florida Senate, and he introduced six separate bills that I neither wanted nor needed. Senator Mallory Horne of Tallahassee made statements detesting "the hippies' long hair and dirty words," as did Senator William Barrow of Crestview. Senator Dempsey Barron from Panama City was a Florida cracker and a staunch Southern conservative who was for several years the Florida Senate's most powerful member. While he was viewed by many at the University as an advocate for sterner student discipline measures, this view of Barron was mistaken. He seemed to understand the campus issues, including the need for the University to advance the interests of black students. I regretted that he was so often misunderstood and unappreciated by many on our faculty.

When it came time to respond to requests from legislators

that we get tough with protesting students, Bickel was a shrewd counselor. We tried to state our position politely but firmly: You (legislators) have seen no one on our campus get hurt, no significant property damage, no interference with the orderly processes of education, and the authority of the President has never been successfully challenged. What more could you expect? And please note (again, to legislators) that in all of this there has been no instance of anyone's freedom of speech being abridged. We've respected that most sacred document, the Constitution of the United States; and if we hadn't, how could we face the people of Florida and honestly claim to be a university?

The close alliance between the university president and the general counsel is now seen to be all but indispensable in most universities. Lawyers must be involved in the contractual and regulatory aspects of federally funded research, in equal opportunity matters, in employment and admissions, and campus safety and security issues.

Not everyone in the academic community is enamored of the prominent place lawyers now have in university governance. Occasional critics among the faculty have emerged, often claiming that lawyers have too prominent a role in decision-making. Those involved in the administration of higher education would do well to counter such claims and to respond vigorously to attempts—well-meaning but often misplaced—to neutralize the role of the university's legal counsel.

My work with General Counsel Bickel evolved into a close, mutually respectful relationship that helped to guide the policies of the administration through this period. Bob Bickel was a man of well-founded principle: He seemed to know how my office should respond to most of the disruptions, and he was skillful with words—he could help craft just the right legal language to describe our policies to the media and legislators. His cordial relations with student groups and individual student leaders helped to establish our credibility—in other words, they trusted him. It can be said that Bob Bickel's counsel was important in preserving order and guaranteeing freedom to all, and his efforts surely helped to prevent damage to property and injuries to people on the FSU campus.

The President's Special Assistant For Equal Opportunity

With the tumult that swept the nation in the sixties and seventies, providing equal educational opportunity for students and equal opportunity in hiring and promotion for staff members became a major challenge for the University administration. Opportunities that were decidedly unequal kept appearing at a disturbing rate and demanded the President's attention. I noted the progress on race in other segments of the social order—most notably the public schools—and I felt uneasy about what seemed like foot-dragging in higher education, including, unfortunately, my own University. While there were a few institutions in higher education that were developing forward-looking, well-reasoned efforts, there weren't many. By 1972, the situation at FSU required that something be done, and a solution, with the good fortune that often seemed to characterize my administration, appeared.

Dr. Freddie Groomes, who was then Director of Institutional Research at Florida A&M, called me to express her interest in coming to FSU and creating an office that would set the course in race relations and give day-to-day direction to our efforts in "affirmative action" (a suitable name for the program, but one that would soon become politically tainted). She was to report directly to the President, she would be a member of the senior administrative group, and I let it be known to the administrators—meaning vice-presidents, deans, and department heads—that we had embarked on a new course in opportunities for minorities.

FSU was the first university in the State University System to establish such an office, and our decision was noted by the Board of Regents and the other universties. Dr. Groomes's office became the model for the system, and the FSU program was the impetus in 1974 for the establishment of the State University Coordinator For Equal Opportunity who reported to the Chancellor. Minority student enrollment at FSU in the years following was considerably larger than at any of the other state universities.

The U.S. Department of Education (DOE) had taken an aggressive stance on equal opportunity for students and the Department's Office For Civil Rights established goals for colleges and universities. In DOE's first institutional evaluation, the top three universities in the country were FSU, Harvard, and MIT. No, they did not rank order those three.

Dr. Groomes continued to provide sound leadership in race matters throughout my presidency and for at least a decade thereafter.

CHAPTER 5
SDS: Its Origins, Influence and Decline

Students for a Democratic Society (SDS) attracted more attention on the FSU campus during 1969 and 1970 than either its numbers or its programs might have warranted. The same was true on the national scene, where news stories and editorial comment in newspapers all across the country gave the impression that SDS was a large and powerful organization. The facts are that the organization had modest membership and a limited role in the broad national movement to advance student rights and participatory democracy. But that did not mean that SDS was not a major disruptive force on many campuses, for indeed it was. In this chapter we will look carefully at the SDS—at its origins, its programs, and the feelings it generated on the campuses and with the press and the public.

The SDS at FSU managed to muscle its way into many of the protests and demonstrations in ways that generated headlines throughout the state and made believers of many on campus. In the early days, I followed the course of the organization's activities on other campuses and developed a genuine apprehension about the members' ability to be disruptive, so whether or not SDS had real power as a national organization was somewhat irrelevant to me. The organization created sufficient disturbance on our campus through its always dramatic protests, demanding enough of my time and attention to be in fact a force to be reckoned with.

The disturbances caused by SDS and other closely related student groups also occurred elsewhere in the state university system. At the University of Florida, the Southern Students Organizing Committee (SSOC) sought to be recognized by the University, but was not successful. SSOC representatives announced that they had dropped their SDS affiliation, but University authorities seemed not to believe them. The SDS name conjured up images of militant protests, including in the halls of Congress. Representative Richard Ichord of Missouri, Chairman of the House Committee on Un-American Activities, said that the first order of business for his committee would be to investigate SDS. He said he was concerned about reports of the increasing militancy of the organization and its conduct of classes in sabotage, how to make Molotov cocktails, and violent guerrilla tactics.[1]

At the SDS annual convention in January 1969, the organization moved to broaden its membership by moving into high schools, trade schools and the armed forces. Bernadine Dorn, Inter-Organizational Secretary, said that high schools would be the main thrust of their efforts and that they are nothing more than "baby-sitting jails."

The SDS role in the uprising at Columbia University in 1968 was followed by continuing threats of violence there and at other Eastern universities.

Carl Davidson, an earlier Inter-Organizational Secretary, had spelled out the organization's goals with respect to military recruiting on the campuses. He announced that the SDS must stop military recruiting: "We have to stop that even if it means going to the point of suppressing what is an organically democratic point of view... they have to be fought by whatever means we have to do it... as long as the institutions have authority in the eyes of the people that are underneath them, people will not move against those institutions. The institutions have to be stripped of their sanctity, so that they reveal that they are nothing but naked power... the university in this society is a service station, a developer of manpower for capitalism."[2]

On the FSU campus, SDS pressed hard for powers that would have transformed the University. One of the demands it made on President Champion in January 1969 was the following: "Faculty-student committees, must be given powers to hire and fire faculty and administrators, plan courses, and adjudicate individual faculty-student disputes."[3]

While I did not spend the time or the effort then to learn about the origins of SDS, I have found it of sufficient interest now to justify some research in the preparation of this book. Readers who recall the ways SDS became newsworthy in 1969 and 1970 may share my interest in its history.

As an organizational entity, SDS was born in 1962, but its origins go back to the latter part of the 19th century. The anarchists of those years and the Bolsheviks of the early 20th century formed what became the stereotypical student protester of the 1960s. Organizations such as the Intercollegiate Socialist Society and the League for Industrial Democracy back then trained young disciples on college campuses to work for "participatory democracy." They urged students to participate in the administration of the universities, involve workers in the management of factories, and undertake efforts to overthrow "the establishment." Use of student protesters as "detonators" in revolutionary circles was not a new idea, but it found new opportunities on the campuses in the 1960s.

The organization's founding document—the Port Huron Statement—was drafted at the first SDS convention at Port Huron, Michigan in 1962. It's an idealistic document that calls for the New Left to transform society; it rails against the apathy of the people and cries out against their helplessness and indifference. Its tenets spawned violence on many university campuses as students were seduced by the Port Huron promises. It became the holy writ for student members and an important recruiting tool.

The principal author of the statement was Tom Hayden, then a student at the University of Michigan—the same Tom Hayden who later married Jane Fonda, the famous anti-Vietnam War activist. Hayden made no secret of his revolutionary intentions. Gregory Calvert, the national secretary for SDS, reflected the revolutionary character of the organization in 1967 when he said, "We are working to build a guerrilla force in an urban environment. We are actively organizing sedition."[4]

In 1969, the SDS proclaimed a role for the organization that concerned many Americans and surely those who were trying to limit their activities and their influence on the campuses. In March at their national meeting in Austin, Texas, national secretary Mike Klonsky identified the organization's primary task as "building a Marxist-Leninist revolutionary movement" and advanced his plan to transform the movement into a working class youth movement. He proposed sending groups of students into major industrial centers to take summer jobs and influence the worker's movement in a revolutionary direction. Revolutionary Youth Movement (RYM) also used its strength to pass a resolution identifying the black liberation movement as the most advanced element of the U.S. revolution and the Black Panther party as the vanguard of that movement. At about this time, the SDS attempted to establish links with other revolutionaries elsewhere in the world, including the German SDS, Vietnamese groups in Paris and Hanoi, Arab guerrillas in the Middle East, and some of the Cuban leaders.

In June 1969, the SDS began to split apart. The two factions were the Progressive Labor (PL) and RYM, and they had members on various campuses including Florida State.* The RYM attempted to counter PL's influence in the South by sending representatives on speaking tours, including both Florida State and the University of Florida. Secretary Mike Klonsky

---

*The PL was the Progressive Labor faction, and it was a Maoist organization whose objective was a working-class revolution. In light of this, the PL sought for students to make alliances with workers to further the cause of revolution. The RYM was the Revolutionary Youth Movement, and it identified "the youth" as a distinct class and hoped to awaken middle- and working-class youth to be the vanguard in a violent revolution. The RYM was more closely allied with the black liberation movement.

spoke to some 200 students at FSU on April 10 on the lawn of the Bellamy Building, predicting that the South would soon resume its "historical role as a focal point of protest."[5] Klonsky called on students to reject middle class affluence and also the hippie lifestyle in favor of a true communist revolution. Tension between the two branches of SDS continued, arousing fear among authorities on several campuses.

Protests at FSU continued. At a demonstration at an Army recruiter's table in the Union on May 14 of the same year Sanford was arrested for "profane, inflammatory, and obscene language."[8] Several days later, SDS activist Rick Johnson was arrested for a similar offense. Officers also arrested SDS member Sue Brasswell for interfering with police officers when she tried to pull Sanford out of a police car in which he had been placed. Other students kicked the car and stood on its hood. These arrests and related incidents caused a sizable uproar on campus, and caused students and some faculty members to join pro- and anti-Marshall forces.

In late May, protesting students and faculty formed a new organization—the Committee Against Repression (CARE)—that included radical students but also some liberal elements. CARE held a teach-in on May 19, and the following day, they held a March to the Capitol by some 400 students to present demands to the Governor and the legislature. A line of highway patrolmen formed a menacing presence in front of the Capitol. The crowd began to cheer "Lock up Hamlin," "Lock up Campbell!" and "Put Tanner away!" as an expression of its opposition to the police.[6] A series of speeches was given by CARE members, some faculty members, and SDS representatives as well.

These activities by students angered many in Florida, as might have been expected. Still, I am mildly shocked today to read the vehement news reports and especially the editorials on SDS at FSU in the state's newspapers of that time. The *Orlando Sentinel's* views were similar to those of many other papers.

In an editorial on January 15, 1969, *The Sentinel* wrote:

> THE FIRST – and somewhat mild – effort at
> disrupting the Florida State campus came last year in
> a silly ruckus over the use of four letter words in a
> college literary magazine.
>
> A few immature students and some other equally
> naïve teachers... forced the resignation of FSU's
> President John Champion.
>
> The people of the state led by 40,000 Central
> Floridians who responded to a *Sentinel* petition en-
> couraged Champion to change his decision. The cur-
> rent episode appears far more serious.
>
> The FSU administration must stand firm. It must
> continue to refuse to sanction the SDS. And it
> should expel promptly and permanently anyone who
> joins in the disruption of the normal campus life.[7]

The determination of the SDS students to have their chapter approved as a registered student organization could not be
ignored. The same week that the *Sentinel* editorial appeared
(January 12-18, 1969), the University requested an opinion
from Attorney General Earl Faircloth as to whether FSU officials were required to recognize SDS as a campus organization. President Champion (he would remain president for another month) first asked University Chancellor Robert Mautz
for an opinion, but Mautz referred the question to the Attorney General. The request was made after some 200 students
demonstrated outside of the Westcott building demanding that
the administration recognize the organization. *The Flambeau*
editorialized: "Some of the SDS's demands (a most unfortunate word) aren't legitimate: others are mere 'scatter gunning'
efforts to include many of the moral and ethical problems affecting the entire nation." The editorial continued, "If SDS is

desirous of seeking solutions to some of its listed demands, the proper course to take would be through the city and county commissions and state legislature."[8] These were the same guidelines I followed when I sought an injunction to prevent the SDS's occupation of the University Union on March 4: The proper course of action, I believed, was through the existing legal structure.

The *Flambeau* advocated for recognition of the SDS on occasion in its editorials. But I believed the editors and reporters missed an important point: That the SDS wanted no support from the usual leftist students and faculty, however liberal they might have been. Such support would only have served to dilute their efforts to overthrow the whole societal structure. For that reason, SDS members and many other activists wanted no help from the liberal elements who might have been expected to support them. Their liberal supporters on campus didn't get the SDS message: Those in power—all of them—must be overthrown.

The *Tampa Tribune* in an editorial on January 18, reported that the SDS's national convention in June 1968, called not only for aiding draft resisters and defectors from the armed forces, but also for infiltration of the armed services "to initiate and support activities directed toward creating a radical political consciousness among members of the Armed Forces. You can translate that into one word—mutiny. " The same editorial noted that an FBI report revealed that the SDS held a workshop on sabotage and how to make bombs and Molotov cocktails (firebombs).[9]

Enough was known about the SDS at the national level and on other campuses that John Champion and his fellow administrators, in January 1969, must have looked hard for legitimate ways to hold the organization at bay. Board of Regents' policy on student organizations really left them no choice on the question of recognition, but recognition wasn't the whole story. Champion must have hoped that SDS would never attain the same standing among students as other student organizations had, and indeed that it would soon be a victim of its own extremism. But that didn't happen. The SDS played a leading role in much of the turmoil at FSU during 1969 and to a considerable degree in the next two years. So it is useful, as we review the history of campus events in those years, to look into the early history of the organization at Florida State.

Origins of the SDS at FSU

On October 7, 1968, student Mary Kelly Price filed an application for approval of SDS as an official university organization, claiming that it came into existence at FSU in 1965. Her application was accompanied by copies of the FSU chapter and the national SDS constitutions.

On November 2, the Student Senate approved the application. On November 30, Acting Vice President Jack Arnold advised President Champion of the Student Senate's action, but said he believed the SDS was in violation of the BOR policy that prevented recognition if the organization has a purpose, either in name or in fact, of advocating the overthrow of the government by force or other unlawful means. Champion delayed an official ruling, hoping that the Board of Regents policy would soon be clarified. On December 8, the administration advised Miss Price of its decision to deny recognition.

But Michael Klonsky, the national secretary of SDS, declared the SDS chapter would be officially a part of the national organization even though recognition had been denied by the University. Miss Price then announced that "it's a dead issue" and that the SDS, on the basis of approval by the Student Senate, was a fully approved student organization.

On January 13, 1969, the SDS held a rally in front of Westcott presenting eight demands to President Champion. The demands included the following: that SDS be permitted to use campus facilities without restriction; that all University employees be given time off to hear a speech by Conrad Lynn, an SDS activist, on January 16; that all University documents and correspondence be open to inspection by any member of the FSU community; that no narcotics agents or political spies be allowed on the campus; that a department of Afro-American studies be established; that the University cease its plans for expansion into Frenchtown, an African-American neighborhood just north of campus; that the university bookstore be made into a nonprofit organization operated as a student-faculty co-op; that faculty-student committees be given the power to hire and fire faculty and administrators; and that the University stop providing draft boards with information on students. Following this rally, President Champion sent his request to the Chancellor and the Attorney General for an opinion on the disputed clause in the Regents' policy.

The next day the Faculty Senate voted to recommend to the President that University policy be changed to neither approve nor disapprove student organizations. The same afternoon, January 15, a crowd gathered in front of Westcott at about 5:30 for an SDS rally. They decided to participate in the picket line that had already been planned for 7:30 that night in Westcott for the Arthur Goldberg speech. At about six o'clock a group of students brought picket signs into the second-floor lobby and were told by a student affairs officer that they were in violation of University policy against carrying signs into buildings. Frank Schrama, a 25-year-old senior from Tallahassee, tried to force his way into the auditorium carrying a sign, but was prevented from doing so by an assistant dean of men and Chief Tanner. He was then arrested and was advised by Arnold that he could take his choice of being charged at the Tallahassee police station or through the University courts, and he elected the former. Later that evening, another student, Wayne Wittgenstein, a 21-year-old junior from Panama City, was arrested for carrying a placard into the Longmire Building, where a reception was underway for Ambassador

Goldberg following his speech. Student Jon Madsen was also arrested for creating a general disturbance at the Goldberg lecture, using profanity, and for boisterous harassment. His case was referred to the student honor court for adjudication.

The SDS members met on February 10 and announced that they had prepared a comprehensive list of names of "narcs" (narcotics agents) and spies working for the administration. They said they would not release the list until they were more certain of the identities of those named. They also announced a plan to distribute literature to local high schools, particularly Leon High School in Tallahassee, and they announced plans for an after-school rally at Leon on February 20. Phil Sanford told the group that the state ACLU Executive Committee supported the SDS case for recognition. The group also went on record as protesting the recently announced resignation of Vice President Chalmers.

In March, soon after my appointment as Acting President, SDS conducted a guerilla theater performance on Landis Green, using humor as a way to get their message across. I was portrayed as a human puppet whose strings were being pulled by the regents and the power structure. Sheriff Hamlin was represented as a cigar chomping cowboy, calling the students "dirty, long-haired hippies."[10] The closing act was a funeral scene with the burying of a coffin marked "Free Speech."

In a position paper SDS attempted to distribute at the AAUP meeting that they disrupted in April, titled "Who Runs Florida State University?", the SDS charged that the Board of Regents was comprised mainly of "big business and their stooges."[11] The paper asserted that upon orders from the University administration, faculty were allowed to teach only within the framework of corporate-approved guidelines, and the purpose of higher education was "to instill in the children of the ruling middle- and working-classes the skills and attitudes necessary to maintain the corporate empire." The paper went on to say that the ruling class needed the universities to supply them with manpower to fill positions in the corporate and military bureaucracies and "social and military techniques to pacify external colonies in both the third world and the 'internal' colony or black community in the United States."[12] The SDS paper also depicted student government as the tool of the university administration. By that point, the SDS had angered many at the University, and its tactics had begun to produce a negative response. Sam Miller, editor of *The Flambeau*, wrote that SDS had greatly damaged itself.

In July 1969, SDS set up picket lines at Publix Supermarkets in Tallahassee in support of a strike against one of the suppliers of Publix meats. On September 24, some 500 members of the International Woodworkers of America struck the Elberta Crate and Box Company, which had factories in Bainbridge, Georgia, and Tallahassee. The one in Tallahasssee was located on Lake Bradford Road adjacent to campus, and the company was owned by the Simmons family—distinctly old Tallahassee. SDS members were quick to join the picket lines. The union had struck for better pay and benefits, including improved safety and sanitary conditions along with an end to alleged racial discrimination in hiring and promotions. Picket lines were manned mostly by black workers and their student supporters from the campus. White workers crossed the lines in order to keep the plant running.

The strike brought about many incidents of vandalism and violence. Tallahassee police arrested several students on charges of disorderly conduct and obstructing traffic in and out of the plant. Jack Lieberman and several other students were named in the Elberta lawsuit requesting an injunction to prevent picketers from interfering with plant operations. The strike ended in early November with a negotiated settlement for improved wages and working conditions.

As SDS continued to weaken, the Progressive Labor arm of the group became a growing faction within SDS and the Revolutionary Youth Movement had also achieved considerable strength. The PL group was a distinctly Maoist organization whose members believed that the working class was the primary agent of revolution and emphasized a need for students to form alliances with workers. The two factions became highly contentious. RYM stressed the need for armed struggle to achieve a revolution and encouraged the black liberation movement as part of revolution, while PL favored alliances with the down-trodden and oppressed.[13]

But the SDS was involved in other activities in 1969. SDS members participated in a major riot in Chicago among ghetto residents; they had demonstrators at large rallies on Easter Sunday in New York, Chicago, and other cities; and there was the occupation of Harvard's University Hall by hundreds of students in which 200 were ejected and 30 injured.[14]

Parr comments on FSU's becoming known as "Berkeley East," pointing out that radical students came from other campuses to learn more about the successes of the radicals at FSU. The FSU chapter of SDS sponsored a southern regional meeting in October, attended by about 150 persons.[15] The Progressive Labor party was the main Maoist organization within SDS, but the Revolutionary Union and the October League were also represented. The Stalinist-Communist party and the Trotskyist Spartacist League and Young Socialists Alliance were involved as well.

By the fall of 1969, the SDS at FSU began to decline as SDS continued to weaken at the national level.

Several writers point out that the real SDS revolutionaries were a rather small number, and that the SDS at Florida State did not cause the kind of violent uprisings that had occurred in other parts of the country. Parr ascribes this to the "relative moderation of a student body in the south." Parr, I believe, was partly right, but only partly. As others have noted, the stand taken by the University administration—"hard-nosed," it was sometimes called—in the winter and spring of 1969 had a salutary influence on the protesters' behavior at the University in those troubled times.

CHAPTER 6
The Protests Continue

The mood at FSU in the period following the highly charged events of the first six months of 1969 was much like that at universities all across the country. We had witnessed the armed takeover at Cornell, the violent protests at Wisconsin, Michigan and Syracuse, the insurrection at Columbia, and the Night of the Bayonets at Florida State. There were literally hundreds of campus protests, and they would continue for the nearly three years, but with notable changes by the protesters in both strategy and tactics. The form of the protests at FSU varied with the sponsoring organizations, the cause, the date, and above all, the opportunity the protesters saw to gain public notice; the press, after all, was in many ways the handmaiden of the protesters, and they were always alert for opportunities for some free ink.*

In this chapter we will view the continuing campus events and activities as they were seen by students and by the people of Florida, most of whom had developed a strong interest in campus goings-on.

The Anti-War Movement

Young men of draft age were in the forefront of the growing number of Americans who demonstrated against the war in Vietnam. Our students found ways to express themselves, and the protesters were by no means limited to those in league with SDS. In the latter part of John Champion's administration, black students had begun to press for recognition, and not the least of their concerns was the war and the numbers of black soldiers who had been drafted for service in Vietnam.

---

*With the advent of television as the main agent of on-the-spot news coverage came the use of "media" as the descriptor for radio, TV and print, but in the '60s and early '70s, the news was reported mostly by newspapers.

Anti-war demonstrations were a frequent occurrence on the campus during the winter and spring of 1970. In January, the FSU chapter of the National Student Mobilization Committee (SMC) joined the national organization in calling for the immediate withdrawal of our forces from Vietnam, banning military recruiters from the campus, ending ROTC, and ending all war-related research, including project THEMIS, in which the University's physical scientists had a contract with the Department of Defense. Jack Lieberman was invited along with other anti-war activists to go to Vietnam at the invitation of President Ngyuen Van Thieu.

FSU's SMC conducted several events as part of Antiwar Action Week during April 13-18. The SMC organized a campus referendum on the war: A march from Landis Green to the Capitol with participants from SDS, Women's Lib, the Black Student Union, and several local clergy. The crowd was estimated at 350 FSU and FAMU students. A member of the Malcolm X United Liberation Front spoke, telling the crowd that "no Vietcong... ever burned a church in Mississippi... and (or)... call themselves the Ku Klux Klan." One of the most active of the SDS students, Tweet Carter, called for the group to support a Vietcong victory.

But conservative students were not to remain silent. On April 13, another Landis Green rally was held, this time by the Committee on Responsible Student Action, which was an offshoot of the Young Republicans Organization. They were joined by fraternity and sorority members and representatives of some of the churches. Their purpose, they said, was to try to counter the image held by many Florida legislators and other Florida citizens of college students as long-haired protesters and hippies. They called themselves the New Party and they wanted to project an image of conservatism and patriotism.

CPE and Radical Jack Lieberman

In the spring quarter 1970, FSU students with the support

of student government, established the Center for Participant Education (CPE). It was a matter related to Lieberman's participation in CPE that resulted ultimately in his dismissal from the University.

The idea behind CPE was for students to teach their own courses in whatever they thought would be of interest to other students. They would be noncredit courses—not really courses in the usual academic sense, but group meetings in which the teacher—or leader—would conduct the class pretty much in the way he or she chose. There were classes in macramé, motorcycle repair, women's issues, meditation, the philosophy of anarchy, and other things that students would not find in the university's course offerings.

CPE was an innovation I liked from the beginning and tried however I could to encourage and support. I suppose I should have seen the potential for problems from the SDS, but in the early days I didn't. Not until Jack Lieberman offered a course advertised as "How to Make a Revolution in the USA" was I able to see the potential for problems with the new CPE program. Lieberman was widely described in the media and on campus as "Radical Jack," a nickname that he seemed to like and one that suited the protesters' purposes well. His course was soon followed by two courses on homosexuality. Steve Buchanan, student director of CPE, stated in September as the fall program got underway that he foresaw no problems, the administration was not expected to interfere, and the biggest problem was the "lack of student support from most students."[1] CPE and the administration had gotten into a controversy back in the spring when the Board of Regents and the legislature had raised questions about the courses mentioned above. Why should state tax monies and state buildings be used for courses in the study of homosexuality and making a revolution, they asked. Given Radical Jack's record for fomenting trouble, I could understand why they raised such questions. The agreement we had reached with the CPE Board of

Directors was for the instructors to submit their course outlines to the Vice President for Student Affairs, and that office would check to see that there was nothing in the courses that would violate state or federal laws, and that was all. We believed this would address legislators' and regents' concerns and not hamper CPE.

In the rush of the opening of school, Vice President Steve McClellan's office was unable to review all of the outlines in the time agreed upon, and we asked for a one-week delay in starting the program. The CPE board agreed. Jack Lieberman initially said he would respect the delay in starting his course because "we don't want to break any rules,"[2] but a few days later, Jack announced that he would teach his course, ignoring our agreement for the week's delay, and he would deny the University the right to review his syllabus. In *The Flambeau*, Lieberman stated that he was not looking to break any regulations but would exercise his democratic right of free speech. The CPE board joined again in asking instructors to observe the delay.[4] Editor Sam Miller wrote that "President Marshall has backed CPE, every edu-group in the program, all the way down the line. He can be credited with saving CPE more than once." In my continuing controversy with Lieberman, Jack and I agreed on the rights of free speech and assembly for CPE, but not on student control. Jack was unwilling to accept any role for the administration in the use of university facilities or resources. "Students," he said, "must have absolute and complete control over the CPE program..."[3]

So Radical Jack did as he said he would do. He taught his class despite the ban, telling his students that the meeting was not an official CPE class, that they were "just a group of students using a university room for a discussion."[4] The administration was not buying his lame exception to the ban, and we responded by placing Jack and another instructor, Claire Cohen, on interim suspension, which meant that they were to appear for a hearing before the University's student judicial officer.

The next step in this drama was a lawsuit in which eight students filed suit in federal court, asking that the suspension of Lieberman be lifted and the two CPE courses be reinstated. The students were represented by Tallahassee attorney Kent Spriggs. The result was a setback for Lieberman. The administration conducted an administrative hearing, which found that the interim suspension should not be lifted, and U.S. District Judge David Middlebrooks ruled that the ban of the two courses and the suspension of Lieberman would stand. But Lieberman's case was then heard by the Student Honor Court, where he was acquitted of all charges. *The Flambeau* reported that speculation abounded over the possibility that President Marshall might use his final review authority to rule on the case. Pending action by the President, Lieberman's student status was restored while his case went to the Student Supreme Court for review.

The last chapter in the Jack Lieberman story was his dismissal as a student, and that occurred on Sunday, November 7, 1971. The order Lieberman violated had been issued by me on September 16, delaying the start of the CPE program and temporarily denying university facilities and funds to CPE. The facts before me in my review clearly indicated that Lieberman had been aware of that order, and he willfully disobeyed it, announcing in advance his intention to do so. He had distributed a statement questioning the right of the University to regulate CPE in any way, and stated that he would lead his discussion group at the specified time and place, delay or no. I emphasized in my review that the content of Lieberman's discussion group was not at issue, that the issue was Lieberman's conduct in openly and willfully defying a valid order of the University President. And so I ordered that Jack be permanently suspended, that he be separated from the University in which he had enrolled as an 18-year-old freshman three years earlier. It was a decision from which I took no pleasure.

Reaction by student leaders was as expected: Student body President Ray Gross and student Supreme Court Judge Wayne Hogan affirmed my authority to overrule the student courts, but expressed their objections to my having done so. They called my decision "a blow to honor court and student government."[5] I released a statement on November 9, explaining the reasons for my decision to expel Lieberman. I said that I had conducted a thorough review of the case and that Lieberman was notified in advance of the time, place and date and format for my review. He elected not to appear, but was represented by Richard Shapiro, a law student, and Tallahassee attorney Kent Spriggs. I determined that Lieberman was guilty of both charges against him—failure to comply with an official order of a university officer and the intentional disruption of and interference with the functioning of the University. An additional factor in my decision was his disciplinary status at the time—he was on administrative probation as a result of a previous finding of guilt by the Student-Faculty Committee on Student Conduct in 1970, on charges of disruptive activity.

Jack Lieberman's departure from FSU was not a cause for rejoicing by me or any member of my administration. Dismissal of a student for any reason is an occasion for sadness, and my feelings were tinged with a certain hard-to-explain fondness that I had developed for Jack. I found him to be a person of principle who really believed in the causes he supported, even if his methods were often unacceptable. And while he was often at the edge of the more confrontational activities, he was never at the center. He never, to my knowledge, advocated violence.

The Lieberman story has one final nostalgic twist. One day in the mid-1980s, I was walking south on Biscayne Boulevard in Miami when I saw ahead of me three men carrying placards, walking in the same direction as I. One of those looked from a distance like Jack Lieberman and to my astonishment as I approached, that's who it was. When I called his name, Jack turned and there, once again, was the same dimpled smile and the handshake that Phil Sanford could not this time prevent. We greeted each other warmly as old friends and Jack introduced me to his comrades as "my old college president." They were headed for the Intercontinental Hotel with their signs, a few blocks farther along where a meeting was taking place by some organization that they opposed. I smiled as I walked on ahead, having seen once again that Jack was still true to his principles, as I expected him to be.

The Kent State Tragedy and its Aftermath

What was probably the most significant event in this whole period occurred in April 1970 when President Nixon ordered the invasion of Cambodia. Angry demonstrations erupted on campuses all across the country, and on May 4, National Guard troops shot four students to death and wounded nine at Kent State University in Ohio. The troops had been harassed by a crowd of some 600 students who were shouting obscenities and throwing rocks at the troops, who opened fire despite having no orders to do so. It was a tragedy that shocked the nation as no other event or events had done since the student uprisings began.

The shootings occurred on Monday, May 4, and during the rest of the week college campuses across the country exploded in furious indignation. Police were called out to control rioting at the University of Maryland, and at Syracuse University students broke windows and blocked faculty from entering classroom buildings. Similar protests took place at Stanford, Wisconsin, Berkeley, and at least a dozen other universities. ROTC buildings were attacked on 30 campuses, and some 200 incidents of arson occurred, both on college campuses and at corporate offices.

At the University of Florida, thousands attended rallies at the Plaza of the Americas and marched on the ROTC building and Tigert Hall, the administration building. At the University of South Florida 1,000 people attended a memorial service for the Kent State victims and many students then observed a one-day strike. Demonstrations were also held at the University of Miami and at Florida Presbyterian College (now Eckerd College), Florida Atlantic University, and Florida A&M in Tallahassee.

Students at Florida State were also quick to act. They held a mass rally on Landis Green on Wednesday, May 6, and called for a moratorium on classes on Friday. Student body president Chuck Sherman announced that student government had arranged for rides to Washington for students to participate in a nationwide rally on the following Saturday, and student editors at a number of Northeastern universities joined together to publish an editorial that was endorsed and reprinted by other student papers throughout the country, including *The Flambeau*. The editorial called for "militant, immediate and continued opposition from all Americans to stop the war." It argued that all elements of the University including students, faculty, and administrators should focus on that as their primary task. "The significance of classes and examinations pales before the greater problems outside the classroom... within a society so permeated with inequality, immorality and destruction a classroom education becomes a meaningless and hollow exercise."[6]

On Tuesday evening at FSU, a large group of students had marched to the President's home to demand that he cancel classes on Thursday and Friday. I addressed the crowd, saying that events at Kent State "bring sorrow and shame on all of us," and "symbolize the anguish of our country, and dramatize in a tragic way, the frustrations all young people feel so deeply," but then I denied the request that the administration cancel classes. I stated that class participation would be an individual matter between professors and students, and professors should feel free to use class time to discuss student concerns. I continued to be stubborn on the matter of closing the University.

Early Tuesday evening some 250 students marched to the ROTC building, where they occupied the first and second floors, lowered the American flag to half-staff, and engaged in debate with two ROTC officers. Many of the demonstrators evacuated the building when the sheriff's deputies arrived; the deputies blocked off the doors to prevent further entrance to the building and ordered any remaining students to leave. There were no arrests. Wednesday evening another rally took place on Landis Green, resulting in pushing and shoving between students and police. At the ROTC building, some objects were thrown and several windows broken. The protesters then marched on to Westcott where about 300 occupied Ruby Diamond Auditorium and disrupted the showing of the movie *The Graduate*. Sheriff Hamlin's deputies again cleared the building, and afterwards several hundred students staged an all-night vigil on the Westcott Lawn

On Thursday afternoon I called a faculty meeting, which was also attended by a large number of students. The auditorium at Westcott was filled to capacity and as I walked to the front of the auditorium preparing to preside, I observed a Vietcong flag hanging from the balcony. I faced the demonstrators and asked that the flag be removed, explaining that it would not be appropriate for the University to hold an official meeting in the presence of that symbol of our country's enemy, regardless of how we might feel about the war, and I was prepared to call off the meeting. After an interval of perhaps three minutes—a very tense three minutes, during which I stared at the flag holders and they stared back—the students holding the flag folded it up and carried it from the balcony. I then called the meeting to order.

This meeting had been announced as a called meeting of the Faculty Senate, but I knew that many of the general faculty and students would be present. I had chosen this to be the opportunity to make a statement about Kent State and to respond to the calls for me to close the University as a symbolic gesture, as university presidents elsewhere had done. I had no doubt that my meaning was clear in the Vietcong flag matter—that I would cancel the meeting if the flag were not removed. As I thought of doing so, I looked out over a group of tense, sweaty faces (the auditorium was not yet air conditioned and this was a warm May day) and I thought I saw frustration and anger of a kind I had not seen before. I have a distinct recollection that I thought we were closer to violence at that moment than we had ever been. If I had adjourned the meeting and walked up the aisle toward the doors in the rear, I believed then, and I do now, that my path would probably have been blocked, and then what? It's a question that, thankfully, never required an answer, and Florida State once again had dodged a bullet.

I have thought many times about that meeting, and the what-if possibilities, and I've reviewed the moments before the flag was removed. When I saw the flag hanging over the balcony, my reaction was a mixture of anger and fear. I was angry that a group of FSU students—our students—would show such disrespect for their country and their University. I was repulsed by their act, and I suppose it showed. I was also genuinely fearful that those who were so defiant might carry their defiance to another level, meaning violence. Then I looked down at the front row of seats where my vice presidents were seated, and I saw the need and the opportunity for some advice on how to deal with a situation we had not faced before. I walked down to where they were seated, leaned over to whisper, "What do you think?" and of course, they knew what I meant. Each of the three turned his head to look at the packed auditorium behind them and their response was unanimous: Go ahead with the meeting, they said, and I walked back up to the podium intending to do just that.

But when I turned to face the flag something that defies explanation prevented my doing so. I just couldn't call to order a meeting of the Florida State University with that symbol hanging over us all. These are our students, I thought, and I can't really believe that this display represents their true feelings, so I'm going to try again to appeal to their better natures. I understand your feelings about the war, I said, but I cannot and will not conduct a meeting of this University in the presence of that symbol, and I appeal to you once again to remove it from the room. You have three minutes in which to do that, and you must do so if this meeting is to take place. Slowly the hands that held the flag pulled it from the edge of the balcony and carried it out the doors in the rear, and with that the meeting was called to order.

On Thursday evening after the faculty meeting, police faced protesters at the ROTC building for the third day in a row. They had marched around campus gathering students as they passed dormitories and fraternity houses. There were some 1,500 students in the line when they reached the ROTC building. Over 100 Leon County and university police officers surrounded the building and the crowd decided to disperse.

The Governor Visits Campus

Governor Claude Kirk had expressed his interest in events at FSU on several occasions, and I was pleased that he was content to leave matters to those of us on the campus. He often described himself as the "education Governor," and he was a major figure in the teachers' strike in 1967. He had also traveled to Gainesville to confront disruptive UF students there.

The Governor, at the invitation of student body President Chuck Sherman, came out to the campus in May, 1970, at about seven o'clock on a Thursday evening and took up a position seated in a wicker chair on Landis Green. I took a position at another point on Landis Green, to discuss various issues with students as the Governor was doing. I went home at about ten o'clock, but Kirk stayed throughout the night.

The Flambeau reported that the atmosphere was laid back with students sitting at Kirk's feet, the Governor shunning the microphone for a quieter area of the rally on Landis Green. Jack Lieberman taunted the Governor, which prompted other members of the group to shout "Jack off campus!" In response, another group replied with cries of "Kirk off campus!"[7]

Editor Gary Smith editorialized about the night's events. He objected to "the actions of those students who tried to prevent Governor Kirk from speaking to students last evening…Whether his motives were pure or merely political is not the point. The point is that he did present himself to students on their territory; he did listen, and many students had the opportunity to express their concerns and ask him very pointed questions. Those students who attempted to put the governor in a position of mass confrontation were merely interested in embarrassing the Governor and provoking an emotional response."[8]

In an exchange I had years later with a student who had sat all night with the Governor, the student recounted his most lasting impression of Claude Kirk. "The guy sat in that wicker chair all night long and didn't leave to go to the bathroom once."

The Movement Begins to Weaken

The week of protests ended on Friday, May 8, with about 1,000 demonstrators marching to the Capitol to present a petition to the House of Representatives demanding, among other things, that campus police be disarmed. A delegation of members of the House of Representatives accepted the petition, and student body president Chuck Sherman, along with several faculty members, gave anti-war speeches on the Capitol steps. The national protests climaxed on Saturday, May 9, with a demonstration in Washington by some 60,000 people, organized by the New Mobilization Committee to End the War in Vietnam. Members of the Nixon administration and the Cabinet met with students in groups near the Capitol and on the lawns in Washington, using the same tactic that Governor Kirk had used a few days earlier in Tallahassee. About 100 students from FSU attended the Washington protest.

Things returned to normal on Monday at FSU, but the protests continued in other places. Some 1,000 students were reported to have fought National Guardsmen with rocks and bricks at the University of South Carolina, where they broke into administrative offices and destroyed furnishings, scrawling obscenities on the walls. Violence occurred on May 14 at Jackson State College in Mississippi when state troopers fired into a women's dormitory, killing two students and wounding 12. Rallies were held in Atlanta on Saturday, May 23, to protest the "shoot-to-kill mentality in America." Speakers included U.S. Senator George McGovern; Black Panther David Hilliard; Ralph Abernathy, who was then president of the Southern Christian Leadership Conference (SCLC); and Jesse Jackson. FSU students were represented by Jack Lieberman and a group from the Black Student Union. I sent a telegram to the president of Jackson State, expressing Florida State's "sorrow and sense of deep regret at the tragic events."

The tragedy of the student deaths at Kent State University has weighed heavily on people in higher education for years. How could "normal student protest" have resulted in such a senseless tragedy, and wasn't there anything the University administration could have done to head off the whole sorry episode?

Those student protests weren't really so normal. Hundreds of students racing across the campus hurling missiles and insults at the National Guard troops should somehow have been prevented. Those men in uniform who fired their weapons were not murderers—they were citizens of Ohio who had not been trained to react to that kind of attack by students or anyone else. What they did was to respond under great stress, and the results left deep scars on both the Ohio National Guard and Kent State University.

Could the tragedy have been prevented? That's the question that has not been answered, and it never will be, but this much we know: Students at Kent State and a good many other universities defied normal student behavior. They chose their own way to protest Vietnam and racial injustice and the sins of "the establishment," and at Kent State they did whatever felt good. In all of this they defied authority—or what should have been the authority—of the University, and the freedoms they exercised turned out to be very costly. I'm sure there were parents of those students who wished the University had taken steps to prevent the undisciplined actions that cost their children their lives. College students in that period often made much of their standing as adults, but making that claim did not by itself convey adult behavior. There was still a place for institutional order, and some universities, regrettably, failed to establish it.

The protests surrounding Cambodia and Kent State were the high point in the antiwar movement, which continued until the war ended in 1973. The decline in the number and intensity of protests was due in part to federal, state, and local suppression of the New Left, and there were also internal differences in protesting organizations such as the SDS and SNCC. As those organizations became more militant, the more moderate members fell by the wayside. There was also a growing group of Americans who supported Nixon's call for law and order, and who disliked the antiwar protesters as much as the war itself. On May 8, during the Kent State protests, some 200 hardhat construction workers attacked an antiwar rally on Wall Street in New York City, injuring seven student protesters.

The positions taken by the New Left at Florida State in the early 1970s were similar to those elsewhere. Parr reports that "a major difference between the Old and the New was the former's advocacy of class conflict and the latter's emphasis on ethnic and national liberation. The New Left got much of its impulse and inspiration from the civil rights and black liberation movement"[9] and expanded further into feminism, gay rights, and the American Indian movement. It benefited from political and consciousness-raising efforts among a wide range of ethnic groups.

But the general decline in activism did not entirely quiet the several interest groups on the campus at FSU. The most conspicuous of those still had causes to champion, and those are discussed in the sections that follow.

Black Student Concerns

Notable progress in race relations at FSU began to take shape in the early sixties. The first black students to enroll at the University were a group of junior high school science teachers from Broward County who came to participate in a 1962 Summer Science Institute funded by a grant from the National Science Foundation. It was a program I conducted then as head of the Department of Science Education. My department also awarded the University's first doctoral fellowship to a black student, Robert Mitchell, a high school teacher in Duval County. Mitchell went on to a distinguished career in education, including service as the President of Edward Waters College.

The concerns of our black students were rooted in the civil rights movement as it took shape in Tallahassee. National figures such as a Ralph Abernathy, president of the Southern Christian Leadership Conference (SCLC); Bayard Rustin, founder of the Congress of Racial Equality (CORE); and even Martin Luther King Jr. had come here to advance the interests of local blacks as they fought to integrate public swimming pools and restaurants. Leon High School was integrated in 1963, with other public schools soon to follow. The Tallahassee bus boycott attracted national attention in 1956 when students from Florida A & M (FAMU) forced the city to abandon the practice of segregated seating. Florida State University accepted its first full-time black students in September 1962, and our admissions policies from that point on made it clear that race would not be a factor in admissions.

By 1968, at Florida A&M, both students and faculty, assumed a more aggressive posture to expedite change. Adam Clayton Powell, former U.S. Representative from New York who also served as minister of a large Baptist Church in Harlem, spoke at a rally on the FAMU campus. He urged white students to join blacks "against the white power structure." He also spoke out against the Vietnam War, calling for the immediate withdrawal of all troops, because as he said, "I cannot dig the scene of black men fighting colored men to win a white man's war."[10]

Fears by Florida A&M faculty and students that their university and FSU were about to be merged also surfaced in 1968. Some legislators could not see why Florida needed two state universities only two miles apart. A student leader at A&M said the students would "burn down every building on the campus rather than allow the merger to take place."[11] But Charles Wright, a leader of Florida's Black Power group, told students they needed a unified effort to cure the inherent ills of our community, proposing this as an alternative to civil disorder.

On the campus at FSU, things were heating up. The Afro-American Student Union (AASU), in October 1968, presented to President John Champion seven demands for immediate consideration. Some 50 black students walked into Champion's office to present their demands, which included, among other things, that black security officers be added to the FSU police force, that more black professors be hired, and that "Dixie" not be played at campus events. Champion responded by telling the students that he would assign members of his administration to investigate each of the claims and make recommendations on needed changes.

The playing and singing of "Dixie" became an issue not just for black students but also for others among our students and faculty. It was the subject of many letters to *The Flambeau* from partisans on both sides. A tradition had been established at FSU for the song to be played by the band at football games, and as a longtime spectator in the stands, I sensed resentment coming from the student section at the stadium. This feature was quietly dropped during the football season of 1969, my first as President. To my great relief, the "Dixie" proponents made no protest.

Black students became more active on the campus in early 1970. In January the Black Student Union (BSU) asked me to call a special session of the Faculty Senate to consider several issues that they believed had not been addressed by the administration. BSU President John Burt said that the situation regarding black students was "rapidly deteriorating," and in early February, the Faculty Senate met in a special session at which 31 proposals were presented by the BSU. They included demands that the University "hire more black administrators, faculty, students, doctors, nurses, house managers, resident counselors."[12] They also wanted a black barber and a black beautician at the University Union, a daycare center for non-academic employees of the University, and a building named after a prominent black.

Tallahassee also had a local version of the Black Panther Party (BPP). It was based in Frenchtown, just north of the University campus, and they urged the adoption of a social services program, including breakfasts for school children, a security escort service in Frenchtown, and education programs on sickle-cell anemia and black history. They organized under the banner of the Malcolm X United Liberation Front (MXULF) and remained independent of the SDS, believing that blacks and whites should organize separately and each group pursue its own interests. The MXULF said that they agreed with the Black Panthers' philosophy, and its leaders regarded the Panthers as their vanguard. In late February, they sponsored a march and rally from the FAMU campus to the St. Mary's Primitive Baptist Church on Call Street to commemorate the 1965 death of Malcolm X. MXULF leader Raleigh Jugger organized a group to protect blacks from police brutality, to establish a "liberation school," and to provide tutoring service for black children. Jugger announced his intention to spread his plan throughout the South.

An event that caught the eye of the public was the unscheduled gathering of a group of black students in my office in April 1971. I did my best to avoid thinking of it as an occupation, but that was the way it was seen by many people at the time.

I looked up from my desk in Westcott to see a large group of black students enter my office, having walked past the receptionist in the outer office. I recognized several of them as students I had met with in earlier meetings, including John Burt, who was a prominent black student leader and a varsity basketball player. Their purpose, they said, was to talk to the president about the lack of progress on several issues they were concerned about. They mentioned what they regarded as unfair treatment of black cheerleaders, and they wanted me to dismiss charges against two black students who were charged with an assault on a white student, a football player. I believed then that they had noticed they were getting less attention in the media than other protesting groups, and they wanted to do something to change that. In my office, they were essentially non-confrontational—that is, they spoke forcefully about their concerns, but they did so with what I thought was an acceptable level of decorum. I concluded that this was not really a building occupation but rather a sort of conference-on-demand, and I could accept that.

What the students who had marched into my office did not know was that Sheriff Hamlin's deputies were assembled just off campus. The Sheriff had been alerted by Chief Bill Tanner, who knew I was serious about our policy of no occupation of buildings, and he thought from his vantage point that this looked like one. The sheriff awaited a call from my office before moving in for the arrests. After about an hour, the students left as they had entered, by simply walking back out through the reception area, and the Sheriff received no call. There was a report the next day that the students had somehow received word from the A & M campus that their protests could be counterproductive to merger opponents, and they should leave the office. Whether that report was factual, I still do not know.*

Women's Issues

Women's concerns did not generate the same interest at Florida State as those of black students or the anti-war movement or the role of students in university governance. Nonetheless, *in loco parentis* as a way to regulate student conduct was simply unacceptable to many students, and their absence from the marches and demonstrations did not mask the depth of their concern. A major victory was won in May 1970 when all curfews for women were abolished in accordance with a decision two weeks earlier by a student Supreme Court ruling that curfews were unconstitutional. This decision was based on a policy of non-discrimination on the basis of race, creed, color, or sex as required by the Civil Rights Act of 1964. So it was the federal government's action on Civil Rights that ended curfews and ushered in a new era of freedom for women.

The Women's Liberation movement found other ways to

---

*Sometime about 1998, I was asked by the District Governor of Rotary to suggest a speaker for the annual conference of the Rotary clubs in North Florida and I recommended former astronaut Winston Scott, then the FSU Vice President of Student Affairs. He was invited to speak, and I was asked to introduce him. In my introduction, I mentioned that he had been an astronaut and after he had left NASA he came back to FSU, and I painted him to be the famous and distinguished scholar-astronaut that he was. When he took the podium, he thanked me for the introduction and added that there was "something about me that Dr. Marshall does not know." He said that he had been one of the black students who occupied my office back in 1971, and then he paid me what I thought was a nice compliment. He said, "Dr. Marshall treated us like a bunch of 17-year-olds, and we left."

express its concerns. The organization maintained a literature table at the University Union, but wisely denied any affiliation with the SDS. A leader of the movement, Laurence Coe, described the women's goals as equal and independent opportunities for women at the University, the establishment of a medically-supervised program of birth-control at the University Health Center, an end to male-chauvinism in course content, more women's athletic programs, and an end to *in loco parentis*. Ms. Coe also advocated for a "policy of equality for black people and an end to the imperialist war against the Vietnamese people."[13]

Environmentalism

FSU's participation in environmental concerns occurred mostly through the Environmental Action Group (EAG), which sponsored participation in the second Earth Day in April 1970. EAG was founded by Senator Gaylord Nelson of Wisconsin and Representative Paul McClosky of California in 1969 as a way to direct youthful activism to oppose pollution and the destruction of the environment. Earth Day was observed at some 2,500 colleges and universities and several thousand high schools. Demonstrations occurred at a number of Eastern universities along with major rallies in New York and other cities.

Senator Nelson came to FSU in May to participate in a campus program to encourage FSU students to petition the legislature. EAG asked the legislature to support several environmental bills and to request the major broadcast networks to devote airtime to problems of overpopulation, pollution, poverty and the destruction of natural resources. EAG also sent a petition to President Nixon calling for an end to the supersonic transport (SST) program. A separate request was made to the FSU health center for birth control devices on request. I was asked in April that the University either cancel classes or discuss environmental issues in class on April 22, Earth Day, and once again, I refused to call off classes. The

EAG also sponsored concerts, folk bands, and poetry readings to call attention to its demands. The turnout for Earth Day at FSU was not what sponsors had hoped, with only a few hundred participating. Nevertheless, EAG continued to play a role over the next few years, organizing demonstrations and sponsoring recycling projects.[14]

Legislative-Campus interactions

A continuing challenge for me was finding a middle-ground between faculty members—meaning the activists mostly in the Faculty Senate—and angry legislators who held the faculty largely responsible for the student insurrections. A few members of the faculty seemed to delight in demonstrating to legislators that academic freedom extended to their support of any cause that appealed to them, whether or not it was related to their specialized knowledge. If doing so put them on record in opposition to prevailing opinions in the legislature, well... so, what's the problem?

The disturbances at both UF and FSU caused legislators to initiate new efforts to investigate radical student activities on the campuses. Bills were introduced in both the House and Senate to set up investigation committees that would require college students to sign loyalty oaths and permit presidents to expel students convicted of interfering with "peaceful conduct" at state universities. Representative Don Reed, of Boca Raton said that he suspected that universities had more autonomy than they really deserved, and Senator C.W. "Bill" Young of Pinellas County said that legislators were only responding to the requests of the people of Florida who were "demanding a cure" on behalf of the 99% of students who attended the universities to get an education and not to agitate. At the national level, President Nixon proposed cuts in federal grants and loans to college students who were convicted of taking part in disorders. Florida Representative Paul Rogers proposed such a bill in response to the uprisings at San

Francisco State. Representative Reed later introduced a bill to allow any university to fire any professor or expel any student who occupied or obstructed access to a campus building, or damaged university property. He stated that attendance at a state university was a privilege, not "an unqualified right." Reed also sponsored a bill requiring any person suspended, expelled, or dismissed from one university to obtain presidential permission to visit another campus on the grounds that it might be unconstitutional since campuses were public property.

Later in the legislative session Senator Young introduced a package of six bills to clamp down on dissent. This was the same Senator Young who had grabbed a bullhorn at the demonstration on Landis Green where he was harassed and shouted down by students—and the same Bill Young who has served with distinction in the United States Congress for 30 years. My response to all of the above was to send to the faculty and staff a message emphasizing that FSU was not San Francisco State, Berkeley, or Columbia, and that our students were serious about obtaining an education, and that they had not engaged in the destructive behavior that had been seen on some other campuses, and of course, I expected legislators to get my message. I assured legislators that existing regulations would be enforced, and we would keep tight control on the campus. I wanted to avoid new legislative initiatives that were not needed, and I hoped the faculty would listen up. In March, the House Higher Education Committee defeated a bill sponsored by Representative Jim Tillman of Sarasota to set up a special investigation committee to study campus disorders.

In Tallahassee, legislators saw and heard up close the activist students and faculty, and that worked both ways. In students such as Lyman Fletcher, Ray Gross and Chuck Sherman, they saw student leaders who were basically responsible and respectful of the system even though to maintain their campus political clout, they were often required to pretend otherwise. But unfortunately, legislators had occasional contacts with students and a few with faculty members about whom no such claim for respect and responsibility could be made, and that made our relations with legislators a near-constant challenge to the administration. So, my job was mostly to act as a peacemaker between the two factions. It was easy for me to describe the large numbers of students who were engaged in useful pursuits at any point in the day or night—studying in the library, going to band practice, working at part-time jobs—while a very small number were engaged in disruptive activities.

Leaders of both bodies in the legislature were usually people I had come to know personally; many had become my friends, and they were often inclined to cut me some slack. They knew that I understood the need for them to do some grandstanding for the benefit of their constituents, and they often seemed to look for ways to show me they understood the role I was trying to play. In May 1971, I was summoned to testify before the Senate Committee on Higher Education, chaired by Senator Bob Haverfield. He had probably been the most active legislator in calling for me to get rid of the troublemakers: Just dismiss them, which you have every right to do. In my testimony, I explained as tactfully as I could that yes, I found the protests troublesome, and I knew of my powers to dismiss students. But there is the U.S. Constitution to take into account, I reminded the senators. It covers the matter of free speech pretty clearly, and if we don't teach respect for the Constitution at the University and act on those principles, I don't believe we have a legitimate right to call ourselves a university. One of the senators later assured reporters that President Marshall would not succumb to pressures from the legislature. The same sentiment was expressed by Senator William Barrow during his testimony in the lawsuit challenging my dismissal of Lieberman (discussed earlier in this chapter). Lieberman's ACLU lawyer claimed that I had dismissed Jack in response to pressure from the Legislature, to which Senator

Barrow replied, "Marshall indicated he would not in any way be influenced or intimidated by the Senate."[15]

"Taxpayers' whorehouses"

In loco parentis was a concept that gave university authorities powers that went beyond the U.S. Constitution. It seemed to say that students were not full citizens and that higher education was not a right but a privilege—a privilege that could be denied by the authorities for any or no reason.

Among the elements that made up student life on campus, the regulations that governed student housing were among the most objectionable to the students. One of the reasons that students then—as well as before and since—went to college was to get away from their parents, and those of us who worked and lived with students were nearly as eager as they were to shake the parental role and let students be students.

Curfews for women students were strictly enforced on most campuses before the protests. The operating principle seemed to be that if the girls are in, the boys will be too. As late as February 1969, women at FSU were still required to sign out at the front desk of their dorms anytime they wished to leave campus and to provide an estimated time of return. Disciplinary action was taken against a student in February 1969 when she failed to sign in upon her return to the dorm. She appealed the decision, and the Student Supreme Court ruled that the stated time of return was non-binding. That was a major defeat for *in loco parentis*.

Dorm visitation rules were revised the same year. The presidents of Kellum and Smith Halls and the Dean of Women Katherine Hoffman worked with student body president Vince Rio to design a policy allowing co-eds to visit male students in the lounges and study rooms of their dorms.

The general liberalizing of the rules and customs of student conduct made many parents uptight—not just parents, but taxpaying citizens who thought they should have a say in whatever took place on the campuses their tax dollars provided. "I hardly think it necessary," wrote one angry mother, "to point out that parents do not expect that the university should be run and regulations should be established by the students.—Perhaps I am old fashioned," she continued, "but I hardly think young people are privileged to make decisions relative to campus living until they accept the responsibility of adulthood which includes paying one's own way—all of it."[16]

If boys and girls—OK, men and women, today—were going to misbehave, I doubted that both sexes living in the same dormitories would make much difference. High school students, I remember saying to some of the regents, go on class trips where boys and girls stay overnight in adjacent hotel rooms, and we don't get uptight over that. The analogy was imperfect I realized, but I was trying to make the point that men and women living in the same building, on different floors or in different wings, but with visitation hours in each other's rooms, was no assurance of immoral behavior.

When co-ed dorms were first set up, students were quick to point out the benefits. Men and women students were able to relate to each other in more natural, more family-like settings. Guys seemed more relaxed, reported one dorm counselor. It just seems normal to have them around was a sentiment expressed by many women. Men and women did all of the normal student things together—they studied, watched TV, played ping pong, and had ice cream parties.

The rightful place of America's youth was much on the minds of the people and not just those concerned with administering our universities. Often there was intense debate; the 26th Amendment to the United States Constitution was ratified in July 1971, lowering the voting age to 18, a move that was controversial. In many states, the age for legally consuming alcohol was also lowered to 18, although this action in several states was later reconsidered. So the sentiment on the part of many students was that we're old enough to vote and to fight for our country—and you're going to continue to play mommy and daddy to us in college? We're not children, and we don't like regarding university authorities as our parents.

In May 1970, the university administration agreed to end all curfews for women living on campus. The earlier ruling by the Student Supreme Court was based on a BOR policy of non-discrimination in accordance with the Civil Rights Act of 1964. The administration agreed with the Student Court and thus was ended one of the most despised features of *in loco parentis*.[17]

Regent Elizabeth Kovachevich, who was appointed to the Board of Regents by Governor Claude Kirk, took a decidedly dim view of students' clamor for relaxed visitation rules and said so in a speech to the Clearwater Rotary Club in May 1971. She had heard reports that women who attended the nearby University of South Florida were making trips to New York for abortions, and she agreed with the irate parent who called her to say that "college dormitories are becoming tax-payers whorehouses." The *St. Petersburg Times* headlined the story, and other state papers picked it up.

BOR Chairman Burke Kibler took exception to Kovachevich's comments, calling them "unwarranted" and "without basis in fact." Governor Reubin Askew said that her remarks were out of line, and the student body presidents at all of the state universities were deeply offended. They accused Kovachevich of using "good old public relations and salesmanship" to oppose the open visitation policy, which she disliked.

The students had a delightful time with the issue, mining all of its possibilities for humor. At FSU, sorority "girls" posed in front of their house to beckon "customers." They wore provocative clothing and posed before a sign advertising "special rates for BOR"—the picture appeared first in *The Flambeau* and was widely distributed. In another, a male student lay in bed with folding money in both extended hands as he beckoned two scantily clad females. "Please pay when served" read the sign the girls displayed.

But the Kovachevich statement did not in the end have much effect on the move to relax student regulations. Curfews were ended, housing rules relaxed, and students—both men and women—were looked to by both the administration and the faculty to accept greater responsibility for regulating their own behavior. And in the end, I believe most parents thought we were moving in the right direction.

Yippies

Two of the SDS's major national figures were Abbie Hoffman and Jerry Rubin, who gained national attention at the 1968 Democratic National Convention. Their idea was to bring the nonconformist lifestyle and counterculture into the political agenda of the Left. They nominated Lyndon Pigasus Pig for President and created general havoc among delegates to the convention. Both Hoffman and Rubin were charged by Democratic Party officials with conspiracy to disrupt the convention and in the weeks to follow, they they founded a new movement, The Yippies.

By spring 1970, the Yippies' appeal had spread to the campus, and its disciple at FSU was student Jeff Savlov. Jeff saw the possibilities for humor in the protests and found many opportunities for hilarity. He declared himself to be the "non-organizer" who persuaded other students to join his "nonchapter." In March he issued an invitation to "all who want to join the revolution for the hell of it...." He said that FSU needed the Yippies to counteract those who were "intellectualizing the revolution too much...they are quoting Mao and Marx all the time."[18] He announced that his purpose was "to use levity to stop the war, to show the irrationality and absurdity of the war and to confront

---

* Jeff Savlov, after graduation, attended law school at FSU and now heads a successful Tallahassee law firm. Savlov &Anderson advertise regularly on the radio and every time I hear Jeff's name, I remember and I smile.

the authorities but not to antagonize them."*[18]

On March 4, 1970, the first anniversary of the Night of the Bayonets, the Yippies held a celebration in the Union. Rick Johnson, one of the SDS activists, came disguised as Sheriff Hamlin. They said they would practice Arapaho fertility rites and that Alice B. Toklas would supply the brownies. Their "mystery guest from Massachusetts" turned out to be a jar of Boston baked beans.

The Yippies provided opportunities for levity and fun with the University administration too. They organized the Pigs Bowl touch-football game between the "Freaks" and the "Pigs" (students and campus police), refereed by President Marshall. Satire and humor came to be used more frequently by protesters in the early seventies. The Committee for Immediate Action (CIA) held anti-military balls in imitation of the ROTC's traditional formal events. At one of the balls they elected a King and Queen and, in deference to Women's Lib, required that bras be checked at the door. The organizations that co-sponsored these events included CIA, SMC, Women's Liberation, and Vets Against the War.[19]

At a small conservative student rally in April 1970, Jeff Savlov said that his group "infiltrated" the rally and carried signs proclaiming such sentiments as "Kill a Commie for Christ." Savlov and the Yippies had an unusual sense of humor, at best. But at least their antics were always light-hearted and not intended to disrupt the University's educational endeavors.

Those of us who lived and worked with students tried never to lose sight of the fact that young people—and college students especially—are fun to be around; and even in the confrontations between protesting students and the authorities, there were moments of mirth. When students would march on the president's home at night, which they often did, my standard response was to step out onto the front porch, to face the crowd on the sidewalk with a big smile and clap my hands together and say "Okay, boys and girls, what ch'all wanna talk about tonight?" With that, the anger faded from many of their faces and the hard-liners had a harder time generating an angry crowd reaction.

The Flambeau cartoons by student Doug Marlette (who went on to win a Pulitzer Prize as a nationally syndicated cartoonist) were a genuine delight. He drew me, featuring the nose, of course, in ways that I found delightful. He was never spiteful or mean, and his cartoons often conveyed a message that I could understand and appreciate.

The Yippies and the tone they set may not have done a lot to aid the revolution, but they surely made it more enjoyable.

Stephen Parr writes that we were fortunate that FSU did not become another Kent State, Berkeley, or Wisconsin. I have never downplayed the role of good fortune in my personal and professional experiences, but as I wrote earlier, this was more than good luck. The police played important roles in events on many campuses including Florida State, and the police presence at FSU was surely a factor in the relative tranquility we enjoyed. Campus Police Chief Bill Tanner and Leon County Sheriff Raymond Hamlin, in my opinion, were exactly the kind of police officers we needed. Both were thoughtful, temperate officers who understood the issues that troubled our students, men who did not need to be reminded to be firm but fair. That was their mantra, and they lived by it.

Streaking

When people all across the country think about FSU, what comes to mind is. . . well, Bobby Bowden and Seminole football are up there, but so is streaking. Yes, it's true. Streaking is believed to have started at FSU, then caught on at several other universities, but we get most of the credit for initiating the practice.

It all started on the night of Thursday, March 7, 1974. According to *The Flambeau* whose male reporters seemed to have followed the action unusually closely, "... a small band of divested adventurers flashed through the tree-lined way separating Salley and Kellum Halls."[20] The commotion then brought residents outside and soon there were at least 300 intensely interested male observers.

Flambeau reporters, Richard Lee and Tom Kirwan described the scene:

> As darkness crept over the campus, a full moon revealed that the flashing streaks were becoming more numerous. And then it happened. The first woman bared her bod in shameless disregard of the fact that she was violating the laws of indecent exposure.
>
> Over 750 people watched as the dauntless young Ms. swept through the tennis courts and on to the Mabry Heights buildings. An enthusiastic gang of males cornered her by a house where she began to cover up, but after the men gave her rousing ovation, she ran bare-assed back to Salley Hall.
>
> Later, two nude motorcyclists appeared out of nowhere, converged in the middle of the road, shook hands and sped away as quickly as they had come. After a few more detours, the word went out that President Stanley Marshall's home was the next destination. The crowd trudged through a construction lot and stopped traffic on Tennessee before it was discovered that police had encircled the President's residence.
>
> At one point, a Domino's pizza truck made its way onto the grass and began giving away free pizzas to streakers while a nude coed danced on top of the truck.
>
> By midnight most of the activity was over, although isolated reports of streakers continued until about 3 a.m.[21]

As for their plans to make a pilgrimage to the President's home, which I later learned was thwarted by the police... well, of all the treks students made to our home, this was one I would surely have enjoyed more than most others.

The variety of modes of streaking and the creativity of the streakers showed the best of our students' creativity. America's first blind streaker sauntered across the grass, wearing only his shoes with his cane to guide him. Three students claimed to have set a marathon streaking record when they ran five miles over a measured course. Another attempted the difficult job of shimmying up a lamp post and one hopped on his motorcycle for a tour of the campus not totally nude—he had strapped on his gun belt and holster.

Why did they do it? I could find no words to explain this strange manifestation of student life, and I don't think I tried very hard. It was just happening, that's all, and after the angry, tense confrontations of the past, I found it hard to object—or at least to do so with a straight face.

A mythical student identified as "Suzy N.York" wrote an essay in *The Flambeau* that may have said it best:

> Freedom is a word I seldom use, but recently I found I was free to be free. Like a child unburdened by the conventions of society, I ran free. Free of everything, I romped up and down the hills of this fair city covered by a grin and tennis shoes.
>
> The realization that the guys I was surrounded by were naked never occurred to me. They were simple free spirits, like Shakespeare's nymphs in *A Midsummer Night's Dream*. Magic filled the air with sparkle and glitter that went unmatched by anything I had ever seen.
>
> No one was leering at the bodies that ran because the energy was too electric. Whether it was shock or astonishment is questionable, but it was un-

forgettable.

The spontaneity of the streaking made it a pure experience. Nothing dirty or disreputable touched me as I streaked from place to place in open innocence.

It was after the huge crowd of gawkers gathered to jeer that the innocence left and I must have experienced what Eve felt when she was expelled from the Garden. The memory of my new-found freedom is just as strong today with my clothes on as it was without them.[22]

Charlie Barnes, the well-known and widely popular Executive Director of Seminole Boosters, has spoken many times of his experience that night, and I asked him to record what he remembers. Charlie had only recently returned from service with the Army in Vietnam. I think his account adds luster to this history of Florida State University.

I was in my last semester at FSU in March of 1974, and the more exuberant excesses of college life in the 1970s were nowhere more in evidence than in Tallahassee, Florida. It was a wonderful spring.

I had just finished giving a presentation in advertising class and was walking home to my fraternity house, dressed in a coat and tie. The sun was almost down; the dying light mixed with the street lamps along Jefferson gave a soft yellow cast to everything. I walked east along the quiet street. The air was sweet; I was going to start work for Procter & Gamble in April so this was my last few weeks as a college student.

I was on Jefferson, near Dorman Hall, when I noticed a sheriff's car, at the intersection ahead. At first I thought he was just waiting to turn, then realized he was blocking the street. Other figures began to appear, and I kept walking, keeping an eye on the growing barricade up ahead. I was all alone.

Then I heard something behind me, almost like the sound of wind rustling through the brush.

When I turned and looked behind me, I saw a solid wall of naked people, running. They were running toward me. The leader was a short young woman wearing nothing but a pair of shoes and a very serious expression. They ranged from sidewalk to sidewalk, and as far back as I could see.

I was wearing a vested suit and tie, and I was carrying a briefcase. For just a moment, I had a vision of being drawn in like a pebble along the banks of a flood, torn into the raging current. At first I was worried, "Does this have anything to do with *me?*" I covered myself with my briefcase—not being of a frame of mind to be unclothed in public at the moment—and watched the torrential column of hundreds of naked people fly past me on their way to the barricades.

I can't tell you what happened at the top of the intersection; I was too engrossed in the surreal experience of being the only man wearing clothes in a sea of naked people. In that quick moment on Jefferson Street, I saw the end of my youth. "Well, that was college," I thought, and I smiled.[23]

Streaking was an event whence the University president could take a small measure of joy (from observing, please understand, not participating), along with many others in the University community. But the joy was short-lived and the heavy hand of authority was soon to descend. Early the next morning, Chief Bill Tanner came to my office to report. First he showed me a series of photographs taken by his officers the night before, which revealed more intimate behavior behind the bushes than we had thought was going on. Then he told me that the police in the area had been alerted to widespread interest on the part of the citizenry including those in the rural areas outside of Tallahassee and in south Georgia. He said we could expect to see lots of visitors from those areas tonight and that crowd control could be a major problem. We were fearful that the festival of the night before could turn into something other than good, clean (well, mostly) fun, and the word went out from the President's office that any streakers from that point on would be arrested on site. There might have been a few isolated instances of bared bodies sighted around campus during the remainder of the year but most of our students put on their clothes and went back to the books.

The Carswell Affair

Richard Nixon left his imprint on Tallahassee in at least two ways. He came here during his campaign for re-election as president in 1972, stopping at the Tallahassee airport where he made a short campaign speech, but his nomination of Harrold Carswell to be a justice of the U.S. Supreme Court got far more notice.

The vacancy Carswell was to fill was created by the resignation of Justice Abe Fortas in May 1969. Nixon nominated Clement Haynesworth of South Carolina for the seat, but he failed to get the Senate's confirmation. In January 1970, the president then nominated G. Harrold Carswell of Tallahassee, who had served for the past seven months on the Fifth Circuit Court of Appeals, which sits in New Orleans. When questioned about his Supreme Court nomination of a judge whom he had never met, Nixon said that he was familiar with Carswell's record and had studied some of his more important decisions.

Many people in Florida were pleased to have one of their

own about to join the Supreme Court. The reaction in Tallahassee was strongly in support of the man who was for many a
friend and neighbor. His friend, Malcolm Johnson, editor of
the *Tallahassee Democrat* called him "an honorable man, a re
spectable neighbor, a federal judge of a dozen years who is as
close to the people as he is to the law...Naturally, we are pleased
that one from the Southeast is chosen because our part of the
nation has had a dearth of representation on that court for
many years." The general sentiment in Tallahassee and much
of Florida was that he should be confirmed by the Senate without delay.[24]

Former Governor LeRoy Collins testified before the Senate Judiciary Committee in support of his friend and former
law partner. He said he knew Carswell and believed him to be
no racist or segregationist "...I believe him to be qualified to
make a fine justice on the Supreme Court," Collins said. The
Senate was then divided evenly between Republicans and
Democrats.

U.S. Senator Ed Gurney of Florida first suggested Judge
Carswell to Attorney General John Mitchell, who had presented
his name to Nixon. Gurney was a strong Carswell supporter in
the Senate debate.

The attacks on the nominee were not long in coming, for
he had given his critics more than enough grist for their mills.
He had stated in a speech in 1948 that he was "...a Southerner
by ancestry, birth, training, belief, and practice, and I believe
that segregation of the races is proper...I have always so believed, and I will always so act."[25]

Nixon was believed to be following precedent set by President Eisenhower in infusing the government in Washington
with the "conventional values of American life." It also fit
Nixon's "Southern strategy," in which he was compelled to
strengthen the southern base of the Republican party.[26]

But Carswell's record was hard for his friends to defend.
The Dean of the Yale Law School said that Carswell "pre-

123

sents the most slender credentials of any man put forth in this century for the Supreme Court."[27]

Students rallied to protest the nomination. At a large anti-Carswell demonstration on the lawn outside Moore Auditorium, student body president Chuck Sherman said that President Nixon was "asking for more serious problems than demonstrations," saying that "we must give this country back to the people...Thank God the people care enough." Reverend C.K. Steele also spoke, telling students, "It's good to see you here making a massive effort to keep a racist off the Supreme Court."

In testimony before the Senate Judiciary Committee, Carswell admitted his part in trying to "fix up the little wooden country club." That was the Capital City Country Club, whose officers made no secret of their intention to remain racially segregated when the city-owned golf course was transferred to a group of local citizens. Carswell was shown to have been one of the incorporators.

The University was drawn into the story by the release of a letter to President Nixon protesting the nomination and signed by nine professors from the FSU Law School. They urged him to "... withdraw the name of Judge G. Harrold Carswell and to submit to the Senate the name of some truly distinguished Southern jurist." The Florida reaction to the professors' letter was pretty intense, especially in government and business circles. Burke Kibler, chairman of the Board of Regents, scolded Josh Morse, Dean of the Law School in a letter which said in part, "It is a little sad that these professors cannot take pride in the fact that a fine honorable Floridian has been nominated to the highest court in the nation." Kibler reminded Morse that such "imprudent actions" make it harder to get adequate funding for the University and more difficult to "successfully oppose the repressive legislation... that is introduced in every session of the Legislature."[28]

The defeat of Carswell by the Senate on April 8, by a vote

of 51 to 45 probably took some of the heat off the law school. Most of the professors who signed the letter remained on the faculty, and several completed their careers at FSU and are remembered as some of our best professors.

But there was another chapter in the Carswell Tallahassee legacy, one that involved the University in a way I would never have expected.

The Carswell defeat in the Senate was a bitter pill for his friends and supporters, of whom there were many in Tallahassee. They resented in particular the part played by Senators Ted Kennedy and Indiana's Birch Bayh.

In late summer of 1970, plans were underway for Homecoming, and alumni groups were making preparations for their annual banquet. An officer of the Alumni Association, entirely on his own and for reasons he could not explain, had issued an invitation to Senator Bayh to be the Homecoming banquet speaker, and Bayh accepted. Only after the fact was I informed of this. The disappointment—and yes, some anger—that I felt, was shared by everyone in the administration, but the deed had been done.

I knew that leaders in Tallahassee—bankers, real estate people, professional people, some in government—would regard this as a needless affront, and I decided they should hear it from me. Accordingly, I arranged to meet with about 20 people I considered "Tallahassee's elders" in the board room of the then Tallahassee Federal Savings. I told them what had happened, that I regretted it greatly, and I was really not seeking their advice but just informing them that I would try to handle this embarrassing situation as best I could, and we would proceed with Homecoming.

Most of those present were as unhappy as I was about the invitation but were resigned to seeing it through—all but one: E.C. Allen, a generous friend of the University and a man who was well known for speaking his mind. "Here's what I'm going to do," he said. "I'll rent the county fairgrounds for that night and bring to town the most famous speaker I can find, and we'll see who draws a crowd." Well, calmer heads prevailed, and E.C. was persuaded that there might be a better way.

The sad end to the story came when the Senator's wife was diagnosed with cancer the next week, and he cancelled all of his outstanding appointments. Sadder still, Mrs. Bayh died a short time later.

Student Protests at FSU

SDS protesters hang President Marshall in effigy—he said he hoped they didn't really mean it.
Photo courtesy of Tally Ho Yearbook 1970-71, v 24.

SDS leader, Abbie Hoffman speaks at FSU.
Photo courtesy of Tally Ho Yearbook 1970-71, v 24.

Students March on the Capitol, 1969.
Photo courtesy of Florida Archives.

FSU students respond to Regent Kovachevich.
Photo courtesy of Florida Archives.

Radical Jack (rear) at a Women's Lib rally.
Photo courtesy of Florida Archives.

Black students occupy the president's office.
Photo courtesy of Tally Ho Yearbook 1970-71, v 24.

The Westcott Fire

Student volunteers save valuables. *Photo from the personal collection of Stanley Marshall.*

President Marshall gives instructions to Director of University Relations Mike Beaudoin.
Photo courtesy of the Florida Flambeau, Strozier Library Special Collections, Florida State University.

FSU President Marshall and Sheriff Hamlin—was it arson? *Photo courtesy of the Florida Flambeau.*

Fighting the Westcott fire
Photo courtesy of Florida Archives.

A Tallahassee firefighter douses fire in an attempt to save the Westcott Building.
Photo courtesy of the Florida Flambeau.

Celebrities Come to FSU

Burt Reynolds greets Shirley Marshall.
Photo from the personal collection of Stanley Marshall.

Jane Fonda.
*Photo courtesy of Florida
Archives.*

Joan Baez.
*Photo courtesy of Tally Ho
Yearbook 1970-71, v 24.*

FAIR, WARM

No rain expected through Friday. Highs today and Friday 90, low tonight 64. Southeasterly winds, 5 to 15 miles per hour.

65th Year, No. 113—32 Pages

Tallahassee

Florida's Capit

(Democrat Photo by Sage Thigpen)

FSU President Marshall with actor Tony Randall at intermission of world premier performance of Menotti's "The Leper".
Photo courtesy of the Tallahassee Democrat.

Streaking—As Seen By The Flambeau

Everybody's doing it!
Photo courtesy of the Florida Flambeau.

They said it couldn't be done.
Photo courtesy of the Florida Flambeau.

Looks like the whole fraternity showed up!
Photo courtesy of the Florida Flambeau.

The Florida Flambeau's photographers caught the Free Spirits.
Photos courtesy of the Florida Flambeau

Students Find Humor In Whorehouse Charge

The "Ladies" of DeGraff Hall beckon customers.
Photo courtesy of the Tally Ho Yearbook 1970-71v 24.

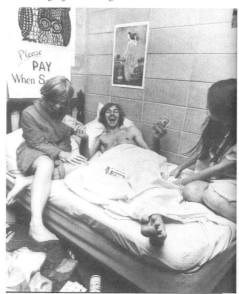

A "customer" is expected to pay.
Photo courtesy of the Tally Ho Yearbook 1970-71 v 24.

Cartoons by FSU student Doug Marlette, a future Pulitzer Prize winner.

"Your mission, Mr. Marshall, will be to discourage campus dissent by any means at your disposal. Should you or your team of crack administrators fail, the Board of Regents will disavow all knowledge of your existence!"

"Now you're not going to hold me to everything I say, are you, boy?"

The Lighter Side of Student Life

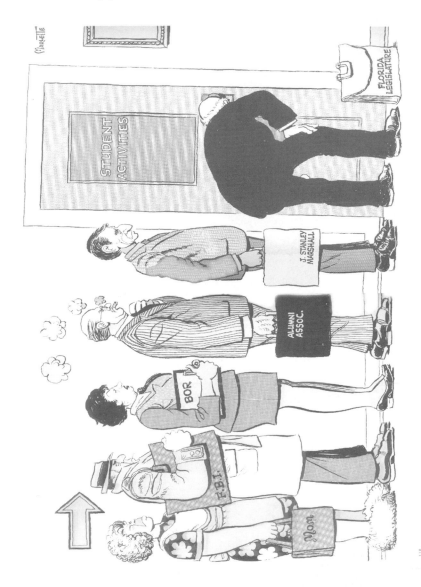

Doug Marlette's view of interested parties peeking into students' lives. *Artwork on pages 139 and 140 courtesy of the Tally Ho Yearbook 1970-71 v 24.*

Refereeing the Pigs versus Freaks football game, surrounded by some of the "radicals".
Photo courtesy of the Tally Ho Yearbook 1970-71, v 24.

Flag football with students.
Photo from the personal collection of Stanley Marshall.

FSU's sorority girls serenade the Marshall family with Christmas carols.
Photo from the personal collection of Stanley Marshall.

King Hussein Becomes an FSU Alum

The Marshalls join Queen Alia and King Hussein to admire the FSU
Marching Chiefs at the Royal Stadium in Amman, Jordan.
Photo from the personal collection of Stanley Marshall.

At lunch in Tallahassee with Jordanian Army Chief of Staff, Shirley
Marshall, and King Hussein.
Photo from the personal collection of Stanley Marshall.

Jordan's King Hussein receives honorary degree in Westcott ceremony.
Photo from the personal collection of Stanley Marshall.

Being welcomed by the Jordanians in Amman.
Photo from the personal collection of Stanley Marshall.

An Honorary Doctorate for a Most Honorable Lady

President Marshall and Helen Hayes.
Photo from the personal collection of Stanley Marshall.

The MacArthurs at FSU: (from left to right) Jamie, Helen (Hayes), John D.,
President Marshall, and Jamie's wife, Melody.
Photo from the personal collection of Stanley Marshall.

Florida Governor Claude Kirk with FSU and UF Presidents Stan
Marshall and Steve O'Connell.
Photo from the personal collection of Stanley Marshall.

FSU students demonstrate during a campus visit by Governor Kirk.
Photo courtesy of the Tally Ho Yearbook 1970-71, v 24.

The Florida Congressional Delegation discusses campus dissent with President Marshall, (1969).
Photo from the personal collection of Stanley Marshall.

The Marshalls are greeted by Happy and Nelson Rockefeller.
Photo from the personal collection of Stanley Marshall.

At the FSU Presidential Inaugural: (left to right) Presidents Campbell, Blackwell, Champion, and Marshall.
Photo from the personal collection of Stanley Marshall.

Florida State College for Women Alumna Beth Moor and Senator Claude Pepper.
Photo from the personal collection of Stanley Marshall.

The President's wife is forewarned.
Photo from the personal collection of Stanley Marshall.

Izzy Hecht gives FSU our first major gift.
Photo from the personal collection of Stanley Marshall.

President Campbell counsels the new president.
Photo from the personal collection of Stanley Marshall.

CHAPTER 7
The Role of the Faculty Senate

Faculty Senates as Institutional Entities

The faculty senates in many American colleges and universities have attracted attention to themselves in a variety of ways. During my time as a member of the Board of Trustees at FSU (2001 - 2005),* I got to know and observe several senate presidents. I thought they were worthy representatives of the faculty as they attempted to give the general faculty a voice in university governance. The FSU Faculty Senate in this period had competent leadership, people who seemed comfortable in working with the administration and who found no reason to seek an adversarial relationship.

But it was not always so. The Faculty Senate at FSU—and more particularly, the Senate Steering Committee—often assumed a role during the period of my presidency as a persistent antagonist to the administration and a frequent critic of the President's policies. The positions members took on many institutional issues seemed to be motivated by the members' wish to assert what they believed to be their rightful place in managing the University. Whether the University would be well served by the actions they proposed often seemed to me less important than making their voices heard and proclaiming to the general faculty that they would not be taken lightly by the University administration, the Board of Regents, or the legislature. It seemed to me that what they really wanted was power, and they were determined to have some.

The faculty senate as an entity on the higher education

---

*I was appointed to the Florida State University Board of Trustees when the board was established in 2001. My appointment to the Florida Board of Governors in January 2005 required that I resign from the Board of Trustees.

scene in this country has an interesting history. In the 1950s, university faculties across the country came to see the need for collective strength within their institutions as they resisted the loyalty oaths and other repressive anti-Communist measures that were part of the so-called Red Scare of that period. By the mid-1960s, faculty senates were taking an active and often vociferous role in university governance. The Faculty Senate at Berkeley for example, in 1964, weighed in forcefully on the Free Speech Movement on several occasions. The Senate passed resolutions that put it in direct conflict with the policies of the administration, thus forming a tenuous alliance between faculty members and activist students. During the Sproul Plaza rallies in 1964, Berkeley's Faculty Senate overwhelmingly passed a strongly worded resolution condemning President Clark Kerr for calling in police to restore order. Following adoption of the resolution, members of the Senate were cheered by student demonstrators who had gathered outside their meeting room.[1]

The Senate at UC-Berkeley also adopted a highly controversial ruling that seemed to be aimed directly at President Kerr's efforts to regain control of the University. At a University-wide meeting of the students and faculty, Mario Savio, leader of the Free Speech Movement, moved to take over the lectern from President Kerr, but was prevented from doing so by police. The Faculty Senate saw this as a blatant denial of free speech, and on the following day the senators passed a resolution affirming that "free speech or advocacy should not be restricted by the University."[2]

This is not to say that the entire faculty at Berkeley supported the actions of the protesters. Two of the faculty's most outspoken critics were Berkeley's celebrated professors Seymour Martin Lipsett and Philip Aultbach. They published a paper titled "Student Politics and Higher Education in the United States" in which they lamented the lack of opposition from the "elite" of the University—meaning the faculty—who by their silence provided some legitimacy to radical causes. Students were then struggling to gain more authority in student affairs, especially in regard to *in loco parentis* policies as they were carried out on many campuses. Student governments often passed resolutions to express their collective voice, and together with some faculty members, they struggled against the centralizing tendencies of university bureaucracy. Increasingly, however, faculty senates found themselves less concerned with actual university governance and more involved in campus politics. The two groups—faculty and dissident students— seemed to make comfortable bedfellows, because in the words of Kenneth Mortimer, both groups saw "existing governance structures as nonrepresentative [*sic*], and therefore illegitimate."[3] It is probably not an overstatement to say that many members of both groups operated on the basis of a kind of fundamental truth: the world—in this case, the university—is an imperfect place, and somebody is to blame. Most often that somebody is the person or the organization in charge.

When I assumed the presidency of Florida State University, I had been a member of the FSU faculty since 1958, and I identified clearly with other members of the faculty, many of whom were close friends and respected colleagues. Thus, I naturally looked to fellow faculty members for counsel and support when I found myself suddenly in charge. I had followed the protests closely at other universities where violence had occurred, more closely, it turned out, than most other faculty members. I felt frustration and indeed sometimes anger when I learned of the disruptive activities at Berkeley and Columbia and especially Cornell, where one of my sons was then a student. It was almost incomprehensible to me that members of the faculties at those places would permit such atrocious behavior, much less participate in it. So it was that in following events at other universities, I developed an interest in their governance structures. My investigations then, and now my research for this book, have brought to light useful and revealing information about faculty senates.

The performance of faculty senates in the decade following the well publicized events surrounding the Free Speech Movement at Berkeley in 1964 was the subject of many studies in the years following those events. One of the best known was performed by John B. Millett, then a highly regarded leader in higher education for the past 30 years. In his report, published as *New Structures of Campus Power*, Millett described the purpose of his study as "not to analyze the student revolution, but to analyze experience with campus-wide governance."[4] One of his early observations was that the student revolution seemed to be an excuse for, rather than the cause of, new forms of governance. He wrote that faculty members, "generally tended to perceive presidents, administrative officers, and boards of trustees as somehow not fully cognizant of or properly deferential to the new faculty power of the postwar era ... student unrest and student disruption provided faculty members with the opportunity to push their claim."[5]

Millett pointed out that by 1975, sufficient time had elapsed following the protests and demonstrations to determine the effects of new forms of institutional governance. The method employed by Millett and his associates was to conduct 30 case studies at particular colleges and universities. A number of questions were to be answered in those case studies; reduced to the simplest terms, the researchers wanted to know what the new governance structures looked like and how well they worked.

Millett observed that conflict had been building in many colleges and universities during the decade of the '60s, eroding past patterns of accommodation and trust. "Civility and social discourse and etiquette in personal relationships," he wrote, "gave way to impolite language, strident demands, and disruption or violence."[6]

In this study and others, various writers emphasize the role that faculty attempt to play in governance. Historically, boards of trustees were never intended to be the only authority in all decisions about academic matters, including establishing degree requirements, the development of curricula along with instructional objectives and course content, the evaluation of student achievement, and many other things that make up the academic enterprise at most institutions. In time, the scope of matters considered academic expanded to include the recruitment and selection of faculty, decisions about tenure and promotion, and, of course, faculty compensation. While these matters remained in the official province of the boards of trustees, such matters became of strong interest to faculties acting in an advisory capacity but one often having substantial influence with the boards of trustees.

At FSU, the faculty members were no doubt reading about events at other universities, and their attitudes about their own role in governance were surely influenced by what was happening on other campuses. I've found it instructive to study models of faculty government at three elite universities during that period and to try to discern how those efforts influenced university governance in the long term.

Columbia University

Governance at Columbia University in the years following the protests on that campus in 1968 was described in the Millet study. The University Senate was established by the Board of Trustees in May 1969, in the aftermath of the campus student revolt in April 1968. By 1975, the Senate was reported to be operating smoothly even if it was a somewhat inconspicuous element in the University's governance structure.[7]

Prior to 1969, the only university-wide agency of governance had been a University Council that was established in the 1890s. The Council was comprised mostly of deans and other administrative officers along with two elected faculty members from the University's 15 schools and colleges. It met once each semester, usually for less than an hour. The faculty as a whole did not meet; yet, faculties of particular schools and colleges met on occasion. The faculty lifestyle at Columbia "...emphasized individual commitment to scholarship and public service, but not commitment to the university as a community."[8] The University President was the presiding officer, and he set the agenda, an arrangement that was viewed as a means of ensuring presidential interest in and acceptance of the Senate's role.

The Senate at Columbia did, on occasion, address matters of concern to the faculty and make useful contributions. But the Colombia case study reported that by 1976, the senate was "perceived as a useful but not spectacular addition to the governance of the academic community."[9] It was easy to see that faculty members with national reputations were more likely to accept election to the Senate in the early days, but before long, they tended to drop-out because they considered attendance to be a drain on their time and energies.[10]

The University of Wisconsin

Until 1970, the entire faculty of the University met periodically in a town meeting format, but only a small fraction of the faculty attended the meetings. This changed in the 1966-1970 period, when the University was beset by student demonstrations that resulted in substantial property damage and the death of a graduate student. In that period, most of the faculty attended the meetings. Plans were initiated in 1970 to establish a Faculty Senate, and the faculty voted in 1973 to make the newly established Senate a permanent body.[11] It was chaired by the University's Chief Administrative Officer, the Chancellor. Its task was to consider academic matters of campus-wide concern and to submit its recommendations to the Chancellor. It dealt with a wide range of campus concerns including the academic calendar, admission standards for foreign students, and a code of ethics for faculty behavior.[12] Throughout this period, the faculty at the University of Wisconsin at Madison, historically the state's premier university, wrestled with the Wisconsin legislature's determination to create a state-wide higher education system with the Madison campus as the senior unit, but nonetheless only one unit in the system. That change was made over the Madison faculty's objections.

The University of Wisconsin faculty's interest in university governance was in most ways similar to those at other universities. The faculty wanted to be seen as playing a role, and they did so in the years when the University was under siege, but they seemed to have trouble defining a useful and productive role in the years that followed. The Senate has persisted and as with most other universities, has had a limited role in university governance.

Cornell University

The Cornell story is one of the most revealing and saddest in the Millett study. That such abdication of leadership by the administration and many of the faculty could have occurred at such a distinguished and highly regarded university was deeply troubling to many Americans. The drama of the takeover by black students was reported at length and in detail by the national press, causing Cornell University to be disparaged throughout much of the country.

Cornell University consisted of 11 colleges, each headed by a dean and each with its own separate faculty and its own educational policies committee. New students were admitted not to the University but to the individual colleges. The faculty of the University met periodically as a governance structure of sorts, but the meetings were poorly attended. There were several faculty committees, but in general, the administration paid little attention to the faculty's role in student life.

In April 1969, some 100 black students undertook a series of protests and demonstrations that turned violent. Willard Straight Hall, which housed the student center, the campus radio station, and other offices, was taken over by students wielding rifles and shotguns. Leadership from the central administration was lacking by most accounts, and a constituent group of faculty and students emerged and undertook to draft a constitution for campus-wide governance. The President was replaced by the Board of Trustees before the fall semester started in September 1969.

The new Senate began to operate in the fall of 1970. The domain of the University Senate was broader than at any other university in the Millett study. The constitution declared that the Senate was to be "the principal legislative and policymaking body of the University in matters which are of general concern to the University community." It had responsibility for a wide range of nonacademic matters and had the power to formulate a statement of the principles of academic freedom for students. In addition, the Senate had the power to recommend legislation to the general faculty and the Board of Trustees. It also had the power to examine short- and long-range plans of the University, including broad allocation of the University's resources and the power to participate in any presidential search by the Board of Trustees.[13] It would have been hard to find any phase of the life of the University that was not included.

In practice, however, things worked out differently. The Senate was largely excluded from any real influence over most of the University's academic affairs. The trustees had not approved the constitution that founded the Senate but only "recognized" it, and the board soon made it clear that it retained the authority to veto any Senate action. Over time, the University Senate found it more difficult to determine precisely what its role was to be. It was reduced to dealing with action on such issues as equal access for men and women to recreational facilities and discussion of the University's chapel service, resolving that the University would not sponsor "worship services," but only "convocations with speakers rather than preachers."[14] Senators debated at length on the use of

Christian symbols at Christmas time.

During the 1975-76 school year, about half of the meetings of the Senate were held without a quorum. In March 1976, the President established his own commission on University governance, which was advisory to the President. In March 1977, the University President recommended that the Board of Trustees abolish the University Senate and replace it with a Campus Council of 21 members, including seven faculty members and seven students.[15]

The FSU Senate's Role in the Events of the Day

My views on the role of the Faculty Senate at FSU are based to a considerable degree on a frequent and continuing relationship with the Senate over a period of nearly eight years. I should like to say once again that the Senate at FSU, and probably at many other institutions during the turbulent sixties and seventies, exhibited behavior that would not be emblematic of faculty senates in most of the years since then.

It must have been clear to everyone during the first three or four years of my presidency that the Faculty Senate and President Marshall were often at odds. But despite the tensions, I felt that I owed the Senate the recognition and respect merited by an official body of the University, and I did my best to fulfill that obligation. I recall no instance when any faculty member, including those in the Senate, ever indicated that I had not done so.

The views expressed by the Senate Steering Committee from the early days did not really surprise me, as the committee was dominated by a handful of members from the College of Arts and Sciences, which had been assuredly, if not formally, in support of Larry Chalmers as the University's next president. Larry was still in office as Academic Affairs Vice President in winter and spring of 1969—he was not to leave for Kansas until the end of the academic year—and I felt that many of the A&S faculty still flew his flag, so I didn't expect their enthusiastic support. But neither did I expect the Steering Committee to be such consistent opponents of my actions as I tried to establish order following the turmoil of John Champion's two resignations.

After the Night of the Bayonets on March 4, the Senate majority, again speaking through theSteering Committee, made its position clear: it believed that my decisive actions in handling the occupation of a building were inappropriate—"beyond the pale of propriety," they said. It felt that I should have granted recognition to SDS, and it let me know that it did not support many of my policies for governing the University.

No special analytic skills were required for me to understand the stance taken by the Steering Committee. I could easily think of several reasons for its opposition to my administration, including the following:

- The universities where the most serious disturbances had occurred were some of our most prestigious institutions: Berkeley, Cornell, Wisconsin, Columbia, and if the faculties at those institutions were sympathetic to the student demonstrations, well... why not FSU?
- John Champion's style was not such as to relate well to faculty members who had a taste for action and maybe even a slight urge for confrontation. John was not given to reaching out to faculty members, to asking for their advice on administrative decisions—and if we're going to try to change that, why not start with the new guy?
- The Board of Regents was generally remote from things on the campus, witness my appointment as Executive Vice President, and then as Acting President with no involvement by the Faculty Senate. To those who thought the faculty had a rightful place in such decisions, this was an un-

pardonable act, one they liked to believe would never happen at Berkeley, Columbia, or any of the other elite institutions that they thought FSU should emulate.

- Almost everything about the incident on March 4 went against the grain of Steering Committee members: my going to court for the injunction, the order from the President delivered by the Chief of Campus Police for the SDS to vacate the building (any *order* by the administration to students or faculty to do anything would have been abhorrent to some faculty members.)

Nonetheless, the Senate and I had to coexist, and the remarkable thing about our relationship in this period may have been that we were able to do just that. I continued to preside over the Senate at its monthly meetings (an arrangement I thought to be uncomfortable for both the senators and me, which was changed at my initiation in 1974 when the Senate came to elect its own presiding officer); and I met regularly with the Steering Committee. The constitution of the University decreed that the agenda for each Senate meeting was to be drawn up in advance by the University President and the Steering Committee jointly, a practice we followed carefully until the first meeting of the 1974-75 academic year. The full Senate seemed to me to be more tractable and to have a better grasp of campus problems than the Steering Committee, and I was gratified that that body never took formal action to oppose any of the policies of my administration. I also took note of the support for my actions expressed by many of the faculty's most respected, senior members, and it gratified me.

Nor do I wish to convey the notion that I did not look to the Senate to play a role in university governance. The minutes of the Senate meetings during the period report action on a number of academic matters, and some non-academic, that the administration took to heart. There were numerous issues on which I recognized that I needed broad faculty input. Two of the Senate's committees, the Academic Affairs Committee and the Faculty Professional Relations Committee, in particular, dealt with matters on which the administration should—and did—look to the Senate for guidance. They recommended that the much discussed requirement for physical education, specifically that the three-course requirement for non-majors, be deleted. The Faculty Professional Relations Committee made recommendations on appointments to a variety of committees that dealt with such things as transfer credits by junior college transfers and the number of credits that must be earned for graduation at a senior institution in the State University System. The Senate advised me on how we should deal with the devastating library budget cutbacks in 1969, a reduction of one third over the previous year's budget. Considerable Senate time was given to the discussion of a more refined grading system than A thru F; students had expressed their interest in a pass/fail system rather than letter grades. And the Senate, of course, engaged extensively in discussions of faculty salaries and fringe benefits.

Still, the agenda of the Senate throughout this period was dominated by discussions and debates on what senators saw as the Senate's rightful place in the selection of John Champion's successor and the appointment of other university administrative officers including vice-presidents and deans. Clearly, the Senate wanted a greater role in the appointment of administrative officers than I was willing to concede, and that remained a sticking point in our relations throughout my presidency.

At the last Senate meeting of the year on May 22, 1969, student Rick Johnson was granted the privilege of the floor to read a statement he said represented the views of the student Committee Against Repression (CARE). Johnson, a well-known activist in SDS and leader of student demonstrations, advised the Senate concerning what it ought to do to oppose the "repressive fascist actions" of the University. "The repression must be fought at every turn," he said, "and a revolutionary class unity must be forged between black, brown and white revolutionaries who see that this repression reflects the deepening crisis of U.S. imperialism and the desperate efforts of the ruling class to maintain its oppressive control over the millions of people all over the world." It was not obvious to me why Mr. Johnson was accorded a place on the agenda of the faculty's most important deliberative body.

The Standley Influence

Feelings were strong and actions by the Steering Committee and especially by Committee Chairman Fred Standley of the English Department strained our relationship many times. There were two incidents, both well-documented, that illustrate Standley's attitude concerning the role of the Senate and his approach to the administration. Both deserve to be described in some detail.

The Senate met in special session on October 2, 1974, for its first meeting of the new school year. This was a special meeting called by the Senate Steering Committee supposedly to organize the body for the year ahead, thus there had been no meeting with me to establish an agenda. Senate President Standley opened the meeting by saying that the Steering Committee had decreed that he should say something—a kind of "state of the senate message," he said. And so he thought he would "engage in some philosophizing and sermonizing." He stated that James Baldwin, in one of his essays, said that where there is no vision, the people perish. Standley suggested that this ought to be applied to the 1974-75 year, and he thought that Baldwin's words should be transposed from "where there is no vision, the people perish" to "where the faculty have no vision, the University will perish—languish first—then perish."[16]

Standley went on:

The faculty, you and I, we must—as in the past—accept responsibility for the academic and intellectual vision of this University. Why must we fashion a vision for the University? Because the faculty is the only stable component in the life of the University—the stable entity, who can hold together simultaneously those considerations of the past and present and the future.

...Administrations, too, are a reality in the vision of the University, but administrators come and go— passing into oblivion with little significant impact for good or ill (some of us have been here for 12 years, and we have had three administrations; we are still here, they are still going; and many of you have been here longer than that).

...Long after the professional managers and administrators are gone from the scene—the faculty of this institution—the academicians, the researchers, the teachers, the intellectuals—will still be here; and the students will be here, (though in flux)." He concluded his "philosophizing and sermonizing" by saying "... let's inform those who have not had faculty responsibility and experience: what we have as a faculty for the University is a vision of excellence and service within the context of the public good... What we want to discuss and promulgate: what is true and beneficial not what is pseudo and trivial, what is of quality and value and not what is shabby and shoddy..."[1]

7

I did not know how Standley's remarks were viewed by others, but to those of us in the administration who were clearly the people to whom his comments were directed, they sounded pretty vitriolic. "Shabby" and "shoddy"? What had any of us done to warrant adjectives like those? Despite sharp differences on many issues, none of the parties had to this point engaged in rhetoric of that kind, and I found no one who could remember such attacks in the recent history of the University. My reaction approached disbelief—I had heard Fred's words, but had difficulty understanding what had caused him to abandon the civility that mostly characterized our relationship in the past. I believed that many in the Senate were embarrassed by their presiding officer's conduct.

In the weeks between that first meeting of the year and the second meeting scheduled for mid-October, I prepared to respond, as I knew I must. It was not hard to reply to Standley's charges in a way that would reveal just how hollow they were. So when the Senate met on October 16, I addressed the body with the following remarks:

> I believe that I must take vigorous exception to Mr. Standley's statement that "administrators pass into oblivion with little significant impact for good or ill." Only those who do not know their history would believe that intellectual freedom in this State would have arrived at its present condition had it not been for the courage and strength of President Conradi, or that this institution would have ever gained the statewide support it enjoys without the efforts of Doak Campbell, or that President Strozier, even in his brief term, had no impact on the University's standing and its respect nationally. I had lunch last Thursday with Karl Dittmer and three of his fellow administrators at Portland State. They told me of the strong influence Vice President Dittmer has had on the program of research and graduate study at Portland State during the past half dozen years. At the same meeting I saw Chancellor Werner Baum of the

University of Wisconsin, Milwaukee.* How many of our faculty would say that Dr. Baum had little significant influence for good or ill on the development and growth of Florida State University?

I then recounted the names of about a dozen faculty members who also served as administrators—deans, heads of departments, directors of research centers—and challenged Standley to deny the enormous contributions to the growth, the prestige, the well-being of Florida State University. And I told him that it was "both inaccurate and unfair to say that they pass into oblivion with little significant impact for good or ill."

As for the durability of administrators, I told senators that such a question is related more to science than opinion. In the 22 years from the University's founding in 1947, we had had four presidents, which averages to about 5.5. years per person in the office allowing a little time for acting presidencies. Some of those presidents, I reminded senators, had enjoyed long service in both teaching and administration, and it would be difficult to deny them strong roles in the evolution of this institution.

"Not all administrators are great," I added, "but neither are all of them insignificant. And even though the glory of a university is always in the distinction of its faculty, that glory is often heavily dependent on the vision and support of the president and other administrators."

Marshall's "Offer to Resign"

The other issue that Standley seized upon in subsequent attacks on the President was the resignation that I supposedly

---

* Karl Dittmer was then serving as the president of Portland State University, and Werner Baum as president of the University of Wisconsin at Milwaukee. Both had served at FSU as faculty members, department heads, and as vice presidents of academic affairs.

offered at a meeting in early November. The setting was a small conference I participated in by invitation entitled "Humanizing the University." It was a rather informal conference; we sat in a circle in a small conference room—there were not more than two dozen people present, mostly graduate students. Hettie Cobb, a reporter from the *Tallahassee Democrat*, was also present, and she asked me if there were circumstances under which I would consider resigning. The question was out of order in this meeting, but I felt I should give a polite response. I dismissed the question by saying that if I thought a majority of the faculty really wanted me to, I would probably step aside, but I was satisfied that there was no such feeling among the faculty. The discussion on humanizing the University resumed with no further comment on my "resignation."

To my considerable surprise, the *Tallahassee Democrat* carried a major story the next day with a headline about Marshall's resignation—by Hettie Cobb, of course; and that was to become an over-riding interest of the Senate Steering Committee for the rest of the year. Fred Standley, aided by *The Flambeau's* editors who featured the resignation issue in news stories and editorials, missed no opportunities to use the matter in his continuing attacks. He told the Senate at its meeting on November 20, "…the question of resignation is a question the President has to struggle with. No faculty member made the suggestion initially; rather, President Marshall did so. If he wishes to conduct a referendum on the administration's performance of its duties, then the faculty senate, if it chooses to do so, will consider helping him to implement that referendum."[18]

Of special interest in this matter is a letter I received from Peter A. Butzin, director of United Campus Ministries. Mr. Butzin had attended the meeting on Humanizing the University and had heard the exchange with Cobb, "I deeply regret the way your statement last Tuesday has been taken out of context and exaggerated," he said. He enclosed a copy of a letter to *The Flambeau* in which he said that "Dr. Marshall never suggested that he might resign in response to a haphazard poll among faculty...President Marshall opened himself up to any and all questions from the group. Although this question did not naturally grow out of Dr. Marshall's prepared introductory remarks, he responded freely, yet carefully...There were no follow-up questions from the group...Our concern is for the protection of free speech, and for our own announced purposes: Humanizing the University."

In his letter to *The Flambeau*, Mr. Butzin said, "we are distressed by the response of *The Flambeau* to a brief exchange which took place as a part of our open discussion with President Marshall last Tuesday afternoon." He continued, "the result of your attempt to sensationalize may be that no university administrator will feel free to speak openly and informally in a public forum...We must all work to avoid character assassination." In a later communication, Mr. Butzin complained that *The Flambeau* had not acknowledged or published his letter. The editor replied that their failure to do so had been due to lack of space.

Faculty Senates: Some Reflections

I was asked occasionally during those times if I was tempted to reply to some of the Steering Committee's intemperate statements with intemperance to match theirs, and why I did not give in to the urge to assassinate some character myself. There are two important reasons why I felt I must not do so.

One was that I did not wish to raise the level of tension between any of the faculty and the legislature. It was to the University's benefit to have legislators' anxieties reduced if we were to avoid seeing punitive laws passed to control dissident faculty and students, laws that I neither needed nor wanted. Calling attention to the strident behavior of the Steering Committee and its Chairman would, I thought, be seen by some legislators as yet another instance in which those troublesome "degree-laden professors" should be brought into line by laws designed to broaden the university president's powers and perhaps to move some of those powers to the legislature.

Another reason, more influential than the first, was my belief about what a majority of the faculty expected me to do. You're the President, I could almost hear them say; we expect you to maintain order, to keep the University open, to guarantee the constitutional freedoms to all, and to maintain conditions that will allow us to teach and do our research free from the political intrigue that we read about in *The Flambeau* but want no part of. Dealing with that is your job, not ours. Just do not let this place become another Berkeley, Wisconsin, Michigan, or Cornell. And as student Will Bray said in his letter of support, if things on the front get too tough, we'll come to your aid.

But there was also a third reason: Responding in kind would, I thought, have been beneath the dignity that I felt the President owed the university community and the people of Florida, and I was determined to remain above the diatribes.

And there was something else that surfaced occasionally in my reaction to the Senate and those who made it up. On more than one occasion, when the time came for me to go to late afternoon Senate meetings during the time I was its presiding officer, I would remark to Ruth Wester, my long-time Executive Aassistant, "Well, I'm off to the Senate—it's the children's hour," a devilish thing for me to say, and a remark that overlooked the fact that the Senate contained many "grown-ups" with whom I had continuing good relations. But Longfellow's poem just kept coming to mind, and I couldn't resist. Why do I now relate this bit of silliness? Well, as I said, history is history.

The literature on university governance contains more criticism than praise for faculty senates, and this may be due in part to the natural inclination of writers to write about things that are easily described. It's easier to find examples of the irresponsible antics of the Senate at Berkeley than to delve into the useful and productive things it might have done. The over-reaching Senate at Cornell and its inevitable demise made good copy, even for scholars who might have wanted to support faculty senates.

But the senates themselves did not help. I have a feeling, mostly intuitive, that the senates achieved more good than one can easily find in the literature. It would have helped if, in those stressful times, the senates had acknowledged their role to be advisory to the university administrations and had organized themselves to do that effectively. I believe they could have brought faculty values and ideas for dealing with specific issues into play in ways that would have reduced the antagonisms and the stress on all of the participants—and just might have avoided the lasting damage that accrued to some of the universities.

My feelings toward our Faculty Senate at FSU were decidedly mixed. I was disappointed in some of the actions of the Steering Committee members and wondered why the full Senate did not show greater interest in calling them off. I had high regard for and close personal friendships with many of the Senate's members and I waited for them to display the mature judgment and concern for the University's welfare that I knew they sincerely felt. But what I hoped for was not to be found at FSU or at most other universities for reasons that are easier to discern now than they were then. Many faculty members were affected by the same concerns that troubled students: the war in Vietnam, racial tensions, and a growing discontent with "the establishment," whether the person in authority was president of the country or of the university. It was time for change, and they were determined to bring it about, and if doing so meant things were going to be uncomfortable for those in charge—well, that's just too bad.

One of the writers commented that the best reason for the existence of faculty senates was simply that faculty members wanted them to exist. Their actual accomplishments might not be all that important. Some faculty members I've talked to seemed to endorse that thought: Don't expect the Senate to have a specific role; just let it exist.

Is it possible that their efforts to oppose and discredit administrators as the Senate sometimes did at Florida State, served a useful role by preventing those of us in the administration from resorting to more autocratic policies or more centralized decision making generally—to keep us in line, so to speak? Maybe so. I don't believe the record at FSU would support such a claim, but I may not be the best qualified person to address that question. My best answer is that whatever mistakes the administration might have made and wherever the President might have fallen short of what was expected, the fact is that Florida State University survived this difficult period with no disruption of its educational function, no significant property damage, no loss of life, and no denial of any of the constitutional guarantees. A good many other university presidents during that period would have liked to make such a claim.

CHAPTER 8
Reflections on The Sixties- What Did We Learn?

"Someday we may look back on these times and laugh, and then again, we may not."
                              -Jesse Kornbluth, activist, 1968

There is no shortage of literature on the period generally referred to as "The Sixties." The term is shorthand for about a decade covering mostly the campus disruptions that started at UC Berkeley in 1964 when student Mario Savio launched the Free Speech Movement. It's hard to say when it ended, but it was undeniably slowed in the first half of the '70s when Congress passed the Equal Rights Amendment (ERA)* and our troops came home from Vietnam. But scars remained, and those of us who witnessed student activism up close could easily identify burning issues on the campuses throughout the 70s and beyond. The use of drugs, disenchantment with government at all levels, Richard Nixon's resignation, a relaxation of sexual inhibitions, continuing racial strife, and a serious economic crisis—remember "stagflation"?—these and related concerns have worried many Americans until the present day. I'm reminded once again of the statement by Terry Anderson, a highly respected student of social activism, whose writings provide as insightful an analysis of those times as I've seen. Those young Americans, he told us, have called into question the very meaning of America, and some of those questions are still in need of answers.

---

*The ERA later failed to be ratified by enough states to ensure its adoption.

Major writers on that period have fallen into three easy-to-identify categories: Those who supported the protesters and their causes, those who opposed them, and those who took a largely unbiased view and tried to analyze events dispassionately. I've read accounts of all three kinds and have relied more heavily on the third group (Anderson, for example.) But I've gained much from the others as well, especially the first group (Todd Gitlin, professor of journalism at Columbia may be the best known), and they have caused me to think hard about the motives and the consequences, both positive and negative, of the student protests—outcomes that it was often hard for me to see in the heat of the controversies.

In reviewing and assessing the effects of The Sixties, I have chosen to separate the events at FSU from those that might be considered national in scope. What happened at Florida State University was in many ways a part of the national protests, but at the same time, the FSU story is distinctive enough to be described separately. Let's examine the national picture first.

Across the Country....

Anti-war protests

Young people all across the country expressed their objections to the war in Vietnam and nowhere more than on the college campuses. Peace advocates were joined by the counterculture in sometimes violent protests. Actions by the Nixon administration—the Cambodian Invasion in 1970, covert activities directed against various student groups by the FBI and CIA, exhortations to support the war by Secretary of State Henry Kissinger and Defense Secretary Robert McNamara—all raised the level of concern by students who had the most to risk—being drafted to go to Vietnam.

Some university administrators took actions and made statements that seemed to encourage violence. Their anti-war sentiments were understandable but there was no requirement that university administrators give vent to their feelings in ways that raised student anxieties on the campus while contributing nothing to the peace effort. The office of the President of the University of Wisconsin told a group of students:

> We clearly oppose the U.S. involvement in Southeast Asia and the murder of over 500,000 Asian civilians, We also oppose the increasing repression of legitimate dissent ending in events like persecution of the Black Panther Party and left leaders and the Kent State massacre.[2]

The number and vigor of the antiwar protests no doubt affected the attitudes of those in government, especially in Congress. Long-term effects? The unconventional methods employed by the most aggressive protestors (who, of course, got most of the headlines) made their message less acceptable to the establishment, and that resulted in actions by government that many students believed to be oppressive. But despite the harsh language by President Nixon and others, no repressive measures of lasting importance were enacted.. Yet the vigor of the protests, I believe, very likely has caused national leaders ever since to be more sensitive to the opinions and attitudes of young people, not just in military matters but in many other things as well.

Civil Rights

The message of Martin Luther King Jr., resonated with college students and energized them to work for advances in human rights. They pressed for more vigorous enforcement of the Civil Rights Act of 1964. The report of the Presidents' National Advisory Committee on Civil Disorders rejected the idea that the race riots in several American cities were caused by some nefarious conspiracy. The Kerner Commission's report warned that unfulfilled promises of equal rights for blacks threatened serious national disorder. Students on the campuses took heart from such bold statements and from programs such as Head Start and a variety of job training, inner-city economic development projects and need-based financial assistance for college that benefited many black students.

An unpleasant facet of black student activism was the part the Black Panthers played in the protests. The organization was mostly controlled by extremists who seemed to be more interested in committing acts of terror than in advancing civil rights. Their methods were so extreme that most people came to dismiss them as a fringe group with no lasting appeal to Americans of any race or color.*

The Women's Movement

While campus activists for women's issues got relatively little coverage in the late sixties and seventies, substantial changes were made in many matters that affected women's lives. Women's Liberation did however attract attention and support on some campuses, and the changes that were initiated then have been extended and strengthened in the years since.

Women have career opportunities they could only have dreamed of in 1970. Incomes of women have approached if not yet equaled those of men. On the personal side, gender roles are still observed, but America has surely become a more androgynous society. Many colleges today have women's studies programs, and female university presidents are more common. Working mothers, and on some campuses student mothers, are offered child care and a variety of other programs to facilitate their active participation in their studies or their ca-

---

*"In 1969, 348 Panthers were arrested—not for political transgression, which might have made them martyrs, but for rape, burglary, and robbery." from John C. McWilliams *The 1960s Cultural Revolution*, (Westport, CT: Greenwood Press, 2000): 88.

reers. Thus, we can say with confidence that the concerns expressed by young people contributed substantially to the women's rights movement.

Environmental Concerns

The fragile condition of the environment concerned people during this period, including many students. Membership in such organizations as the Audubon Society and the Sierra Club grew rapidly. In April 1970, million of Americans celebrated Earth Day. Hippies were said to have politicized the ecology issue as they called attention to the abuse of animals by their fellow Americans. People worried about the disposal of toxic waste and the threat of global warming, issues that have recently re-energized those concerned about the environment.

Most of the impetus for change in this area came not from the universities but from non-campus organizations and from people active in civic affairs. It is relevant, however, to note that the values and some of the information that such groups relied upon could be traced back to their college experience.

Still Other Concerns...

Anyone who visited the college campuses in this period couldn't help identify issues that some students would add to this list. The winds of change had caught many people, not all of them young, and the America in which the baby boomers had been born was no more.

Many personal habits and traditions had given way. Marriage was becoming an institution that was optional for cohabitation. Homosexuality continued to be a volatile subject for much of society, but same-sex relationships didn't create the attention they once did. Recreational drug use was accepted by a sizeable segment of society. Religious organizations became more concerned about social ills and more involved in community problems. The variety of religious beliefs and organizations increased. What constituted legitimate corporate behavior regarding social and civic responsibilities was widely discussed. And the rights—indeed, the obligations—of the people to expect and to initiate change became a way of life. It's safe to say, as many students of social behavior have, that at no time in the twentieth century has change been so constant a factor in the lives of most Americans.

Meanwhile, on the Campus in Tallahassee...

Challenging Authority

The practices against which most of the protestors vented was the refusal of authorities to grant them the influence they wanted in matters of university governance. Decisions that affected their lives were too distant and often made by people who, students thought, wouldn't listen when they spoke.

Students had had quite enough of rules and regulations they did not like and could see no reason for. In 1968, the FSU president censors a story in a student publication for reasons many students did not like. Along comes the next president, and he refuses to recognize a controversial student organization. The Attorney General and the Board of Regents support those decisions, and what's worse, so do the majority of their parents and others who are in charge of things. What's a person to do who really believes there's a better way?

The obvious thing to do was something that would get the attention of those in charge. It never works to go through channels, they said, and to try to operate within the system. If we take to the streets and make threats, maybe they'll listen. So that's what they did, and I am quite willing to say that it worked. Well, in a way it did. That approach got our attention all right, and those of us in the establishment responded by making some of the changes that the protesters demanded. We sought and received more active participation by students in decisions of many kinds through such vehicles as the Board of Student Publications, the Center for Participant Education, and others. We made real efforts to reduce what students thought of as a kind of campus imperialism.

But the vigorous student protests had another outcome, one that might have had an impact on students in a way that had not occurred to any of us. The posture of the President's office along with others in the administration, including especially the University Police, might have sent a message to students that young people needed to hear: There must be a place for discipline and order in any community including a university. Spontaneous expressions against the status quo have their place, but if order is to be maintained, those in charge must, on occasion, establish regulations and see that they are enforced. Anarchy may be fun, but it has its limits. Resolute leadership is sometimes required to vouchsafe institutional welfare, and the leader sometimes has to go on his own instincts and values. That has always been a requirement of leadership, and the opportunity that our students had to see it in action might have been a useful lesson—or in the current educational jargon, a teachable moment.

Race Relations

At FSU, we avoided any serious confrontations due in part to the leadership of our black students, who were mostly responsible young people who were here for essentially one purpose: To get a good education as quickly as possible. Those of us in the administration thought we made important strides in the march for equal rights for black people on the campus, both students and employees.

The absence of any real threats of violence on the part of black students drew upon a long, rather positive record by my administration in race relations. As a department head in the School of Education in 1960, I hired the university's first black secretary and awarded the first doctoral fellowship to a black graduate student the following year. The first black students to set foot on the campus were science teachers from Broward

County who attended a 1962 Summer Science Institute conducted by my department under a grant from the National Science Foundation. Black schoolmates of my children attended parties and overnights at the President's home, and that might have been noticed. I sensed that our black students knew something of my record on race relations, and that seemed to help.

What we did was to establish the first Black Student Union (BSU) in the State University System, set up a black students' center, and undertake vigorous recruitment of black faculty members. FSU was known to be the most progressive institution in race relations in the State University System in the early '70s. Relations between our administrators and black students were generally cordial, and that was due in no small part to the mature understanding by the black student leaders—such as John Burt and Winston Scott (his story is told in a footnote on page 107). Those students seemed to be eager not to be seen as allied with other student protest groups whose goals were never well defined. The black students knew what they wanted and it didn't serve their purpose to be seen as in league with the SDS and other opportunistic protestors.

I felt some regret then, and still do, that those of us in the administration were unable to convince the black student leaders to adopt a more inclusive stance in the changes they sought. The BSU served a need, but it also tended to set black students apart from the main student body. I managed to persuade their leaders not to press for a black studies major, and through backyard social events at the President's home, I tried to establish their place in mainstream campus life. I knew they felt like the minority group that they were, and I wished we could have found more ways to create a single, inclusive student body.

So, while we made substantial progress in advancing black students' interests, we probably didn't do enough. How could we not have identified Winston Scott as a young man of promise and somehow make sure that he got tapped for some student leadership role? Yes, we did have a black Homecoming Queen, but we somehow missed Winston Scott—and I'm sure there were others like him who passed through unnoticed.

So what did we learn from the students whose demonstrations and protests gave the sixties a special place in the history and the culture of our country? The answer, I believe, is a whole lot, and some of the most useful lessons might help our leaders as they contend with similar protests today.

PART II

The remaining chapters of this book, unlike the earlier ones, are not about the turbulent '60s and '70s at Florida State University. That story has been told and readers, I hope, have been rewarded by my accounts of those historic events—or if the readers are younger people, they have perhaps been informed of events about which they have occasionally heard from their elders.

The following chapters will address events at the University that were different from those wrought by a radical movement—these are events of another kind. They too helped to make history of sorts—a history that shaped the University and its place in higher education in Florida and beyond. Members of the FSU community and our friends would surely agree that developments in athletics during the period placed a stamp on FSU that was noticed by millions of people, and not just those in Florida. A visit to the campus by a sitting head of state is historic by any definition. And an enduring love affair between a university—any university—and Helen Hayes is surely historic.

The four chapters to come are intended to give readers a sense of campus life that will, I hope, be revealing and enjoyable. From the vantage of the University President, those events were an undiluted pleasure. My fond hope is that this recitation of the University's history will awaken happy memories in some of the University's alumni and friends who lived in those interesting times.

CHAPTER 9
Big Changes In Athletics

Coach Peterson's Resignation

It was some time before 7:00 a.m. when the bedside telephone rang. "Stan, this is Bill," said the coach's voice, "Can I have my job back?" The call was not totally unexpected. Bill Peterson's call to tell me that he was resigning as head football coach had come late Sunday afternoon, the previous day. I had had calls during the afternoon from Pete's friends and supporters who had gathered at the Petersons' home to talk about the possibility of his leaving. Whether he convinced them or the other way around, I still don't know, but a couple of them called to ask me to do whatever was required to keep Pete. About mid-afternoon, one of the coach's unofficial advisers appeared on the lawn at the president's home; it was Dr. Ed Haskell, a well-known Tallahassee physician and ardent football fan. Shirley and I were engaged in a game of doubles on the tennis court, and Dr. Haskell approached to tell me that he hoped I would make Pete Athletics Director (AD) so he would stay. The doctor said he was representing a group of people who had been meeting with Pete, and he came as their emissary.

I might not have displayed the kind of courtesy to Dr. Haskell expected of the University President, for I had made my position clear to the doctor and the others on more than one occasion: Bill Peterson would not be appointed Athletics Director. He was a fine coach, a good member of the University community, and a person for whom I had genuine affection. And if it were up to me, he could remain head football coach at Florida State for the indefinite future. He had many fine qualities, I had said, but not those required of the University's Director of Intercollegiate Athletics. It was not negotiable.

The doctor left and the tennis match resumed, but in my gut, I felt I had not heard the last of the matter that had commanded the attention of several prominent Tallahasseans on this lovely fall Sunday afternoon. Pete's call came later in the afternoon, and he got right to the point. I've decided to leave, he said. I've accepted the job at Rice, and I'll be going out to Houston to meet with the president in the morning. The conversation from that point went about as you'd expect. I thanked him for the great 10 years he had given us, and I wished him well at Rice. He replied in kind, thanking me for my friendship and the support I had given the football program, and we both expressed the hope that our paths might one day cross again. We then discussed the public announcement and agreed that we would hold the news until Monday morning. He had talked with the people at Rice about the release, and that was also their wish.

It came as a real surprise then, when I heard the report of Pete's resignation on the 11 o'clock news. I had no idea about how the breach came about, but it didn't seem to matter much.

Yet the early morning phone call caused me some anguish. "Marge has been crying all night," Bill said, "she just can't bear to leave Tallahassee. We would like to stay."

I replied, "Bill, that's going to be hard to arrange especially since the news is out and the folks at Rice think you're their coach." While my concerns for Bill and Marge were sincere, I can't deny that I really felt we had passed the point of no return. Pete had been pressing me for the AD's job ever since I became President, and I just felt it was the right time for him to move on and for me to turn the direction of the program over to the new Athletics Director who I hoped would come aboard soon.

Pete's one-year stay at Rice and another year with the Houston Oilers in the NFL was of interest to many in the FSU sports community—people like me, who were fond of

Bill Peterson and wanted him to do well.

The search for his successor began at once as vacancies in head coach's positions always do. I said then, and I'm no less convinced today, that filling the job of head football coach probably caused me to feel more pressure than anything else about my job as President. Sports fans have intense feelings; they rarely lack certitude, and they are usually not shy about expressing themselves. If they have a candidate for the head coach's job, they're going to let you know. The search for a new coach needed to begin at once, and it did.

But the Peterson loss was more than just Bill himself. Marge was the kind of wife you'd hope your head coach would have, given the opportunities those women have to set a tone among the other coaches and their wives and fans generally. The Peterson's four sons were also the kind of boys you would want other kids in the community to emulate. So the regret I felt over Pete's leaving was shared by many in the community and surely by countless football fans throughout Florida. Maybe even by a few Gators.

Bobby Bowden is Almost Hired

Bobby Bowden was no stranger to FSU; he had spent two years here as a member of Bill Peterson's staff in the mid-'60s. Prior to that, he coached at South Georgia Junior College and his alma mater Howard (later to become Samford). After success there and at FSU under Peterson, he went to the University of West Virginia in 1966. Bowden, of course, had heard about the vacancy at FSU, and we were not surprised to receive his application. There was no doubt that he would be interviewed.

The position attracted many applicants including several highly regarded coaches. Among them was Larry Jones at the University of Tennessee, where he directed the defense. The Vols were having an outstanding season in 1970, and the defense had been recognized as one of the nation's best. Jones made his interest known to me, and I quickly came to regard him as a prime candidate.* I had received calls from Texas coach Darrell Royal and other respected men in the football world who said they were sure Jones would become a successful head coach somewhere. Bill Battle, head coach at Tennessee, was effusive in his recommendation of Jones.

But Bobby was very much in our sights, and we set up a meeting with him during his visit with his relatives in Birmingham over the Christmas holidays. He would meet with us only if we gave our assurance that his interest in the position would remain entirely confidential; he was not about to let the people back in Morgantown know he would consider leaving, and we understood that.

The interview took place at a motel in Montgomery, at about 8:00 p.m. on December 30. Bobby had driven down from Birmingham, and the University's Athletics Committee had flown up from Tallahassee. This was two days before New Year's Day, when Tennessee was scheduled to play Air Force in the Sugar Bowl. I had rounded up six members of the Committee for the flight from Tallahassee in a small private airplane that I used from time to time. I really didn't need to explain why filling the coaching vacancy was a high priority for all of us. They knew.

The Chairman of the Athletics Committee was Dean Mode Stone of the School of Education. Professor Dick Baker of the School of Business was also on the Committee, and he recalls, as I do, that we had a bumpy flight to Montgomery in some very heavy weather.

The interview was not quite what I expected. Instead of giving us assurances that he would be the coach "who could beat the Gators" (that was the standard pledge made by every other prospect we interviewed during this and the next two

---

*Vaughn Mancha had resigned his position as Director of Athletics, and the search was on for his successor. That would be Clay Stapleton, who was hired in 1971. So in December 1970, I was serving as my own athletics director.

head coach searches), Bowden spent more time charming the Committee. Of course, he talked football too, but mostly I remember how he captivated us with humorous anecdotes and the funny one-liners for which Bowden, even then, had become famous—and which he delivers as few men can. But at the end of the interview, I still wanted to know just how we were going to beat the Gators.

If I had taken a poll after the interview with Bowden, I believe the Committee would have recommended hiring him. But the Committee members had not talked with Jones and had not heard his great endorsements as I had. I really felt compelled to meet Jones and have the Committee interview him, and I came up with a plan on the spot. Let's try to wind this thing up without further delay, I told the members; that meant arranging for all of us to meet and interview Jones before returning to Tallahassee. As absurd as it seemed, I managed to sell my scheme to the men on the committee.

...Larry Jones Instead

First there was my call to Coach Battle in New Orleans, where his team was to play Air Force in the Sugar Bowl. Will you consent to our meeting with Coach Jones tomorrow morning if he agrees, and if we can work out the arrangements? Yes, he said. Then I called Coach Jones to ask if he would show up for an interview at the New Orleans airport at 5:30 a.m. No problem, he said. That meant getting our group back on the plane that was waiting at the Montgomery Airport sometime after midnight and flying to New Orleans. All members of the Committee agreed to go except one: The senior member of the Committee was Dean Mode Stone, and he had had enough of flying in a small plane through bad weather. He decided to stay overnight and take the bus back to Tallahassee the next morning. He might have had more sense than any of us. Anyway, we landed in New Orleans at about four o'clock and got ready to meet Coach Jones.

That meeting confirmed all of the favorable things I had heard in Jones's references, and he made a very strong impression on the members of the Committee. We asked him to come to Tallahassee the morning after the bowl game (which Tennessee won), and he agreed to do so. Then we released him to go back to his job coaching the Vols defense, and we wished the team well. Larry and his wife Judy came to Tallahassee the morning after the game, where he went through the expected run of interviews. At the end of the day, I offered him the job, and he accepted.

Bobby Says He Wasn't Ready

When FSU people comment to me on the hiring of Bobby Bowden, I find few who remember that I almost certainly could have hired him five years earlier. It's a story without much meaning in the long history of Coach Bowden's time at FSU. There was, however, one wrinkle in the story that came to light in December 1993, when we were about to play for the National Championship against Nebraska in Miami. Tom McEwen, sports editor of the *Tampa Tribune*, had heard something about the Bowden hiring, and he called me for the story. "Sure," I said, "we could have hired Bobby five years earlier." "Why didn't you?" asked Tom. "Well Tom, I thought Bobby showed his skill as an entertainer, and he established great rapport with the Athletics Committee, but what did that have to do with winning football games?" Then I added some ill chosen words as an afterthought: "I thought he was sort of a smart ass." I remember regretting the remark immediately, but I thought that Tom McEwen, whom I knew well and regarded as a friend, would not use my quote—he would surely protect me from my own bad judgment. Of course, I was wrong—McEwen's column contained my exact words.

I was sure that Bobby would read what I had said, and I was genuinely embarrassed. I've never regarded him in those terms, and during his years at FSU had come to recognize in his unique use of the language the real character of the man, and to understand how effective this can be in his recruiting of student athletes and in his relations with the media and of course the alumni.

What to do? Well the obvious thing was to apologize to Bobby, and I expressed my regrets in a letter that arrived in his office upon his return from Miami. I told him that I admitted that I had made the off-color remark, that I had never so regarded him, and I was truly sorry. Bobby replied promptly, also by letter, and his message is yet another reminder of his great skill in human relations:

> Dear Stan:
>
> Thanks very much for your letter, but don't you worry about an apology. I was flattered by the remark. Wasn't exactly what it meant but I felt like somewhere in there had to be something flattering, but anyway, I want to thank you for hiring me the second time. To be honest with you, I don't think I was ready the first time and you were smart enough to see it.
>
> Take care of yourself and sure enjoyed visiting with you in Miami.
>
> > *Sincerely,*
> > *[Signed]* Coach Bowden

I might have worked with people with as much skill in human relations as Bobby Bowden, but if so, I don't remember them.

The First Fiesta Bowl

The Fiesta Bowl is now one of the elite among college football's postseason games, but it was not always so.

The FSU football team of 1971 compiled a record of eight wins and two losses under first year coach Larry Jones. It was a respectable if not phenomenal record with wins over Miami, Kansas, Virginia Tech, and Pittsburgh. The Fiesta Bowl sponsors out in Phoenix, Arizona, were looking for a suitable opponent for Arizona State University, and they extended the invitation to the Seminoles. This would be the second bowl in the past three years that the Seminoles would christen, following Atlanta's first Peach Bowl after the 1968 season. But our acceptance was not a simple matter. Sure it was nice to think of going to a postseason bowl, even to one nobody had ever heard of. Athletics Director John Bridgers and I discussed the matter, considering at length whether we should extend the season for the players by another month and how our participation would be viewed by people in other universities we cared about. My good friend and sometimes counselor President Steve O'Connell at the University of Florida asked me at a Council of University Presidents meeting why we would make a commitment to such an unknown group. My answer was phrased in language Steve understood, "They have given us a guarantee of $250,000," I said, "and unless we discover some fly in the ointment, we'll go." And we did.

The citizens of Phoenix were great hosts. The elite of Arizona were eager to give prominence and credibility to the new bowl. Senator Barry Goldwater was there along with John Mitchell and his wife, Martha. She was the irrepressible Martha Mitchell who had become a distinctive Washington political wife and a recognized doyenne around the capital. (John Mitchell himself, in the year ahead, would become one of the infamous figures in the Nixon administration's downfall.) The people of Phoenix showed that they knew how to host a bowl game, and I believe their impressive performance back in 1972 had something to do with the rapid rise of the Fiesta Bowl to national prominence.

The football game surely helped to establish the bowl's standing with football fans. If you like offensive football, this was your game. The scoring resulted from great execution, especially by the quarterbacks and receivers. FSU's quarterback was Gary Huff and ASU's was Danny White, who later became a highly regarded quarterback for the Dallas Cowboys. Gary Huff had a phenomenal game, completing 25 of 46 passes for 347 yards and two touchdowns. He won acclaim as the game's outstanding quarterback. Receiver Barry Smith also had a memorable performance using his great speed to score after three spectacular catches.

Huff's NFL career wasn't as long or as illustrious as White's but it was impressive. He played for the Chicago Bears, and he had good seasons in 1974 and 1975, throwing for more than 1,000 yards. After playing for the Bears from 1973 until 1976, he was with the Tampa Bay Buccaneers for the 1977 and 1978 seasons.

After the first two quarters of exciting football, no one could have doubted that the second half would be equally thrilling. Well, it was. The teams kept trading touchdowns, and at no time was either team ahead by more than seven points. Whoever had the ball was going to score. The team with the ball in the last 37 seconds did just that, breaking a 38-38 tie, and that team was Arizona State. The final score was 45-38, and if ever it could be said of an athletic contest, there was no loser.

What FSU got out of the game was more than the $250,000 (and in the days when the total budget for intercollegiate athletics was less than $2,000,000, that check meant a lot). The game was televised nationally, and that helped to establish FSU's name in big-time football circles. I'm sure it also did a lot for the confidence of Coach Larry Jones and his staff.

The Larry Jones Years

During his first two years at FSU, Jones showed himself to be all we could have hoped for in a football coach. His team went to the Fiesta Bowl and made a great showing. He hired Steve Sloan to head the offense—the same Steve Sloan who had been an outstanding quarterback on one of Bear Bryant's great Alabama teams. Steve was also a very personable and attractive young man who had great skill in human relations; he was an upstanding citizen of high moral character, and he complemented Jones nicely.

The sportswriters at the time often took note of the rectitude of Jones and his staff and they would sometimes make light of the clean-cut appearance and praiseworthy character of the players. One of Florida's writers—I don't remember who—wrote that Billy Graham would have a hard time trying to find lost souls among Florida State players, most of whom you would like to introduce to your kid sister. Gary Huff in his interviews with reporters always responded with "yes, sir" and "thank you, sir." The same unknown writer added that you have a feeling that he says thank you, sir, to the water boy during timeouts.

Jones was well-regarded throughout the University and was especially popular with students. In the spring of 1972, the University hosted Bob Hope for a show in Tully Gym, which was our largest venue for such performances. During the preliminaries, Coach Jones was introduced to applause greater than Hope received at his introduction. This was noted by the great comedian, who wove it into his lines during the show. Larry Jones's first year at Florida State was a resounding success, and I could not have been more pleased about our choice of a successor to Bill Peterson.

How then did Jones come to such an untimely and unfortunate end? The story speaks loudly for the strange times that befell FSU and many other American universities in that period.

The national news reports had told of American prisoners of war in Vietnam being kept in wire cages by their Vietnamese captors. These reports of such abuse heightened the already strong resistance to the war, and the part about wire cages really caught public attention. In the off-season training program Jones had instituted, he used chicken wire to create a false ceiling about four feet above the floor; the purpose was to force the players to stay in a crouch as they ran through their workouts. No one seemed to think anything about it until Fred Girard, a sports writer for the *St. Petersburg Times*, likened the chicken wire ceilings to the wire cages in Vietnam, and that was all it took.

Well, not really. Jones' players included several who identified with the students who were protesting and demonstrating on campus, and they seemed to want not to be left out. Until Girard wrote the stories, we had no reason to think any player was concerned, but the lurid newspaper accounts seemed to cause some players to protest publicly, and the matter became big news on the sports pages and in some editorial columns. We felt then that it probably hurt the program badly, especially after several players quit the team.

The other problem Jones faced after his second year was a sharp decline in the talent of his players. He acknowledged that he had inherited from Peterson a good crop of juniors and seniors and he relied on them in 1971 and '72. The freshman and sophomore classes were less talented, and Jones expected to spend a year or two rebuilding.

I believe he might have been successful had the chicken wire matter not ensued. The *St. Petersburg Times* articles were sufficiently damaging to the University that I felt we should take steps to clear our name. Whom should I call on to conduct an impartial investigation and to determine whether there was substance to Girard's claims? Why, LeRoy Collins of course. The former Florida Governor was a respected lawyer and a person of unquestioned integrity, and he undertook the assignment without hesitation. When the Collins Report was completed several months later, it exonerated Coach Jones and his staff and exposed the newspaper articles for what they were: Unsubstantiated articles by a young, ambitious reporter who seemed to believe that taking cheap shots at vulnerable subjects was preferable to earnest work as a news reporter in building his career.

The football season of 1973 saw the harvest of the unhappy events of the previous winter and spring. The record was eleven losses and no wins, and the demoralization of everyone associated with FSU football was palpable. After the season ended, I met often with Jones and Director of Athletics John Bridgers. Our thinking was dominated by the need to do something to invigorate FSU football, for it was clear to us that we were at rock bottom. What that something might have been eluded us, and our desperate situation seemed to leave no choice but to find new leadership. The decision to release Jones came in mid-December and made Christmas for me anything but joyous. Firing people is never any fun, but the character and competence of Jones made this one especially painful. I felt that Jones recognized that the coaching profession he had elected to join contained this kind of uncertainty, and I believe he left with as little bitterness as I could have hoped for.

The Darrell Mudra Years

The selection of Larry Jones was an act performed almost entirely by the President and the Athletics Committee. This time, I decided that the search for the next football coach should be conducted by people who had a strong interest in FSU athletics and who had helped to sustain the programs. Who else but the alumni?

Walter Revell, who had graduated in 1956 and had been an active alumnus and a highly successful businessman, agreed to chair the search committee. The University's Athletics Committee would of course play its customary role, but Revell's committee would take the lead in finding the new coach.

Darrell Mudra surfaced early on and captured the Committee's imagination and their interest. He had been head football coach at several institutions whose football programs needed help, and several of his references told us that he had been a "doctor of sick programs." They also seemed to want to call our attention to his having earned a doctorate, and we thought that was an interesting attribute for a football coach even if we didn't see how it would ensure that FSU would "beat the Gators."

Darrell Mudra was an easy guy to like and a hard one to understand. His methods were, to say the least, unconventional in the world of college football. His "coaching" while seated in a box at the press level in Campbell Stadium was, well ... different. Maybe he really coached from up there, but there were just too many stories from people who claimed to have witnessed his casual approach to his job for me not to wonder.

During the team's practices before the first game in 1974—his first year—I received a copy of a letter he had sent to the players. He told the players that the football team was really very much on its own, that it had no support from the administration, and if they were to have a successful season, they would have to do it without the University's help. The parents of one of the players thought I should see the letter. My response was to call Darrell to my office and ask him to explain.

He said that he had studied successful coaches and one he admired was George Allen of the Washington Redskins. Allen convinced his players that the whole world was against them, and to Darrell that meant both the University's athletics department and the University administration, and his players would face the problem, and they would just have to prove us wrong. It was a great motivator, Darrell said, and that's what he was trying to do.

Maybe it would work, I didn't know. Mudra was not without success in some of the big games. The most exciting game, and doubtless the most disappointing, was the loss to Alabama in 1974. With one of the big upsets in college football seemingly in hand, FSU lost on a last minute field goal after leading throughout the game. Coach Bear Bryant commented that he had never before seen a team coached so much better than his team.

In 1975, FSU demolished Clemson 43-7, then fell to Miami 24-22, and closed the season with a surprising victory over Houston in the Astrodome, 33-22. The record that year was 3-8.

The end for Mudra may have come in a small incident in Houston. Bill McGrotha, the sports editor of the *Tallahassee Democrat*, and I stopped in at the coach's invitation during the team's pre-game meal. Mudra was then remarking to the players on the movie "Patton," which had been shown to the team the night before. We were astonished to hear him criticize Patton, declaring that the general's demanding, authoritarian way was certainly not his style, nor would it generate the spirit he wanted to see on his football team. McGrotha and I exchanged glances, each of us unwilling to say what was on our minds. I had earlier that day remarked to several people, including McGrotha, that I was probably going to announce during my interview on the radio at halftime that Mudra's contract would be extended for another year. But on the radio, I made no comment on Mudra's tenure.

If his contract had been extended, there were reasons to believe that he might have turned things around. He had a good recruiting year (resulting in a rather nice gift to his successor, Bobby Bowden) and at times he seemed to be trying to change his personal style to better relate to Florida State fans. But many little things—which mostly weren't so little—added up to a serious misfit of Mudra to FSU football. He was an ardent fisherman who, it was widely reported, sometimes left practice early or came late, leaving his assistants in charge. One of the writers observed that football was not the most important thing in Mudra's life, adding that he shouldn't be faulted for that.

In the end, I didn't feel that Darrell understood or was

understood by Florida State fans, including especially the alumni, and the future of our football program was not secure. A few days before Christmas I told the coach that I had decided to make a change and as was the case in the dismissal of Larry Jones, Christmas was once again not the season to be jolly—not for Mudra and his staff, nor for me.

Bobby Bowden...Finally!

My mind and that of John Bridgers, who was then Director of Athletics, were not filled with visions of sugarplums that December in 1975, as we contemplated the vacancy in the head football coach's position. But this time the name of Bobby Bowden was not just on the list of candidates; it headed the list. It helped that Bridgers had known Bowden as a fellow coach, and he was certain Bobby was the man we needed.

The interview was to take place in Tampa where Bowden was coaching in one of the post-season bowl games. Bridgers was well-known and respected in football circles, and the two of us had an early evening dinner with John McKay then head coach of the Tampa Bay Buccaneers. The interview with Bowden followed, and there is not much to report about our exchange. We wanted Bobby and we made that clear. The only question was, did he want us? He had had several good seasons at West Virginia and was popular with the Mountaineer fans. What we had to offer was a football program that had had only one good year since Bill Peterson left five years earlier and no real reason to believe that we would return to the good days any time soon. Not unless you take us there, we told Bobby, and that was the pitch we made. Here's a program that can only go up, and we'll give you every reasonable support if you'll come to FSU and take over the program. We also pointed out the great potential for success that was provided by the schedule—and this may be the time to tell readers how that schedule came about.

Clay Stapleton had come to FSU from Iowa State University in 1971, where he had served as Director of Athletics and before that as head football coach. He knew other directors of athletics and coaches in that part of the country well, and he came to my office to tell me that he was certain he could schedule football games with those teams if we wanted to. Why we thought we could play with Nebraska, Ohio State and Notre Dame, I'm not sure, and Clay and I laughed as we thought about how foolish that seemed. But we also understood that scheduling teams of that caliber presented a rare opportunity to put FSU on the football map. I told Clay to go ahead and schedule all of the big Midwestern teams he could. That meeting was a big step in the rehabilitation of FSU football that would, eight years later, give Bobby Bowden the opportunity to propel his team into the national football limelight.

Whether the promise of the chance to play in the big time was an important factor in Bowden's acceptance after the meeting in Tampa, I've never known. But we left the interview having been assured that Bobby would give the matter serious thought, and we both believed that he would accept our offer—$56,000 per year, with no perks.

Bobby told us he'd give us his answer after he returned home. His report of his return home—a story he's told many times in the years since—has him walking up the sidewalk to their home with his wife Ann after getting out of the car they had taken from the airport. The sidewalk was covered with ice, and Bobby's feet went in one direction and his body in another. As he hit the ground, "That's it," he said to Ann, "we're going to Florida!"

Coach Durham's Black Basketball Team

Hugh Durham left an indelible mark on basketball at Florida State University. Durham coached basketball in much the same way that he played it. He made up in spirit and aggressive play what he lacked in size: He was always a force to be reckoned with and was looked to as the team leader by the other players. He was hired to coach the freshman team in 1960 just after graduation; he became Coach Bud Kennedy's full-time assistant in 1961 and continued in that post until he succeeded Kennedy as head coach upon his death in 1966. Durham scored 1,381 points in three varsity seasons, two of which were 500-plus point seasons.

Coach Durham knew from the beginning of the 1971-72 season that he had a special group. That team had nine black players, whose presence said two things about Durham: He knew basketball talent when he saw it, and he was not in the least influenced by those who would have delayed the racial integration of college sports. I admired his stand on this and tried to let him know. Those of us in the Department of Athletics and the University administration felt some of the heat, but the protests never had the disruptive character of those generated by the dissident students, and our strong stance on recruiting black players might have helped to convince the University's black students that FSU was serious about racial equality.

Among Durham's personal qualities was a wonderful sense of humor. I asked him one day about basketball fans' reaction to black players, and his reply was pure Hugh Durham: "It depends on how you play them," he said, "one at home, two on the road, and three if you're behind."

The 1971-72 team compiled an impressive 25-5 record and was ranked tenth nationally, earning them a place in the Eastern Regional NCAA Tournament. There they surprised many in the basketball world by beating Minnesota and then Kentucky. This was the last year for legendary coach Adolph Rupp at Kentucky, and beating him must have been a coaching highlight for Durham, who hailed from Louisville. The final score was FSU 73, Kentucky 54.

This earned the team a trip to Los Angeles and the Final Four, which brought a new level of excitement to our basketball fans. We thought we might have a chance to play UCLA, which everyone assumed would be in the finals. We were paired with the University of North Carolina in the semifinals, but of course we were believed to have little chance of winning that one. Durham's upstarts beat the Dean Smith-coached Tarheels by a score of 79-74.

Coach Dean Smith's comments after his team's loss to FSU showed once again the class for which he was famous. He paid tribute to the Seminoles by citing Otto Petty, FSU's point guard, as the player who was responsible for a lot of his miseries, not the least of which was having the Carolina press "broken in about two minutes flat." Petty, all of five feet seven inches, was the quickest player on the floor throughout the tournament by the word of several coaches.

A very good Louisville team had lost to UCLA in the other semifinal game. The consolation game, Louisville versus North Carolina, was played at 5 o'clock, just before the finals, in which FSU was to challenge the mighty Coach John Wooden and his array of stars led by Bill Walton.

I've always had great affection for UNC (one of our sons later attended the University and played baseball for the Tarheels), and never more than when I heard their pep band play the Seminole fight song during the warm-ups for our game with UCLA. We had just eliminated the Tarheels, but of course, they stayed in Los Angeles for the finals. Their band stayed too, and the Seminole fans who were there to support our team were positively thrilled to hear those blue-clad Tarheel musicians playing "We will fight, fight, fight for FSU."

But before the teams took the floor, we were involved in a matter that got almost as much press as the game itself. Bill Wall, the basketball coach at Macmurray State College in Illinois and president of the National Basketball Coache's Association, charged that several of the teams in the tournament had gone outside the bounds of NCAA regulations in recruiting players, and for some reason, FSU became his prime target. He had written an article for *Sports Illustrated* several months before in which he blasted his fellow coaches for their unethical behavior. He also condemned the Fellowship of Christian Athletes for their hypocritical stance on issues related to recruitment. Coach Wall was described by one of his critics—a fellow coach—as a figure who had not attracted much attention as a coach and had found another way to get his name in the papers. Wall noted that FSU had been placed on probation by the NCAA for two recruiting violations. (An over- eager fan in Atlanta—a wealthy businessman—flew three prospects to Atlanta from Louisville and entertained them in his box for an Atlanta Braves baseball game; two of these players had enrolled at FSU). Wall apparently decided we were vulnerable. On Friday, the day before our game with UCLA, Wall told a group of reporters that Coach Durham had been caught with his hand in the till, and that FSU had no right to be in the tournament.

Wall had generated a major news story, which appeared in the *Los Angeles Times,* the *New York Times,* the *Washington Post;* of course, most Florida papers gave the story prominent space, too. The coach at Long Beach State College in California had followed up Wall's charges by saying that it was impossible for an all-black team to win the tournament because it would lack the teamwork necessary to do so. Three of our players—Ron King, Reggie Royals and Lawrence McCray—had to meet with NCAA officials and sign affidavits that they had not been in negotiations with professional teams. Players from some other teams were similarly charged and were required by NCAA officials to clear themselves in the same way. The story generated by Mr. Wall was one the sports writers could not pass up, and one that remained in the memories of our fans for years.

I was in Los Angeles with the team, I was sure his charges were baseless, and I felt sufficient indignation to demand a meeting with the Board of Directors of the National Basketball Coach's Association. That meeting was held on Saturday morning, and I had the opportunity to face Wall directly and demand that he provide me with any evidence he had of FSU's improper conduct. I acknowledged the earlier NCAA infractions and pointed out that we supported the penalty imposed by the NCAA and the matter was closed. When I pressed him, Wall admitted before the group that he had nothing to support his charges. I then upbraided the Association and told the directors that I thought they should censure Wall. The board of the Coache's Association said they would consider my request and would take up the matter at a later meeting. Whether they did, I never learned.

I thought it best for Coach Durham to stay out of this one—he was there to coach the team, and he didn't need this kind of distraction, but of course the reporters got to him. He strengthened my hand when he lobbed a shot across the bow of Coach Wall and the board of the Basketball Coaches' Association. "I don't know what will come of it," Durham said, "but I know it's not over. They're not tangling with any lightweight in Dr. Marshall. They're in for a time when they get in a verbal one-on-one with that man."

I then met with the reporters who were there to cover the game, and released this statement: "I believe Mr. Wall has overstepped the bounds of propriety. He has maligned a group of young people and an institution that has made an effort to uphold high standards. We cannot ignore this."

My next step was to call Bob Bickel, the University Attorney back in Tallahassee, for his advice on possible legal action. I was unable to reach Bickel, but nevertheless I told reporters that I was considering a lawsuit.* This made the news, and my vigorous response to Wall's charges may have helped our cause with the media and certainly with our fans. It

---

*Bickel delights in describing my attempts to reach him by phone from Los Angeles. Ruth Wester, my very able executive assistant, said he wasn't available, he was "at the races at Sebring." "Well," I said "can't you have him paged?" Bickel erupts in laughter when he reminds me that Sebring is a twelve-hour race that about 300,000 people attend. "Sure, I'd have called you back," he says, "I just didn't hear the page."

caused me to miss the first several minutes of the game; I had been cornered by writers who seemed to think the Wall story was more important than the tip-off. They would not hold that view for long, because the game was a nail-biter from the start.

Bill Walton—the great Bill Walton—Durham knew, would be their major weapon, and we had to limit his scoring if we were to have any chance. Lawrence McCray got the assignment. The 6'11" McCray went man-to-man against Walton, who also stood 6'11" but out-weighed McCray by 40 or 50 pounds. In the first seven minutes, Walton was held scoreless, and FSU led, 21 to 14. Ron King, a 6'4" junior from Louisville, hit four of his first five shots. But McCray drew three fouls, and the loss of our big man midway through the first half really hurt our game, and UCLA led by eleven points at half-time. UCLA led 67-51 midway through the second half, but the Seminoles reeled off nine unanswered points to make it 67-60. The final score, 81-76 was as close as we got as the game ended.

How did the FSU players feel about playing UCLA? Never at a loss for words, Petty had said, "Oh, fine. UCLA's got the greatest coach in the world in Wooden, and the greatest player in Walton. But we're going to give them a game." Reggie Royals said, "I really think we just might upset them. You always have to look forward to playing against number one. UCLA is number one so we're looking forward to playing them." And McCray had this for those who regarded FSU as a decided underdog, "I just wonder how in the heck some of those people figured we got here."

One of UCLA's outstanding players was Tommy Curtis from Tallahassee. He had been recruited by Durham, but he wanted to go to UCLA to play for John Wooden. He was not one of the starting five but was a consistently reliable player, and he probably would have been a starter had he come to FSU.

The players Durham had recruited were, by any measure, a considerable group of young men—talented basketball players, but also fine young men and good students. At the time of the tournament, Ron Harris had been admitted to medical school. The guards were Greg Samuel, Otto Petty, Otis Cole and Ron King. The forwards were Ron Harris, John Amick, Larry Gay, Rowland Garrett and Reggie Royals. Lawrence McCray was the center.

Having a basketball team with nine black players attracted a lot of attention. Other schools, including those in the South, had begun recruiting black players, but none had so many. Our one white player, John Amick, was often the crowd favorite even though he was not a standout player. He wore a long, black pony-tail, which made him even more noticeable. Durham had a great nickname for Amick: Cochise.

Hugh Durham was, by any measure, an outstanding coach. As Jesse Outlar, sports editor for the *Atlanta Journal-Constitution*, wrote, "Even if his Florida State Seminoles had not reached the NCAA finals, Hugh Durham should have been a unanimous choice as College Basketball Coach of the Year."

College Baseball's World Series

FSU baseball has been consistently strong from the early days. Coaches Danny Litwhiler (1955-63) and Fred Hatfield (1964-68) had long careers playing in the National League. Woody Woodward, who signed a lucrative contract with the Milwaukee Braves after he graduated in 1962, made a generous contribution to his alma mater. Jack Stallings took over the coaching duties in 1969 and led the Seminoles to the College World Series in his second season.

The 1970 Seminoles entered the tournament with a 49-9-1 record. They began their quest for the NCAA title with victories over Arizona and Dartmouth. The University of Southern California (USC) had lost the opener but won the next two. FSU was then matched with Texas; both teams were unbeaten, and Texas won 5-1, but the Seminoles beat Texas in the second matchup, 11-2. After USC drew a bye, FSU faced the Californians in the championship game.

The Seminoles led until the seventh inning, when USC tied the game 1-1, and that's the way it stayed until the 15th. In the bottom half of that inning, USC scored, and that was the game and the national championship. FSU pitcher Gene Ammann was named the most valuable player, the first time since 1964 that a player from a team other than the champions had been so honored.

The 1970 team was made up of a group of outstanding student-athletes whose accomplishments after graduation mark them as an unusual class. Ten members of the team went on to play professional baseball. Ron Cash played with the Detroit Tigers for several years, Johnny Grubb played for 20 years in the major leagues, and others who spent time in the majors included Mac Scarce, Greg Schnute, Harry Safewright, Gene Ammann, Mike Slade, Pat Osbourn, Don Harbaugh, and Dave Nichols. Others had distinguished careers in business and the professions: Brothers Greg and Carl Gromek practicing law in Detroit, and John Keith in the sporting goods business in Ohio.[1]

Women's Athletics

Title IX was part of the Higher Education Act of 1972 enacted by Congress, and it had the effect of changing the course of student life for women enrolled in the nation's colleges and universities. It did just that, but not right away.

The predecessor of FSU was the Florida State College for Women which had long conducted strong sports programs for its students, and athletic participation was very much a part of campus life for FSCW girls. Thus, when FSCW became FSU, many of the traditions were carried forward and those included a strong emphasis on sports. Women's athletics at FSU throughout the '50s and '60s earned distinction among such programs throughout the South and in some cases well beyond.

In 1968, four years before Title IX appeared, FSU fielded teams in eight women's sports: Basketball, softball, tennis, golf, swimming, track and field, volleyball and badminton. All of those programs were conducted under the auspices of the Physical Education Department, and the coaches were faculty members and graduate students, none of whom was paid for coaching. The University's Athletics Department was concerned entirely with sports for men, and there was no money budgeted for women.

I have distinct memories of our reactions—the Athletics Department's and the University administration's—to Title IX. How can we possibly organize and operate a sports program for our women students that will provide participation on the same basis as men? Hiring coaches, buying uniforms, providing travel, scholarships—the whole works—it seemed like an impossible task. Like many other presidents, I was less than enthusiastic about the prospects, and I made no secret of my concerns about another case of "government intrusion." I thought that government should have left the matter to the colleges, where we would handle it in our own way. Most of us were unable to see the benefits for female students and to the University as a whole in a vigorous women's sports program, nor could we envision the beauty of women demonstrating their agility and skill in the intercollegiate competition that thrills us today.

The government was better at passing regulations than implementing them, and some six years passed before Title IX had any effect at the campus level. But things did change, and by 1978, FSU had mounted a full-fledged women's sports program, with competition in all of the major areas. Women athletes have brought distinction and honor to the University, and those of us who were skeptical in 1972 can now reflect on the actions of our government and say, "well done." When we do so, we should also say thanks to those members of the faculty and graduate students who kept the spirit alive in FSU's early years. Physical education professor Dr. Billie Jones was the most active of those faculty members, and she was greatly aided by Dr. Ed Cubbon, who, among his other roles, coached the women's basketball team and took a leading role in bringing FSU into the Association of Intercollegiate Athletics for Women (AIAW), where we occupied a prominent place. Eddie Cubbon also hired Marlene Furnell as the first Director of Women's Athletics, and he was active in securing funding for women's athletics from student government. His is another honored name in athletics at FSU.

CHAPTER 10
Marching Chiefs to the Middle East—King Hussein and Helen Hayes Come to Tallahassee

It never fails. I always feel a surge of button-busting pride in FSU when the Marching Chiefs come onto the field at the stadium during football games, and I'm sure nearly everyone else in the stadium feels the same way. As our coaches have always said, the band is an important part of the crowd support that motivates and energizes the team.

So when the Chiefs were invited to travel to Syria and Jordan in the summer of 1974, everyone associated with the School of Music knew that the people in those countries would feel some of the same excitement when they heard the great brass sound that was the Chiefs' signature.

The invitation came from the U.S. Department of State when our country was celebrating the resumption of diplomatic relations with the Arab countries following the 1967 Six-Days War. We had severed relations with those countries, and now seven years later, the new ties were to be celebrated by having one of America's great college bands perform at an international trade fair in Damascus, Syria. We stayed in Damascus for a week, with the band parading and playing each afternoon in a large parade ground in the center of the city and giving concerts in city parks and theaters in the evenings. After the stay in Damascus, our group flew to Amman, Jordan, where arrangements had been made for the band to march and play in Jordan's Royal Stadium.

The trip began with a flight out of Panama City. We made stopovers in New Jersey and Newfoundland, and then on to

Damascus. This was, of course, the first time most of the band members had been out of the country.

The Syrians were an appreciative audience, and the band members responded. Shirley and I went out to the field several times where they would practice between performances, and we really appreciated the rigors under which they performed. Damascus is a very hot place in the summer, and the uniforms the marchers wore must have been oppressive. It was probably much like Campbell Stadium in early September.

The trade fair was about what you'd expect—open-air exhibits of products of many kinds, to be examined and bargained for by merchants who appeared to come from many countries, some well beyond the Middle East.

We met a number of high-ranking government officials, but not President Assad. One of those was the Minister of the Economy, who had an American wife, and that might have helped to account for his reaching out to befriend and accommodate us. He offered—and Shirley and I were pleased to accept—a car and driver who would take the two of us on a three-day tour of the country (while the Chiefs were continuing with their performances back in Damascus). We visited some of Syria's fabulous archaeological sites, including the ancient city of Palmyra which surely ranks among the greatest sites in the Middle East.

After our return to Damascus, the Chiefs still had several more days to fulfill their commitment, so Shirley and I decided to accept an invitation to visit another Middle Eastern country—Iran. I had become acquainted back in the United States with the Iranian ambassador to our country, and I had a standing invitation to visit Tehran at my convenience. Time limitations had prevented my going earlier, and inasmuch as we were in the neighborhood this seemed like good time for the visit. We flew to Tehran and had a fine if brief visit, mostly with people in the Shah's government. It was there that I saw Dr. Amman Birjandi and strengthened a friendship, which is described in the Introduction.

The short flight from Tehran to Amman enabled us to catch up with the Marching Chiefs, who were to present a concert in the Royal Stadium for King Hussein and Queen Alia as part of the Middle Eastern tour. The American ambassador to Jordan was Thomas Pickering (later to become U.S. ambassador to the United Nations and still later American ambassador to the Russian Federation). The Pickerings met us at the airport and drove Shirley and me to the Ambassador's residence, where we spent the next two nights.

The concert was scheduled for the next afternoon, which left the morning free for... well, what else but a visit to the royal palace and an audience with the King. I had met Hussein at a White House dinner (described in "Fond Memories" in the Appendix), and while I'm sure I remember our meeting more vividly than he, the King was as cordial as you'd expect a king to be.

The highlight of the visit to Jordan was the joint performance of the Marching Chiefs and the Royal Jordanian Army Band in the Royal Stadium. As you'd expect, the combined bands played the music of both countries, and I remember the distinct feeling that I had never heard any marching band sound better (the Chiefs might just have been carrying the Jordanians). One of the members of the King's party remarked to me that he had never heard his country's national anthem played so well. Shirley and I were seated with the King and Queen in the Royal Box, which was separated from the general seating area in the stadium only by some fancy decorative ropes and a small fence; also present were several stalwart security men. Several of our students who were, I suppose, band attendants and thus were not out there marching, approached the royal box to get close-up pictures of the royal couple. That seemed to make the security people a bit nervous, and I made some subtle, back-off hand signals to the students, but they didn't notice, and anyway, the King didn't seem to mind.

Hussein was then seen as this country's best friend among the Arab states, and the people of his government that I met gave me a good feeling about their friendship with the United States. (I sat next to the head of the Jordanian Army at dinner following the performance at the stadium, and we talked politics.) Hussein, from then until his death in 1999, was our most reliable ally among the Arab states, and Jordan fills pretty much the same role in that volatile region today.

King Hussein's Honorary Doctorate

Pat Hogan was a multi-talented servant of the University who, among his many positions, served as Executive Assistant to the President.

On the morning of May 6, 1975, Pat was on university business in Washington when he passed a newsstand where copies of *The New York Times* were on display. There on the front page, to his utter disbelief, he saw a photo of his son Wayne, then a student at FSU. Wayne's face was shown full view as was his left foot that was extended into the aisle from his end-of-the-row seat in the auditorium, and on that foot, Pat saw a badly disintegrating tennis shoe. As Pat inspected the photo further, he saw King Hussein walking down the aisle at Ruby Diamond Auditorium past his disheveled son, who just happened to get caught by the photographer's camera. Thus was the world introduced to Doctor of Humane Letters King Hussein of Jordan and Wayne Hogan, junior at Florida State University.

The idea to award an honorary degree to Hussein was born during the band's trip to Syria and Jordan a year earlier. After the Middle East trip, I discussed the possibility with Ambassador Pickering, who liked the idea. So I invited the King, and he accepted. He arrived in Tallahassee on one of the planes supplied by our government and was welcomed at the airport by Governor Reubin Askew and me. The King was as downright friendly and accommodating as I remembered him being in Amman. We entertained him at a backyard luncheon under the big tent behind the president's home, where he mixed and mingled with 50 or so guests from the University and the community.

The ceremony in Ruby Diamond Auditorium went about as such events usually do. There was a formal procession with everyone in the platform party adorned in full academic regalia; the orchestra played, and the King was introduced. I referred to the King's "consistent voice for moderation and hope for a settlement in the Middle East." In his speech, the King addressed the volatile situation in that part of the world. "There is a great reservoir of good will in the Arab world toward America," he said. "You have many friends in the Middle East who are counting on you." He urged the Israelis "to have the courage to make peace" and outlined his view of the historical problems leading to the conflict in the Middle East.[1]

There had been hostilities between Jordan and Israel during the Six-Days War in 1967 and some ongoing tension between Israel and its nearby Arab neighbors after that. At the time of his visit to Tallahassee, the King was rumored to have pledged aid to Arab countries in the event of another war with Israel. He adamantly denied that in his Tallahassee press conference.

Awarding the honorary degree was not without controversy at the University, which didn't much surprise me given the continuing student activism. Student Senate President Doug Mannheimer sent me a letter saying he regarded the honorary degree as an affront to the Jewish community on campus. At the airport, the FSU Israeli student organization mounted a mild protest saying they wanted to show support for peace in the Middle East generally. I tried to deflect the criticism that the honorary degree was a slap in the face to Jewish students by pointing out that earlier Israel's Golda Meir had been offered the same honor, but due to her commitments, she had been unable to accept.

Both *The Flambeau* and the *Tallahassee Democrat* wrote generally favorable editorials on the visit and the awarding of the degree. The *Democrat* urged protesters to act with restraint and hoped they would welcome the visiting dignitary, adding that the Hussein visit might bring FSU some "positive press coverage, for a change."[2]

Helen Hayes Adopts FSU

Florida State University's programs—both academic and non-academic—have often brought people of great distinction to the campus. There have been famous writers, eminent scientists, renowned performers in music and theater, and of course, great athletes. But the group of luminaries from the world of theater who came during what I'll call the Fallon years bids fair to eclipse all of the others.

Dick Fallon was the founding dean of the school of theater in 1972, and he was also the founder of the Asolo Theater in Sarasota. He had come to FSU in 1956 as a faculty member in the Speech Department—we had no program in theater then—who was hired to teach speech to undergraduates. Fallon had a background in acting and directing in New York, and he also served in a Special Services unit of the U.S. Army in England during World War II. There he met and worked with theater people, some of whom went on to outstanding careers—playwright Paddy Chayevsky was one. Many of those men with whom he acted and directed stayed in touch with Fallon throughout his long career at Florida State. Fallon had also served briefly in academic positions in two small colleges in the Northeast, where he promoted closer ties between the academic and professional worlds of theater.

At FSU the new teacher of speech was also permitted to teach a bit of theater as long as its role in the department did not overshadow debate or TV or oral interpretation or whatever else the department had been doing. Fallon saw an opportunity to strike out in a new direction which was to emphasize performance. This would be different from programs at the big name universities—Harvard, Yale, Columbia—which focused on theater history and other academic aspects, but saw professional theater, including performance, to be an inappropriate academic endeavor for a distinguished university.

Fallon began producing plays on the campus in Tallahassee using student actors and also bringing in big name performers to call attention to his productions. Julie Haydon came to act in the first one, Mark Doren's *The Last Days of Lincoln*, which made the Florida papers and convinced the administration that Dick Fallon was onto something.

The University's Art Department had been conducting workshops dealing with the artworks of the masters at the Ringling Museum in Sarasota when, in 1959, the department invited Fallon to present a play in a small theater that was attached to the museum. There Fallon discovered a real gem— a small theater that had been brought over from Italy piece-by-piece and reassembled at the Ringling. This little jewel had been a 17th or 18th century theater in the small town of Asolo, where Robert Browning had composed some of his poetry. After a gala opening, the theater became part of the museum tour and was not again used for the production of plays.

Well, not until Dick Fallon, who knew an opportunity when he saw one, persuaded the folks at Ringling that FSU's theater program should be allowed to use the Asolo theater for plays during the summer. In the first summer the department performed five different plays with some 25 performances, and in 1964, the state legislature showed its appreciation by naming the Asolo "The State Theater of Florida."

In my earliest memories of the Asolo, I see Dick Fallon coming into the President's office to tell me of a serious financial deficit which threatened the existence of the program. Well, I got some money, I'm not sure from where, and financial help from the legislature and the good people of Sarasota. The Asolo program had begun to be noticed by theater people nationwide, who wrote glowing reviews in such publications as *The Saturday Review of Literature, Time,* and *The New York World Telegram.* The result of these early efforts was the establishment of a strong program in theater by Fallon including a Masters of Fine Arts degree that was unique among graduate programs in theater.

The event that really attracted the attention of the theater world resulted from a friendship Fallon had made with Audrey Wood, the famous New York agent for playwrights. He recommended the University give Ms. Wood an honorary doctorate, and he told me that she would attract some famous theater people to Tallahassee. The production to be given on the occasion of the awarding of the degree was to be a new play by Gian Carlo Menotti, who had been persuaded to come to FSU to produce his first non-operatic play, *The Leper.* The play was to be presented in the new theater in FSU's Fine Arts Building. Audrey Wood reminded Menotti that he had a great following of artists and wealthy people in America and Europe, and wouldn't it be wonderful to bring such a group to Tallahassee for his first play? Menotti agreed, and he promptly told his aide in New York to send out the invitations.

Chandler Cowles was a Tallahassee resident who had had some experience as a producer in the New York theater, and he helped Fallon and Wood with the arrangements. Cowles told us that it would not be realistic to expect all those famous people to make their own travel arrangements, that we really should charter an airplane for the trip. I had no money for such an expense when the planners came to me for help. Okay, I said, I'll find the money somewhere to provide the airplane, but what size? They said they expected nearly a hundred people, and that meant a large commercial jet. So, I found some non-state funds, and the deal was made with Eastern Airlines for a plane to pick up the group at LaGuardia Airport and deliver them to Tallahassee. Because of Menotti's standing in Europe, the production attracted international attention, and

Fallon was certain we would have a great collection of the international theater elite and the event would be a feather in FSU's cap.

The planning group raised the matter of accommodations, and we were suddenly faced with providing suitable housing for our distinguished visitors. The solution, engineered mostly by Sue Fallon, Dick's wife, was to invite friends of the University to serve as hosts during our visitors' stay, a privilege each of the hosts would earn by contributing $100, and they would be listed as patrons. We had no trouble lining up hosts.

As the big day approached, I was getting progress reports from Fallon every few days that all was going wonderfully except he could never tell me how many had made reservations. These folks don't think of reservations he said, they just show up.

That didn't satisfy me, and it didn't really satisfy Dick either. I reminded him that I was on the hook for the airplane and he would be on that hook with me if only a few people got off that plane in Tallahassee. The Menotti aide in New York said he just didn't know; there were only six reservations, but he thought there would be more. Eastern Airlines had told me we might get a partial refund of our deposit if I got the request in "right away"—meaning three days before the scheduled departure, which I was of course powerless to do. It happened that a staff member of the FSU Foundation was in New York on departure day, and I got him on the phone. See what you can find out, I told him, and at least let me know how many are on the plane when it leaves.

We had planned a gala luncheon for our guests, and in the belief that they would come, I had invited the Tallahassee hosts to join our guests for lunch in the ballroom of the Union. There the hosts would be matched up with those they were to take to their homes for lodging. I tried without success to reach our man in New York all morning, and when the Tallahassee patrons gathered in the union for lunch, neither Fallon nor I knew who was coming or how many.

Well, the plane landed in Tallahassee, and the visitors were quickly loaded on to buses for the trip to the campus. The luncheon guests, meanwhile, were seated; as they fidgeted over their salads, I was at the microphone telling them nervously that our guests were expected shortly.

With no notice whatever, the double doors at the rear of the ballroom opened and in came the planeload of theater dignitaries. There were about 90. Dick and I searched for words to express our welcome and our relief. I don't remember what I said, but I do remember telling someone afterwards that when those doors opened and the people came pouring in, it made me think somehow of the parting of the Red Sea. Here's how Fallon later described the entourage: "There was everybody who was anybody in society both in Europe and in this country....Tony Randall and every big star, including Helen Hayes." Tony Randall stepped up to the podium and spoke for the group, telling us how pleased they were to be in Tallahassee; then he turned to Audrey Wood to kiss her and congratulate her on her forthcoming doctorate. Tennessee Williams, who had just been released from a rehabilitation center to deal with his alcohol problem, spent the next two days on the campus meeting with students. *The New York Times* gave major space to the Menotti premier at FSU, and Dick Fallon was certain that we had now really arrived in the world of theater.

Fallon was a shrewd fundraiser, and he thought of a way to keep the patrons involved: He called on his friend Milton Goldman, a leading theatrical agent in New York, to help him line up some more big names. They included such stars as Maureen O'Sullivan, who had played Jane in the original Tarzan movies. The list of others who came included Dana Andrews, Barbara Cook, Ossie Davis and Ruby Dee, Jose Ferrer, Burt Reynolds (who came to the campus on many occasions before and since), and Efrem Zimbalist Jr. Such names as these made it easy to keep patrons happy and to continue their donations to the program.

In the next three years, Helen Hayes made five separate visits to FSU. In 1975, the University awarded her an honorary doctorate in a ceremony that attracted more national attention. She was sometimes accompanied by her brother-in-law, John D. McArthur, the brother of her late husband Charles McArthur, the playwright, and sometimes by her son, Jamie McArthur, who was then the star of the popular TV show, "Hawaii 5-0."

Of all the great stars who came, Helen Hayes, I felt, was in a class by herself. She seemed to be completely unaware that she was—well, Helen Hayes. She could not have been more thoughtful or considerate and she was unselfish in her willingness to spend time with our students. I remember clearly one night after attending one of Fallon's productions, she wanted to go backstage to talk to the performers, the director, and anyone else from the production. This went on until nearly midnight. I thought we were taking advantage of this wonderfully generous lady, so I broke in to say "Mrs. McArthur," (that's how she preferred to be addressed) "don't you think it's about time to call it a day?" Reluctantly, she bade the students good night and was taken back downtown to her hotel.

Dick Fallon's goal when he came to FSU was to bring the professional and academic worlds of theater together. Events during the years when I was privileged to be a small part of that effort left no doubt that he had achieved his goal. Dick Fallon has received many honors for success in this and other achievements, and he has earned them all.

CHAPTER 11
FSU's Roots

The Florida State College for Women was established in June 1905, when Governor Napoleon Bonaparte Broward signed into law what became known as the Buckman Bill. The bill established four new state institutions: The Florida Normal and Industrial College for Negroes, the Institute for the Blind, Deaf, and Dumb, the University of the State of Florida, and the Florida Female College.

But our interest in higher education goes back to the middle of the 19th century. In 1851, the legislature established two seminaries. The Seminary East of the Suwannee at Ocala, and the Seminary West of the Suwannee in Tallahassee, which became the Florida Female college.

The first president of the Florida Female College was Albert Alexander Murphree. He had come to the West Florida Seminary in 1895 as a teacher of mathematics. He remained president of the Florida Female College until 1909, when the institution's name was changed to the Florida State College for Women (FSCW).

The succeeding presidents were Edward Conradi, 1909-1941, and Doak Campbell who served from 1941 to 1957. He was succeeded by Robert Strozier, who died during his third year in office. Then came Gordon Blackwell, 1958-1964, and John Champion, 1964-1969.

FSCW was awarded the first Phi Beta Kappa chapter in Florida in competition with the University of Florida, which attests to the excellence of its programs in the arts and sciences.

FSCW's Great Professors

The young FSCW fortunately attracted a coterie of outstanding scholars and dedicated teachers. Dr. William G. Dodd became chairman of the Department of English, Language, and Literature in 1910. Dodd Hall, now home to the Philosophy and Religion Departments, was named for him. In 1913, he was appointed dean of Arts and Sciences and was considered the driving force in many of the academic achievements of FSCW.

William Hudson Rodgers came in 1922. He was a debonair professor who became the campus heartthrob. He was a fine tennis player; he strode the campus in his tweed jacket with a pipe in his mouth and the students swooned. Anna Forbes Liddell came as professor of philosophy, and she became a strong supporter of women's rights. Other distinguished faculty members included Mark DeGraff and Ralph Eyman in education, Earl Vance in journalism, Guy Diffenbaugh in English. Dr. Raymond Bellamy for whom the Bellamy building was later named was head of the Sociology Department and Coyle Moore, later to become Dean of the School of Social Welfare, came to assist him 1928. FSU also has buildings bearing the proud names of Diffenbaugh and Moore.

FSCW to FSU

In 1946, the Tallahasssee Branch of the University of Florida (TBUF) was created to accommodate several hundred male students who could not be admitted to the University in Gainesville for lack of space. The first director of TBUF was Milton Carothers. Coyle Moore served as registrar, Katherine Warren served as Dean of Women, and Otis McBride served as Dean of Men.

On May 15, 1947, Governor Caldwell signed legislation establishing FSU and converting the University of Florida to coeducational status. Student life following the enrollment of men changed; the men of TBUF made an impact even though their numbers were small, but when FSU came into existence in 1947, the male influence made a more serious impact. Intercollegiate athletic teams—men only, of course—were organized and a football field was laid out on the very ground that is now the site of Doak Campbell Stadium.

The Dean of Women needed to consider changes in social regulations for students. The 15-year-old rule forbidding girls to have cars at FSCW was rescinded, but strict social constraints were maintained: the girls who had cars had to have written consent from their parents.[1] Unlimited dating privileges were extended to all but freshmen. Designated smoking areas were established on the campus to accommodate the men, but the dean soon learned that they were inclined to smoke wherever they pleased. Meals became another problem: Men were not satisfied with the size of the portions and the "thin cheese sandwiches, a bowl of rabbit food and a little fruit" were not sufficient.[2]

As commencement approached in June of 1948, it was discovered that the diplomas had been imprinted with the Florida State College for Women designation. An acceptable solution was found by adding to the diploma the phrase, "Issued by Florida State University." That first graduating class in June 1948 boasted 431 female and 12 male graduates, and with that ceremony, history was made.

How did a small, little-known women's college, even one so distinguished academically, move so fast to become a respected, nationally recognized, research oriented university? That's a question Floridians have asked ever since the founding in 1947. And how did the young FSU so quickly develop non-academic enterprises such as intercollegiate football and build a brand new football stadium?

There were residing in Tallahassee businessmen who wanted the fledgling university to grow and prosper because this was a town whose economy had been almost totally dependent on government, and by any measure, government is not apt to be a very powerful economic engine. A new university meant new business. These were Tallahassee business and professional men who had attended University of Florida, and along with many other UF students, they had taken the well-worn path to Tallahassee to find companionship in the FSCW girls. Marriages had bloomed from several of those romances, and the wives of those Gators lobbied their husbands hard for support from their business associates and the community generally.

Present day Tallahassee people remember well several of the early FSU boosters. Rainey Cawthon, who ran a service station and tire store, had captained a Gator football team and was probably the leading FSU booster. Businessman Lou Hill, another big Gator fan, married Mart Pierson, who was president of her FSCW class in 1942 and who has ever since been a strong and consistent voice in support of countless FSU programs and projects. Other names that are familiar to Tallahasseeans today are Charles Ausley, Godfrey Smith, Edwin White, and Frank Moor; all were prominenet in business and civic affairs.

Important things happened quickly at the new university. President Campbell used wisely the generous funding provided by a provident legislature. He recruited from other distinguished universities in 1949 a group of academic stars, mostly in the sciences, who became known as the Forty-niners. But the rapid rise of FSU in national academic circles was due in no small part to the FSCW foundation of academic excellence, and those who treasure our early history acknowledge that. We rode proudly on the shoulders of some great FSCW stalwarts.

Reubin Askew

When Reubin Askew enrolled at Florida State University in 1948, his classmates had no hint that they were in the company of a future Florida Governor.

Askew served as President of Student Government during his senior year and was nothing if not an activist. Those were interesting times at the young University, and student leaders had opportunities to leave their mark. Reubin delights in telling how he broke down one of the barriers that made life difficult for the female students who were still living under many of the regulations that had been carried forward from FSCW days. Women students— girls! — were permitted to wear slacks only under very limited circumstances, and when slacks were worn they had to be covered by a knee-length coat (usually a raincoat, Askew says.) In the fall of 1950, the recently completed Doak Campbell Stadium was ready for our first football game, and student body president Askew appealed to Dean of Women Katherine Warren for the girls to be permitted to attend the game without their coats. Dean Warren gave her consent, and with that, FSU history was made.

Askew became a member of the House of Representatives, then a Senator and President of the Florida Senate, whence he ran for Governor in 1970. He was re-elected in 1974, thus becoming the first Florida Governor to serve two consecutive terms.

One of the Askew's favorite memories is of his commencement speech in June 1974. The ceremony was held outdoors in Campbell Stadium, and I had just introduced the Governor when I was handed a police report of a bomb threat. We had those on a fairly regular basis, and the routine was to clear the area and check out any likely places that might conceal a bomb. OK—all clear, no bomb.

But more excitement was to come. The Governor's security person was one Captain Owen Cason, a former highway patrol officer who had been at Askew's elbow from the first day, and the two had become fast friends. Captain Cason placed himself at ground level in front of the elevated platform, where he had a good view of the crowd when—goodness!—he dropped prostrate to the ground. He had passed out, and the attendants rushed in and lifted him on to a gurney. He was rolled past the platform to a waiting ambulance, and at the point where he passed directly in front of Governor Askew, who was then proceeding with his address, Cason regained consciousness, raised his head, lifted his arm, and gave his boss a snappy salute. Reubin delights in telling this story each time his commencement speech is mentioned.

This wasn't the only bomb threat to bedevil the Governor. At his inaugural ball in January 1971 in Tully Gym (it was the only suitable venue in Tallahassee in terms of size, at the time), we had another bomb alert. It was a cold night by Tallahassee standards, and of course, everyone had to vacate the building. So there we were, women in formal evening dresses and men in tuxedoes, huddled out in the cold while the building was searched. Another of Reubin's vivid FSU-related memories.

During his two terms as Governor, and since, Reubin Askew has been an ardent FSU supporter. Following the great performance of Hugh Durham's "black basketball team" in Los Angeles in 1972, Governor and Mrs. Askew hosted the players and coaches at a reception in the Governor's mansion. Reubin is often seen at University events and has been called on by every FSU president since to lend his name and his presence wherever needed.

But there's more to the Askew story. During the years of my presidency—he was Governor for five of my seven-and-a-half years—he never once joined in the calls for stricter measures against the student demonstrators. His message as I interpreted it was: You're in charge out there, Stan, and if you need help, I'm sure you'll let me know. That's one—but only one—of the reasons why all of the state university presidents in Florida admired him so.

Our Entry into Fundraising

Fund-raising—meaning soliciting money from non-government sources—did not assume the importance on the president's agenda that it does today. Our basic operating funds came from the Florida legislature, but it was increasingly clear that if our aspirations to be a leading American university were to be realized, we would have to find money to add to the legislative appropriations. That was true not just at FSU, but at many other public universities in this period.

Robert Strozier recognized this early in his term as president and proceeded to do something about it. He established the Florida State University Foundation, and this put FSU formally and officially into the business of fundraising. That was 1960, and before he had time to get the Foundation organized, Strozier died unexpectedly in office the same year. The Foundation, like many other new ventures, was put on hold.

During the next decade, plans were made to start up the Foundation but there were other projects underway, and it wasn't until 1972 that the first professional fundraiser was hired. (The operating arm of the Foundation was then called the University Office of Development and the person in charge was the Director of Development.) The first Director of Development was Hal Wilkins, who came to FSU from Illinois State University, where he had held a similar position. We knew precisely the kind of person we needed at FSU, and Hal Wilkins impressed the search committee and me that he was that person.

Before Wilkins took over, the Seminole Boosters had a modest fundraising arm headed by Andy Miller, an FSU graduate and a local boy from Havana, Florida—close enough to be considered local, anyway. Within the first year, The Boosters expanded their operation and named Andy their first president.

Meanwhile, the Foundation had begun to flex its muscles, and FSU alumnus Nelson Italiano alerted us to the interest in FSU of his good friend Isadore Hecht, a prominent Miami businessman. Nelson suggested that Hal and I call on Mr. Hecht at his home on Miami Beach, and the appointment was set. Rarely have solicitors been received with such hospitality. We were invited to play tennis on the Hechts' court, then to swim in the Hechts' pool—this after having breakfast on the Hechts' patio. The right opportunity to make the ask came while the three of us were splashing about.

Izzy Hecht—as he became known to us at FSU—made a

commitment that morning of $238,000, which we used to purchase the house on Call Street that had been the Alpha Phi sorority house. It was remodeled, renamed the Hecht House, and served as the headquarters of the Foundation—in other words, the offices for Hal Wilkins and his fast-growing staff. The Hecht House also served as a reception center for prospective students, their parents, and other campus visitors.

In addition to conducting a variety of fundraising efforts, Wilkins had a very substantial influence on my own fund-raising endeavors. In 1972, we called upon a group of Tallahassee businessmen to establish a discretionary fund for use by the president; we called it the President's Fund for Excellence. Those 20 men made a commitment to contribute $1,000 a year for 10 years, but most gave more than that. The name of the organization was changed in 1977 to the simpler "President's Club," and it has continued to be an effective fundraiser for a variety of needs of the President for which state monies may not be used.

Another sizable gift in that period came from Miss Ruby Diamond—her full name was Ruby Pearl Diamond—a 90-year-old Tallahassee lady who had attended FSCW. Miss Ruby would often entertain Shirley and me in her apartment in the old Floridan Hotel (that's Floridan, not Floridian), always in late afternoon and always over a glass of her special brand of blackberry wine. Her gift of valuable land adjacent to the campus led to our naming the University's main auditorium in the Westcott Building in Miss Ruby's honor.

The University benefited in many ways from the men and women who served on the Foundation's Board of Directors. They were the driving force for some of our most successful fundraising efforts, and they flew our flag far and wide. Because they were people of stature in Florida and often beyond, the University's standing was elevated among people and organizations whose respect we coveted.

Epilogue: Upon Reflection

The Presidency - A Joyful Job

One of the more interesting experiences of my lifetime has been the opportunity to review the life and times of those who were part of the extended Florida State University family in the era now known as the 60s. Indeed, the writing of this book has been a distinctly eye-opening experience that has given me new insights into those events and the opportunity to distill their essence into lessons that have value for me, and perhaps for others.

Why, I now ask myself, has the assignment been so intriguing? What is there about those experiences that have caused the creative juices to flow so freely? While the question has no immediate or easy answer, there are some helpful clues, and a brief review of events may aid readers in comprehending this book's central message. And what, indeed, is the central message of this book? Join me in the search.

At the heart of my dilemma on the morning of February 18, 1969, my first full day in the office of President, was the role I should try to play in healing a divided University while assuring the students and faculty that the University's historic educational mission would be respected and preserved. What does a University President do when the normal operating systems are disfunctional? How does one succeed a President who has found the place to be unmanageable? Is there anything in my background that might be helpful when I position myself behind the President's desk this morning? Could there be anything in my academic training or my work experience or my personal value system to provide insight or guidance—or even comfort—in the demanding days ahead?

I have since thought about UC-Berkeley President Clark Kerr's wry comment about the presidency. It's all about keeping those in the academic community happy, he said—the three

231

major administrative problems are sex for the students, athletics for the alumni, and parking for the faculty. While I did not view the administrative problems at FSU as the whimsical President Kerr did those at Berkeley, there were nonetheless the same three groups in the University to consider. While the actions of the students, whatever they were, weighed heavily at times, they were the reason I had this great job, and I tried not to forget that, for their activities made my life as zestful as it had ever been. As for the faculty's need for parking, that was one I could delegate to someone else, and the alumni's interest in sports—well, that story is told in chapter 9.

Clark Kerr was a much respected University President in the years before the Free Speech Movement in 1964, and criticism of him for his handling of the campus disturbances at Berkeley would at this point be quite unseemly. But from all accounts then and since, his dismissal by the California Regents was related to his failure to maintain order on the campus. FSU's designation as the Berkeley of the South (or East) caused many—especially those in the media—to liken the situations at our two universities and while that created no real problems for me, it did lead occasionally to a comparison of the performances of the two presidents, and that could be awkward. I had experienced some criticism for the way I had dealt with the protesters, and I would certainly not claim that my performance was flawless, but the judgment of my actions as President would, I hoped, be based on the hard evidence: FSU had no injuries or loss of life, only minimal property damage, no loss of instructional time, and no denial of anyone's constitutional guarantees. I believed then, and I still do, that only a few of the FSU students ever protested just to cause trouble; most of the protesters believed that they were pursuing worthy causes, and that tempered my actions.

One of the slogans students used in their protests of the Vietnam war was "make peace, not war," and I thought that would be a promising path for us to follow in the administration's relations with the student insurgents. Making peace I thought, would work better than making war even if it wasn't always easy. The principle that guided the FSU President and the members of his administration was really just an extension of his dealings with students and other young people through a long career in education: Be firm but fair.

What Worked at FSU

The disputatious character of relations between university administrators and protesting students is a sad chapter in the history of higher education in America. While I am in no position to evaluate the actions of those on other campuses, I believe it might be useful for me to describe in simple terms what seemed to work at FSU.

No issue in my opinion was as important in maintaining friendly relations with students at FSU as the President's access and availability. The students' main objection to university administrators generally was their perception that the President was inaccessible, and that was an image of the FSU President that I was determined to change. My message to students was simple and straightforward: I'll meet with you any time, any place, and we'll discuss anything you wish. A group of black students called my office in a state of agitation and asked for a meeting "tomorrow morning." I'm sorry, I said, but I'm scheduled to leave Tallahassee on an eight o'clock flight, how about the next day? No, they said, it needs to be tomorrow. Okay, I said, 5:30 a.m. in the Bellamy Building. I was there at 5:30 and so were they.

One of the students' favorite places to "rap"* was the steps of Moore Auditorium—it was right next to the University Union which housed the cafeteria and the offices of the

---

*"Rapping" was the almost universal word for talking about the issues of the day. It seems to have disappeared from students' vocabularies today in the earlier context. Today "rap" has an entirely different meaning.

Flambeau—and there were frequent requests for me to show up there around noon-time. That location was convenient to students; it was central to the Library and several classroom buildings, and the top step made a good place for me to hear and be heard.

The nighttime marches to the President's home could be a bit annoying, but I tried never to give the students less than a cordial reception. Reporters for several Florida newspapers seemed to believe that we were on the cusp of violence several times, though I didn't think so. There was, however, one gathering at the President's home that might have been closer to violence than we cared to admit. The students gathered about nine o'clock in front of the house, and I assumed my usual position on the front porch. After we had rapped for awhile, the students drifted off, and I prepared to go back inside the house. One of the Sheriff's deputies then appeared from among the trees farther down in the front yard. Our policy was not to have the police interfere with the students as they assembled on the campus and marched across Tennessee Street onto the grounds of the President's home. A lone police officer would, however, sometimes follow the students and remain in the background, unseen by both the students and me. On this particular evening, the officer came forward after the students had left to ask if I had noticed some of the students standing with their hands behind their backs. I had not. The officer then explained why he posed the question. The students, he said, had picked up the paving bricks lining the flower beds in the front yard and were concealing them behind their backs during our exchange. What their intentions were we never learned. That was an event that fortunately did not make the papers or reach members of the legislature; the next day, the University's buildings and grounds people replaced all of the paving bricks with other decorative pieces.

I said earlier that the presidents of our colleges and universities were in a sense part of the problem for the reason that most were by training and experience unfamiliar with the unusual behavior their students suddenly exhibited. Those presidents were good and dedicated academicians, respected scholars who were quite unprepared to deal in any effective way with student behavior of a kind they could never have imagined taking place on their campuses. And the unhappy consequence in many cases was confusion, chaos and serious disdain for higher education in the minds of many Americans.

Searching for Meaning

In any review of events over a long distant past, one looks for strands of meaning, for memories refreshed and lessons learned. And that's where I find myself now in the spring of 2006. I was certain in the ninth grade that I wanted to be a teacher, a science teacher, in the manner of Mr. Blair, who taught me general science that year. During my three years or so in World War II, I ached to get home to finish my bachelor's degree and to begin teaching science. Nothing has changed for me about the lure and the satisfaction of service in education. Not through the years of high school and college teaching and administration, international education projects, research, writing and service on FSU's Board of Trustees, and now as a member of the Florida Board of Governors, which oversees the State University System. Education has always been where it's at for me.

Immersed as I was in events that were life-shaping to many young people and culture-shaping to most Americans during the 60s and 70s, I have searched for those strands of meaning, and I think I've found some. Perhaps the most important lesson learned—or more likely relearned—was that young people—college students—are a priceless commodity of a special kind. They will not always accept customs and practices just because that's the way we've always done it. This attitude often causes those in the establishment to take a new look, often to their discomfort, and it sometimes brings about changes that are overdue. And so it was with us.

The book's initial appraisal of the sixties—the influence of the period on our national culture and our values—has been given in Chapter 8: "Reflections on the Sixties—What Did We Learn?" If I am now to look for a dominant theme, a central focus of the book now as I wrap up the reminiscing and research and writing, it would be expressed in one word: "Listen!" Let us consider for a moment the backgrounds of the protesting students and the climate of the period in which they reached college age.

They were the baby boomers who were born in the years just after World War II. They grew up in an era when parents wanted the best of everything for their kids and for most of them, that's what they got.

But not for everyone. Those baby boomers looked out at the world they lived in and saw racism and poverty. They looked at the administrators of the colleges and universities they attended, and they didn't connect. Then they looked at their government and what they saw warranted their frustration and, for some, their anger. The American presidents for many of the students' early years—Kennedy, Johnson and Nixon—had gotten their country entangled in affairs in Southeast Asia, where many felt that their country had no right to be in the first place. And worst of all, our young men were the ones who had to go and fight in the war that resulted.

Speaking of wars, there are those who believe Americans shouldn't be involved in today's Iraq war protests—protests that bear some resemblance to those in the period we're discussing—nor in the protests over alleged abuses of the environment, of racial injustice, and other troubling issues. And as before, those in authority must contend with the vigorous, sometimes violent demonstrations. Authorities must be mindful of their duty to protect and defend the citizenry against unlawful acts, yet under our system of justice, those who protest must be accorded the protection due all citizens under the

U.S. Constitution.

It Wasn't all Fun and Games

Critics of the protesters often mention the less favorable traits that characterized the students of that period. They say the students were a self-indulgent generation, people whose moral compass seemed to point in one direction: If it feels good, do it. They experimented with drugs; they adopted a style of music that was more protest than artistry; and they adopted many features of a counter-culture that shocked their elders just as it was intended to do. For those of us who lived and worked with young people on a daily basis, they were sometimes hard to take. It wasn't only George Will, who in the 1990s wrote of the "politically barren radicalism of the sixties" when he said "The Sixties are dead. Not a moment too soon."[1] Many respected scholars from our elite eastern universities took vigorous exception and expressed disdain for that generation.

My descriptions in this book of the FSU student protesters and their antics are well-tempered by a kind of enduring affection that accounted for more presidential tolerance than was approved by many of my friends off campus and some in government. Don't you understand what they're doing to our country, they would ask. And aren't you aware of their capacity for violence? The answer to both of those questions was yes, and to the second question, I was more acutely aware of the potential for violence than I thought it prudent to acknowledge publicly. I could have reported on the purchase in March 1969 of two students who bought a British military rifle, and during the same week, of two others who purchased 500 rounds of .22 caliber ammunition along with a .22 Ruger revolver, all bought from a Tallahassee gun shop by four of the most militant members of the SDS. The Tallahassee police kept us informed.

The information the campus police picked up as they followed the most unruly members of the SDS could be pretty alarming. Among the office papers that my staff saved for me are numerous confidential reports from Chief Bill Tanner, and it's chilling now to read them.

SDS bought a series of underground films and showed them to selected members, films that provided instruction on occupation of a building and the use of force to do so. A confidential source inside the SDS told us that one of the members kept referring to "the bomb expert" at their meetings. Some of their meetings were held under tight security—they suspected police infiltrators. We learned of plans by SDS members to follow campus police to wherever they went for coffee, and for one member to divert the officers' attention long enough for another to drop tasteless drugs into their coffee. I took measures to prevent members of my own family from being similarly victimized. FSU police intercepted plans the SDS received from their counterparts at the University of Maine to somehow seduce children of campus police officers and give them drugs. A small fire of unknown origin was discovered by police in the basement of the Williams Building at 1:00 a.m. on May 30, 1969, in an area which housed paint and theatrical supplies. (We suspected arson, but no evidence was found.)

Those were matters that got our attention and caused Police Chief Bill Tanner and me at times to stay in close touch on a daily basis. But I was determined that such threats must not become the focus of my administration of a university that had an important mission—to provide educational opportunites in a reasonably normal setting for a group of mostly earnest young people. I wanted things to look quite normal to most observers, and that, in fact, was the way we determined campus life should be for me and the others in my administration.

The book's central message then is the understanding—the conviction—that the great majority of those young people were a unique subset of Americans whose contributions leavened the national discourse and broadened the American agenda. I speak for most of the students at Florida State University when I state confidently that the causes they championed in the '60s and '70s were motivated by principle even if the principle was not always well stated. They felt the anguish of the downtrodden and oppressed and of their fellow Americans who were denied the full benefits of citizenship because of their race. They attended colleges and universities that denied them an active role in setting the policies and practices under which they lived and studied. Changes in the values and beliefs of Americans down through history have come about through the efforts of many people in many different ways and our young people—the troubled and troubling students of the '60s—adopted their own methods to change the culture of their country, and the results they achieved were both important and long-lasting.

The Most Lasting Thread: Listen to Us

In his award-winning book, *The World Is Flat,* Thomas Friedman tells us how the world has changed during the past four decades. He attributes the enormous globalization movement to the breakthroughs in global communications that have been made possible through the Internet and other instruments of electronic communication. In this profoundly important book, Friedman tells us that it all began with new ways people worldwide found to talk to one another. That's what brought down the Berlin Wall, Friedman says. While I am neither a social scientist nor a student of global commerce, I cannot avoid seeing a connection between the openness that was so actively sought by students in the '60s and '70s and the global communications of today. Talk to us, they said, and listen; we've been cloistered in the tranquil world we grew up in, and we want out. We see things that need to be changed, and nothing seems to be changing. We'll get the attention of those in power one way or another, and they had better listen because the future's going to be different for all of us and for our country.

Listening Works Both Ways

Is there a connection between those protesting students, and the circumstances confronting the authorities today? I am occasionaly asked if I see such a connection and how I think the authorities should respond. I shall not attempt to answer such a question for I lack both the wisdom and the audacity, but I will say that our policy of firmness coupled with fairness achieved my purposes at Florida State University. Whether it would have produced the same results at another university, I have no way of knowing and I'm reluctant to speculate. The difference between FSU and the other more troubled campuses, I believe, was the certain knowledge by the protesters at FSU that there were limits. You have complete freedom of speech and assembly, I told our students, and that means you may do most of the things on this campus that you want to do. But there are some other things you may not do, and if you attempt them, you will be held accountable. You will be suject to disciplinary action by the University and maybe by the courts. That policy was different from those in place at other universities where the use of force—or even the threat of it—was considered unacceptable in a university setting, (as the FSU faculty senate resolved, "beyond the pale of propriety"). Would that assurance given to demonstrating students at those universities have served as an early deterent and thus have prevented the unhappy and sometimes tragic occurences at Kent State and Jackson State and Wisconsin and San Francisco State? I don't know of course, but the record of the 60s at Florida State University is one that my associates in the FSU administration and I are content to let stand.

My final comment in this book will be the same as one finds in the doctoral dissertations submitted by generations of graduate students: not withstanding my findings and conclusions, there are unanswered questions about the Sixties that deserve further study. The impact of the Sixties has been important, and as students of history and human behavior continue to remind us, we still have much to learn about that tumultuous period.

ENDNOTES

Chapter 1

1. Terry Anderson, *The Movement and the Sixties* (New York: Oxford University Press, 1995): x-xi.
2. Stephen Parr, "The Forgotten Radicals: The New Left in the Deep South, Florida State University 1960 to 1972" (Ph.D. diss., Florida State University, 2000): 1.
3. Parr, 159. "Faculty Requests Charges Dropped" *Flambeau,*
4. March 1969. "Senate Resolution Squeaks By," *Flambeau,* 6 March 1969.
5. "Joint Report Blames Faculty for Disruption," *Flambeau,* 20 January 1970.

Chapter 2

1. Lewis S. Feuer, "Student Unrest in the United States, " *Annals of the Academy of Political science and Social Science, Special Issue American Higher Education: Prospects and Choices,* (Nov 1972): 171.
2. Terry Anderson, 140-145.
3. Anderson, Terry 164-5, 299-300.
4. Quoted in Terry Anderson, [*The Movement and the Sixties* (New York: Oxford University Press, 1995)], 296.
5. Anderson, *The Movement and the Sixties,* 294-299.
6. David Frum, *How We Got Here* (New York: Basic Book Group, 1999): 10.
7. "Student Demonstration Continues," *Flambeau,* 15 May 1968.
8. John Champion, "Statement by FSU President John Champion," 13 May 1968, reprinted as "Statements" in *Flambeau,* 15 May 1968.
9. "President Champion Resigns; VP Chalmers Assumes Post" *Flambeau,* 16 May 1968.

10. "Champion Returns; Issues Six Points," *Flambeau,* 22 May 1968.

11. "Students End Week Long Vigil," *Flambeau,* 17 May 1968.

12. "President John Champion Resigns; VP Chalmers Assumes Post," *Flambeau,* 16 May 1968.

13. "Flambeau Forum" *Flambeau* 17 May 1968.

14. " 'Support Champion' Rally Held," *Flambeau,* 16 May 1968.

15. Quoted in Parr, p 92.

16. Ibid, 93.

17. Ibid, 96.

18. Kathy Urban, "Champion Vacillating? Signs Point to Yes," *Flambeau,* 23 May 1968, and Myra Silverstein, "BOSP Evaluates, Seeks New Adviser," *Flambeau,* 3 July 1968.

19. Editorial, *Flambeau,* 15 May 1968.

20. "SDS Demands Presented at Westcott Lawn Rally," *Flambeau,* 14 January 1969.

21. "Faircloth Rules on BOR Policy," *Flambeau,* 15 January 1969.

22. George Waas, editorial *Flambeau* 15 January 1969

23. "Marshall to Fill New Post of Executive VP," *Flambeau,* 12 February 1969.

24. "VP Chalmers Resigns to Head Kansas U" *Flambeau,* 11 February 1969.

25. "Student Body President Calls Prexy 'Frightened'," *Flambeau,* 17 February 1969.

26. D.G. Lawrence, " Champion to Stay As Teacher at FSU; Pressure by Faculty Revealed," *Orlando Sentinel,* 19 February 1969.

27. "Champion's Farwell" Flambeau, 19 February 1969.

28. "Says Rep, Fire Megill or Funds Will Be Cut," 19 February 1969.

Chapter 3

1. J. Stanley Marshall, speech to General Faculty, 27 February 1969.
2. Ibid.
3. The following list of alleged errors appears in Lyman Fletcher, " Carey's Errors ," *The Flambeau*, and it is the source for all quotes in the following four paragraphs unless specifically noted otherwise.
4. George Waas, editorial, *Flambeau*, 15 January 1969.
5. George Waas, editorial, *Flambeau*, 17 January 1969.

Chapter 4

1. Stephen Parr, "The Unforgotten Radicals: The New Left in the Deep South, Florida State University 1960 to 1972" (Ph.D diss., Florida State University, 2000): 178.
2. Parr, 210.
3. Quoted in Parr, 181-2.
4. "Symposium of Student Unrest" *Flambeau*, 16 April 1969
5. "Protest at FSU" Tallahassee *Democrat*, 23 April 1969
6. Michael B. Frost, "Disruptive" letter, *Flambeau*, 28 April, 1969.
7. "'Silent Majority' Makes Presentation" *Tallahassee Democrat*, 30 May 1969.
8. Canter Brown, "The President's Statement" *Flambeau*. 28 April 1969.
9. Joe Savage, "SDSer Arrested for Trespassing" *Flambeau*, 14 May 1969; "The "Disruption" editorial, *Flambeau*, 15 May 1969 as appears in Parr, 194
10. Parr, 196.
11. "Statement by Acting President J. Stanley Marshall," delivered May 19, 1969, Robert Manning Strozier Library Special Collections. Vertical files, Presidents folder.
12. Ken Jones, "SDSer Convicted; More Arrests" 20 May 1969.

13. "Sanford Denies SDS Leader in Interview" *Tallahassee Democrat*, 16 June 1969.

Chapter 5

1. "Question: When is Anarchy Free Speech?" editorial, *Tampa Tribune*, 18 January 1969.
2. Carl Davidson, statement at the National Guardian banquet in New York, December 1967, quoted in "Statement by Vice-President for Student Affairs Jack Arnold" drafted 15 December 1968.
3. "SDS Demands Presented at Westcott Lawn Rally," *Flambeau*, 14 January 1969.
4. Gregory Calvert, SDS National Secretary, 1967, quoted in "Question: When is Anarchy Free Speech" editorial *Tampa Tribune* 18 January 1969.
5. Stephen Parr, "The Unforgotten Radicals: The New Left in the Deep South, Florida State University 1960 to 1972" (Ph.D diss., Florida State University, 2000): 192.
6. Quoted in Parr, 199.
7. Editorial, *Orlando Sentinel*, 15 January 1969.
8. George Waas, editorial, *Flambeau*, 15 January 1969
9. Editorial, *Tampa Tribune*, 18 January 1969.
10. Earl Rickey, "Students Use Humor Not Violence, Score Point" *Tallahassee Democrat*, 8 March 1969.
11. Parr, 183-4.
12. Parr, 183.
13. Parr, 190.
14. Parr, 203.
15. Parr, 214.

Chapter 6

1. "Controversial Revolution" *Flambeau*, 20 September 1971.
2. *Flambeau*, 21 September 1971.
3. *Flambeau*, 21 September 1971.

4. *Flambeau*, 27 September 1971.

5. *Flambeau*, 8 November 1971.

6. "University Must Act Against War," Editorial, 5 May 1970, *Flambeau*, reprinted from *Columbia Daily Spectator*

7. David M. Snyder, "Governor Kirk On Campus," *Flambeau*, 8 May 1970.

8. Editorial, *Flambeau,* 8 May 1970.

9. Parr, 282.

10. "Powell Calls for Revolution of the Youth," *Flambeau,* 3 April 1968.

11. "A & M University Students Protest Phase Out," *Flambeau*, 4 April 1968.

12. Parr, 250.

13. Parr, 253.

14. Parr, 263-4.

15. Ann Frechette, "Senators: No Hostility for Jack," *Flambeau* 4 January 1972.

16. Lillian Musgrove Chason, letter to *Flambeau*, 21 February 1969.

17. Stephen Parr, 253.

18. Parr, 254.

19. Parr, 255.

20. Tom Kirwan and Richard Lee, "Streakers Hit FSU Campus" *Flambeau*, 11 March 1974.

21. Ibid.

22. "Suzy N. York" "Streaking is to streakers 'free and exciting, Streakerette," *Flambeau*, 11 March 1974

23. Charley Barnes, email with author, 29 September 2005.

24. "Neighborly Pride Aside, Carswell is Good Choice," editorial, *Tallahassee Democrat,* 20 January 1970.

25. "Carswell Denies Racist sentiment," *Flambeau*, 22 January 1970.

26. "Carswell May Make Some People Long for Haynesworth," *New York Times*, 25 January 1970.

27. "Carswell Denies he Tried to Balk Golf Club's Integra-

tion; Declares 'I am Not a Racist' "*New York Times*, 23 January 1970.

28. Sam Miller, "By BOR Chairman Kibler, Law faculty Opposition Questioned," *The Flambeau,* 2 April 1970.

Chapter 7

1. Terry Anderson, *The Movement and the Sixties,* 104
2. Quoted in Anderson, 104-105.
3. Kenneth J. Mortimer, "Dilemmas in New Campus Governance Structures," *Journal of Higher Education* 42:6 (June 1971), 473.
4. John B. Millet, *New Structures of Campus Power,* (San Francisco: Jossey-Bass Publishers), Preface, xi.
5. *Ibid,* xi.
6. *Ibid,* 16.
7. Millet, 41.
8. Millett, 43.
9. Millett, 44.
10. Millett, 48.
11. Millett, 50.
12. Millett, 51.
13. Millett, 58.
14. Millet, 61.
15. *Ibid.*
16. Fred Standley, "Address to the Faculty Senate" delivered 1 October 1974.
17. Ibid.
18. Editorial, *Flambeau,* 22 November 1974.

Chapter 8

1. Terry Anderson, *The Movement and the Sixties in America from Greensboro to Wounded Knee,* (New York: Oxford University Press, 1995): 352.

Chapter 9

1. John Keith, catcher for 1970 FSU baseball team, interview with author 1 December 2005.

Chapter 10

1. "Airport Protest Planned; Hussein Degree Sparks Criticism" *Flambeau*, 5 May 1975.
2. Davis Whiteman, editorial, *Flambeau*, 5 May 1975.

Chapter 11

1. Robin Sellers, *Femina Perfecta,* (Tallahassee, FL: Florida State University Foundation, 1995) 270.
2. Sellers, Femina Perfecta, 272.

Epilogue

1. Will, George in *Newsweek*, 25 March 1991, pp 65-66 quoted in Anderson, 412.

APPENDIX

The Appendix contains items intended to provide readers with information beyond that presented in the book's 11 chapters.

There was much about the life of the president and the goings-on at the University over which he presided that was fanciful. Descriptions of those experiences in the Appendix may paint a truer picture of the lives of the president and others during those interesting times.

Three of the author's speeches are included to give readers added insight into the ideas, values, and decisions of the man who led Florida State University during the period reviewed in the book's 11 chapters.

The organizational chart of the University's central administration provides the names of the senior administrative officers during the Marshall administration.

We've included a map to help readers follow the action around the campus.

Fond Memories

In my dealings with those who took exception to the policies and practices of my administration, there were times of tension and stress. But there were also moments of exhilaration and delight, and those far outweighed, both in number and intensity, the contentious times. I've searched my memory and I've reviewed the documents from that period. I've been reminded of the pleasant things that were such an important part of the presidency, of how prevalent and how rich were the experiences that I found to be eye-opening, entertaining, attitude-changing, funny, and above all memorable. What follows are accounts of things that helped to make my job as President of FSU an enormously rewarding experience.

Visitors to FSU

Whether or not FSU deserved to be called the Berkeley of the South (or East) might be answered in part by the attention we received in the national media. Was this a place the activists cared about? Did they want to come here to speak? To perform? To be seen and heard? To engage in political advocacy? A review of the number and variety of visitors to Tallahassee helps to answer those questions.

Hubert Humphrey visited Tallahassee more than once. Both Joan Baez and Jane Fonda came to the University in January 1971, to perform as part of the anti-war movement. William Kunstler, the famous defense lawyer, came to participate in a human rights symposium in February, during which he claimed that "the government's purpose was to frighten and intimidate dissenters into submission as the Nazis intimidated the German citizens during the Reichstag trial era." Other speakers included U.S. Senator and Vietnam War critic William Fulbright, Social Democratic economist John Kenneth Galbraith, civil rights activist Jesse Jackson, along with poet Allen Ginsberg, feminist advocates Gloria Steinem and Dorothy Pitman, Abbie

Hoffman, and Kathleen Cleaver, wife of Black Panther militant Eldridge Cleaver. In September, antiwar Senator George McGovern spoke at the University Union, and after his speech, students burned Richard Nixon in effigy. Lyndon Johnson's former Attorney General Ramsey Clark also spoke on campus, as did Socialist Workers Party presidential candidate Linda Jenness. A prominent leader of the New Left and SDS co-founder Carl Ogelsby came to debate conservative sociologist Ernest Van den Haag. Black militants and Former Chairman of the SNCC Stokely Carmichael spoke at Florida A & M in March.

In January 1972, Shirley Chisholm, U.S. Representative from New York, spoke at Moore Auditorium as part of her run for Democratic nomination for President. In February, Marxist political philosopher from the University of California Herbert Marcuse lectured as part of the University lecture series. Marcuse was widely read by New Left intellectuals.

The speakers list also included moderates and conservatives, including Pepsi-Cola President James Somerall and CBS newsman Marvin Kalb along with John McManus, staff coordinator of the John Birch Society.

Red Barber and the Greatest Inning

After his retirement from broadcasting sports on television and radio, Red Barber and his wife Lylah came to live in Tallahassee. Lyla had been a student at FSCW when Red was a student at the University of Florida in the 1920s, and they had strong ties in the Sunshine State. The Marshalls got to know the Barbers well, and we saw a good bit of them socially.

In August 1974, I asked Red to come to a backyard cookout for the members of the football team and talk to them about his extraordinary career in sports broadcasting. (He had not yet been inducted into the Baseball Hall of Fame.) The football players had assembled early for practice before the students returned for the fall quarter, and Coach Peterson was eager to find entertainment for them in the evenings. I had read Red's book, *1947: The Year All Hell Broke Loose in Baseball*, and I remembered that he had described the ninth inning of the fourth game of the 1947 World Series as perhaps the most dramatic inning in the history of baseball. I asked Red if he would say something about that historic moment, and he obliged in a way that delighted all of us. He pretended that he was sitting before his microphone in the broadcast booth, and he recited the play-by-play of that ninth inning just as he had given it to his radio audience during the game on that day in October 1947. It was a historic moment and a wonderful opportunity for our student athletes to see and hear the greatest figure in the history of sports broadcasting.

A Royal Lady

Helen Hayes visited the campus five times during my presidency (as noted in Chapter Two), and my family and I found her to be as warm and gracious a person as she was a luminary on the American stage. One evening at dinner at our house, we had arranged for her to be seated next to a couple of members of the theater faculty, but in the small-talk before dinner she had noticed our 12-year-old son John across the room, and she made a point of talking to him. As she approached the table, she asked that John be seated next to her, and he was. What happened through most of the meal was table socializing in which she missed no opportunity to bring John into the conversation. Her letter to me after her visit told of how pleased she was to have gotten to know John Marshall, and I had not the slightest doubt that she meant it.

In No Uncertain Terms...

John D. MacArthur was the brother of Helen Hayes's husband, Charles MacArthur, the playwright, and John D. knew of Helen Hayes's close ties to FSU. Mr. MacArthur had come to the campus at my invitation several times, and I made several visits to him at his hotel in Palm Beach Shores. He was widely regarded as an all-time, four-star curmudgeon, and I found reason to believe the reputation had been well earned. On one visit, as we sat at his table at lunch, he was approached by a staff member who had a paper for Mr. MacArthur to sign.

"No, bring the other paper," MacArthur said.

"It's on my desk, I'll go get it," the man replied.

"On whose desk?" demanded MacArthur.

"On your desk. Mr. MacArthur" came the hasty and embarrassed response.

"You're God damn right it is," came the reply, "and don't you forget it!"

My visits to MacArthur were to solicit a major gift to the University, and I failed completely.

Merry Christmas!

The president's home was the scene of many interesting and entertaining events. Among the most enjoyable were the regular visits from groups of sorority girls who came to sing Christmas carols. They would assemble in front of the big white house which was always wonderfully decorated with ribbons and wreaths and bells, and of course my family and I joined in the singing…and well, what a splendid way for the president and his family to join in the university's celebration of Christmas.

Student Loyalties

There's more to the Westcott fire than was told in Chapter Three. The response of students was simply inspiring. They went into the burning building and carried out whatever items they could reach that seemed to be of value. When I got there, several members of my staff and the campus police had arrived and were giving directions to the students. But mostly, it was just a great spontaneous effort by people who were deeply distressed about the destruction taking place before them and wanted to do what they could to save the building's treasures. I have never doubted the loyalty and dedication of our students, but it was wonderful to see those traits so dramatically and courageously displayed at that moment of need.

A Friend in Need

The clock showed 2:00 a.m. when the bedside telephone rang. "This is Chuck Sherman, Dr. Marshall." were the words I heard, "and I have been detained by the police in Gulf Breeze." "So Chuck, tell me more," I said.

The story was simple enough. Chuck who was then SGA President was visiting a girlfriend when his car was stopped for a marijuana search—the cops were suspicious. He asked if I could make a telephone call and try to... Of course I could, and did. And anyway, what are friends for?

Pigs and Freaks

The Pigs (campus police) versus Freaks (students) football game, shown in the photo on page 141, was great fun for the participants and nearly as much for the fans. It demonstrated in the most visible and meaningful way that people in both groups had distinct personal feelings that transcended the issues and events in which they were often adversaries. In other words, we liked one another.

We Play to Win

I received a challenge from Apollo Visko, student body president in 1975, for a touch football game between student government and the administration in the backyard of the president's home. Apollo knew that I regularly invited groups of faculty, students, and friends of the University to play on weekends, and he probably thought those old academic administrators would be easy pickings. Well, I assembled from our regular guys the best athletes I could round up, and we played. Who won, you ask? Do you think I would have mentioned this game if the students had won?

Johnny Bench: Touchdown!

Woody Woodward had been an outstanding baseball player at FSU and had made a generous contribution to the University from the bonus he received when he signed the contract with the Milwaukee Braves in 1963 to play major league baseball. Woody later played for the Cincinnati Reds, and he became close friends with Johnny Bench, the Reds' celebrated catcher. Woody and his family made their home in Tallahassee, which meant that he was available in the off-season to play in the touch football games in the backyard of the president's home. Woody's friend Johnny Bench would visit him in Tallahassee during the winters, and on one occasion, Bench came with Woody to play in one of our more spirited games. All of us weekend athletes learned that Bench could run with and throw and catch a football about as well as he could play major league baseball. Bench was single then, and he was much taken with the beauty of the FSU coeds.

The Senator and the Canal

I had invited U.S. Senator Lawton Chiles to deliver the address at the commencement of our graduates at our center in Panama City, Panama, in 1972. The Chileses and Marshalls flew down together and had an enjoyable three-day visit to the Canal Zone. During our stay, the Senator and I were given a tour of the Canal on one of the ships passing through. Our guide was the general who was the superintendent of the Canal. Of course, he arranged for us to do what every visitor wants to do, place our hand on the big handle and turn it, watching the lock before us swing open. Senator Chiles and I were also given a low-level helicopter tour of the Canal, end to end.

Moral: It's great to visit interesting places in the company of dignitaries who have power and influence.

The (Almost) Mission to China

In the spring of 1972, I was invited by President Nixon to dinner at the White House. The date was March 28, and the event was in honor of King Hussein of Jordan. I arranged to do some other business during the day in Washington, and then I walked over to the White House, not certain of what entrance I should use. As I approached, I noticed there were several large black limousines being processed for entry. The guard told me I really should have used another entrance—this one was for cars—but I showed him my invitation, and he called someone who gave him the authority he needed to admit me. I walked up the sidewalk to the south portico of the White House. There, I joined other guests alighting from their cars, and we were greeted by U.S. Marines in full dress uniforms who escorted us up the steps to the reception area on the main floor.

It was a small dinner as such things go—about 60 people in all—and after we were greeted by the President and met the King, there was small talk in the reception area with the other guests, including several Cabinet members, Supreme Court justices, and prominent people from the business world.

The President made brief welcoming remarks, and then we had dinner. After dinner, President Nixon called on King Hussein for informal remarks in which he told us how important it was for the United States to continue to build bridges to countries in the Middle East, and he assured us that he would help us do so.

After dinner, we adjourned to the East Room for drinks and conversation. I had some relaxed conversation with President Nixon, and I commented on his recent trip to China. (That historic visit had occurred only a few weeks before.) I asked him if he had had the chance to visit any schools in China. "I did not" he said, "but Mrs. Nixon did, and you should talk to her"—and just then he interrupted himself as a new thought crossed his mind.

"We need to know more about education in China," he said, "and I'd like to send... would you be interested, Dr. Marshall, in heading up a delegation of educators to go to China to learn about their schools?"

I remember exactly what I said in reply: "Yes, Mr. President, I would."

"Good !" said the President. "Henry is not here, but I'll have him get in touch with you." Henry, of course, was Secretary of State Henry Kissinger.

Within the week the letter from Secretary Kissinger arrived, and I began to think about identifying some of my associates to join the delegation and to define our task.

A few weeks later my assignment was overtaken by events in Washington that ended the mission before it began: Watergate. From that day in June, the President and those around him were consumed by more urgent matters, and the Marshall mission to China never happened.

Jimmy Carter at the Cape

I attended one of the early space launches at Cape Kennedy sometime about 1971. Shirley and I were walking before the section where dignitaries were seated when we saw our friend Bert Lance seated in the top row with Jimmy Carter, who was then Governor of Georgia. Lance, who later went to Washington with Carter as head of the Office of Management and Budget, was then a member of the Governor's staff, and they had come to witness the shot. (The Marshalls had become friends with the Lances during our visits to Callaway Gardens, where Bert and I played tennis with our mutual friend Hal Northrup, the President of the Gardens.) Bert motioned us to come sit with the two of them, and we did. I talked with Governor Carter and heard some of his views on the space program. No, I don't remember any of them, but I do remember with pleasure the opportunity to watch a space shot in the company of a man who was to become President of the United

States.

FSU One Time!

I have always been a great devotee of band music, especially by marching bands. Performances by the Marching Chiefs have always been a highlight for me at the football games in Campbell Stadium. I learned in the fall of 1969—my first year as university president—that I had access to a grandstand seat to see and hear the Chiefs during their practices. I would stroll over to their practice field across from Tully Gym in the late afternoon, climb up the ladder to the observation tower to watch the marchers go through their formations along with the band director, and to listen up close to that marvelous brass sound that so many of us had come to love.

One more of the great perks available to the university president!

The Kiss That Wasn't

Doby Flowers was FSU's first black homecoming queen in October 1969. She was a Tallahassee girl and a fine young woman who was beautifully attired as she stood on stage before a large crowd in Campbell Stadium. My job was to mount the stage, congratulate Doby and place the crown on her head. Pleasant duty in every way, but then came the moment of truth—can I bestow a congratulatory kiss, as I thought appropriate, or should I just shake her hand? In that moment of doubt, the image that flashed before my eyes was my picture on the front page of every Florida newspaper of Marshall breaking through one more barrier, and I...well, I took the cowardly way out. I've been mildly conscience-stricken about that ever since, and of course I'll never know how the people of Florida, especially Tallahassee, would have accepted such a forward gesture in 1969. I've wondered if Doby noticed my vacillation. She lives in Tallahassee, and we're friends, but I've never asked her.

Education, Not Agitation

The appearance on the campus of our first black students in the Summer Institute for Science Teachers in 1962 made the university administration pretty nervous. As head of the Department of Science Education, I had designed the program and was awarded a rather nice National Science Foundation grant to support it. Neither Education Dean Mode Stone, nor I had run it by President Gordon Blackwell, but we felt sure the president would approve if we got the grant.

Well, he did, but we were all apprehensive. The tensions in Alabama over integration were escalating, and I remembered that Tallahassee was still the Old South.

So the president convened a series of meetings at which we made careful plans. No black students were to be assigned to rooms on the first or second floors of Smith Hall where they were to be housed; we thought missiles were less likely to be thrown through the windows on the upper floors. We believed that various precautions should be taken to head off possible trouble, and we might need help from the police. So, officers from both the Sherriff's Office and the Tallahassee Police Department attended the meetings, and to our surprise, so did Malcolm Johnson, editor of the *Tallahassee Democrat* who believed as we did, that the racial integration of FSU might be a newsworthy event.

Editor Johnson was widely regarded as a staunch conservative, and he revealed his views on such matters as race in his widely read daily column, "I Declare." While I was fond of Malcolm personally, I doubted that he and I would agree on the racial integration of the University and I sat through the meetings in the President's office watching Malcolm writing on his note pad and worrying about what he would write in the *Democrat*.

The students arrived on the campus on Sunday, June 17. The *Tallahassee Democrat* was then a morning paper, and there was nothing on the matter in Sunday's paper, but what, we wondered, might lie ahead? What we read on Monday morning was the lead editorial entitled "Education, Not Agitation," in which Malcolm told *Democrat* readers that Florida State University's purpose was to provide educational opportunity to deserving students, and race had nothing to do with it. How important that editorial was to the people of North Florida in maintaining respect for our efforts we couldn't be sure, but we thought it was huge.

Malcolm Johnson was not much admired by the FSU faculty some of whom probably thought him to be a racist. He and I became close friends, especially in the years after I left the presidency, and he was no racist. Whatever his earlier views might have been... well, I've thought often of the wisdom of FAMU's legendary football coach Jake Gaither. "A converted white man—by that I mean a white man who has made up his mind to be fair—is the best friend a black man can have," the coach said.

The Inauguration

Among the pleasant memories in connection with my inauguration on May 1, 1970, was the gathering of former FSU presidents. I had put off the inauguration for nearly a year following my appointment by the Board of Regents on June 5, 1969, which made it about 16 months after I had assumed the acting presidency—there seemed always to be more pressing matters. Included in this book are a couple of photographs on page 148 of the assembled dignitaries. This was the last presidential inauguration President Campbell was to attend and one of the few remaining occasions for the aging president to be photographed in a university setting.

Sister J Couldn't Make It

In the early 1960s, a series of important changes occurred in curriculum in American high schools. Much of the change was instigated by scholars not from education, but from the disciplines—people from the universities who had not been connected with public education but who had become concerned about the condition of our schools after the Soviet Union launched Sputnik in 1957, which frightened many Americans into believing the Soviets just might win the space race. A group of eminent physicists from Harvard, MIT, and Cornell formed the Physical Science Study Committee (PSSC), and the new course in high school physics that they developed was widely adopted in American high schools. The new course was known by the name "PSSC Physics," and Florida became a leader among states to adopt the new course and to train the state's high school physics teachers to teach it.

As a science educator, I joined in with the PSSC group and worked closely with Professors Gerald Zacharias of MIT and Philip Morrison of Cornell in the implementation phase— in other words, introducing the new curriculum to the nation's high schools. Both had been major figures in the nation's atom bomb project in the early 1940s; they were distinguished and renowned physicists. Another of the scholars in this and other innovations in curriculum was a Catholic nun who had achieved fame as an educational innovator. Sister Jacqueline of the Jesuit Order had been featured in a major spread in *Life* magazine and was much in the news as the president of Webster College in Webster Grove, near St. Louis, where important advances in education were taking place. Sister Jacqueline and I had, through our joint work on the PSSC project, developed a close friendship, and I thought "Sister J," as she was called by the professors, would be just the right person to give the principal address at my inauguration. It happened that she was no longer Sister J; she had left the Order, married a prominent New Yorker, and become Jacqueline Wexler, president of New York's Hunter College. She was invited to my inauguration ceremony, and she accepted. But when inauguration day came, President Wexler couldn't make it; she was being held prisoner in her office in the administration building at Hunter by students on strike over some campus issue. I regretted that I was denied the chance to see my old friend and to have such a distinguished educator participate in the program—but then I remembered this was 1970, and such was life in the American university.

Petersonese

Bill Peterson was, to me, more than a good football coach; he was a good friend, a delightful companion, and a source of abundant good humor. His mangling of the language was one of his endearing qualities. Bill McGrotha, longtime sports editor of the *Tallahassee Democrat*, included some of the best in his daily columns. Pete's malapropisms still produce belly-shaking laughter when I review them with friends. Bill's wife Marge, a beautiful and delightful lady, still insists that he didn't say all those things, and maybe she's right, but I heard him say enough to believe he merited the reputation.

Like his pep talks to his teams:

> You guys can hang your heads high.
>
> If you guys don't go to class, you're going to end up as a bunch of dig-ditchers.
>
> What we need to do is nip that rumor in the butt.
>
> Just let a dead horse rest.
>
> That was a cliff-dweller to end all cliff-dwellers.
>
> He's a good receiver, but he hears footprints.
>
> Fred Biletnikoff, as a receiver, was foot-sure and fancy free.

There were more, like:

> ...Ships that crash in the night.
>
> A good quarterback, who was a trick of all trades.

Prior to the big game, just remember the words of Henry Patrick—kill me or let me live.

Bill McGrotha, writing in the *Florida State Magazine* a few years after Pete retired, put it well: "For 11 seasons, Florida State fans laughed and cried with Bill Peterson, perhaps, as with no other. He had a high talent for making up words and phrases, while challenging individuals—players, coaches, politicians, fans, college presidents—to produce more than they thought they reasonably could."

And in the end it all worked out, for as Pete said to some friends one night, "The greatest thing just happened. I got indicted into the Florida Sports Hall of Fame." And if there were any who wanted the President to speak to the coach about his "problem," well, "why not just let sleeping bags lie."

The Governor's Baseball Dinner

For many years, the Governor of Florida hosted an appreciation dinner for the Major League Baseball teams that trained in Florida. The dinners were held at the end of spring training, just before the teams headed back north to open the season. Governor Reubin Askew invited me to attend the dinner as his special guest in 1971.

The annual event was held in various hotels, this one in Tampa. During the evening, the Governor's party mixed and mingled with baseball people who were usually club executives and some of their outstanding players. On this occasion, I had one-on-one time with several of the stars of the game including some of my all-time heroes, and of course, I got many autographs. The players who signed my dinner program were Bob Feller, Satchel Page, Stan Musial, Yogi Berra, Al Kaline, and of course our own Woody Woodward.

Do I still have the program? Of course I do, and I've resisted suggestions from several friends that I put it on ebay to find out what price it would bring. It's like a priceless work of art—worth more to me and my baseball-playing sons than the dollars it might bring.

Not Really A Fair Exchange

Student government had developed a program called Open Mouth Speakers Forum in the spring of 1974, and I was invited to participate. The Forum was a rather informal setting for students and faculty to speak on any number of topics of current interest. Appearances of this kind gave me yet another opportunity to interact with students, and I enjoyed nearly all of those. Many were intended to be confrontations in which I would be put on the spot by protesting students. After all, I was outnumbered, and I was sure to be asked questions they hoped I couldn't answer, or would be afraid to. Some probably remembered Canter Brown's charge that my predecessor was a "frightened man," and they assumed that the new president would not relish standing before a hostile crowd.

But they did not take into account three things that operated in my favor: (1) I usually had command of the facts related to events and activities under discussion, and they didn't; it was my job to stay informed, and often they were operating from myths and rumors; (2) many of the students I faced were not inherently angry or hostile—they were there largely out of curiosity, and when I spoke openly and with obvious candor, most were satisfied; and (3) the angry ones almost always misjudged the general campus atmosphere, believing it to be more supportive of their position than it was. In this they were surprisingly and consistently misinformed. They had been seduced by the messages they were getting from the radicals on other campuses and believed they had status and strength among the student body while in reality it was at best ephemeral. So I approached most of those open forums confident and relaxed.

I remember some of those with great amusement. In one exchange, the charge was that the administration had plans to move into Frenchtown, the predominantly black section of Tallahassee adjacent to the campus, and to displace the black residents and businesses there. I knew the origin of this charge: Columbia University had expanded into Harlem, adjacent to the campus, and some of those displaced had claimed they were exploited. So if that's what Columbia had done, why shouldn't the FSU protesters suspect their University of doing the same? I remember what I told the students that night. "If we are going into Frenchtown, it will be right after we have completed our occupation of the Appalachian Mountains," I said, hardly able to suppress my laughter.

I remember clearly another interesting and enjoyable exchange. After the administration had moved back into the rebuilt Westcott Building following the fire, I was beckoned by a crowd chanting on the Westcott steps one morning, just below my office, and as usual I heeded the call. "We know what you spent on your office," said the spokesperson. "Your new desk cost $50,000, and it was paid for by our money." Well, they couldn't have tossed me a fatter pitch. "I'd like for a delegation to come up to my office with me, right now," I said. "I want to show you that $50,000 desk." They accepted my invitation, and six or eight students came with me. What they saw was the same desk, now repaired but still showing the scars that Larry Campbell and I had inflicted upon it when he attacked it with a fireman's axe the afternoon of the Westcott fire. The protesting students were embarrassed, and I was amused. That exchange might have turned out more to my advantage than some others, but on the whole, it was not hard for me to leave those "confrontations" pleased that the antagonists who had sought an angry face-off found that it turned out to be closer to a love fest.

So was it fun being president of FSU? Simply stated, it was the second best job I ever had. The first? Teaching high school science, of course!

REMARKS BY STANLEY MARSHALL, ACTING PRESIDENT, FLORIDA STATE UNIVERSITY

General Faculty Meeting
February 27, 1969

The State of the University

It has been a long day and the hour is late. It has also been an interesting ten days for me and for the University. I have gained what seems to me to be an enormous amount of information about the University and what makes it tick. I think I know something about what the members of the University community think on several matters of current interest, and I have a better understanding of the means by which academicians form judgments.

It has been interesting in still another way. The number and variety of rumors that have reached my ears would be sufficient to give all of the clubs and societies in North Florida enough material to last for several months. The number you have heard is probably even greater. I must not fail to take note of the highly creative character of many of the rumors, and I want to pay my respects to the authors of some of these, whoever they may be. At the risk of making things a little less interesting, I shall correct two or three of the most prominent. No, I am not of Lebanese descent although some understanding of Middle Eastern culture might be a useful attribute. Nor

---

*I had been in the office of president only ten days when I delivered this speech to a full audience in Westcott Auditorium. Most of the 1,200 or so faculty members knew me as the dean of the School of Education and I felt an obligation to tell them more about their university's new president and what kind of leadership he would try to provide.

is it true that Governor Kirk will resign as Governor to be named Vice President of the University. Finally, and with apologies to Mark Twain, the report that I am alive and well and living in Argentina is highly exaggerated. That I am alive and well and have managed to survive my first ten days in Westcott should be self-evident.

Let me begin by giving you my assessment of the general situation in the University, now some ten days after Dr. Champion's resignation.

If there was a crisis, I believe it has lessened. If there were members of the academic community poised to make unreasonable demands on the University administration, I have not heard those demands. And, if there were unlawful elements of the community prepared to capture University facilities or otherwise to disrupt the orderly processes of education, they have escaped my notice.

In other words, while there is dissatisfaction among members of the University community—some of it serious—it appears to me to be nearly all constructive dissatisfaction. I have no solid evidence that any segment of the University has adopted destructive or harmful methods, and even if I accept wild rumor as fact, those who would do the University in are small in number and not well organized.

If one is willing to accept rumors as an indication of the magnitude of our problems, however, it is another story. I have made it a point to turn off my hearing aid against most of the rumors that are recited largely because I simply have not had the time to listen. But I cannot resist telling you that it is always a matter of amazement to me that here in the University where we proclaim our devotion to knowledge and truth, we manage to pay so much attention to half-truths, or less. We are no different from others in this, I suppose, but sometimes I wish we were. It may be that rumors and innuendos and half-truths and gossip have a place in the University, but I should like to suggest that we would all be better off if it were a smaller and less conspicuous place.

In any case, we are facing no crisis at the moment. I have received strong and nearly universal support from the students and faculty with whom there has been communication. In some cases I have not agreed with the views of my colleagues, but I have nevertheless appreciated them and could only regard them as sincere and constructive statements intended to improve the situation. This is not to say there are not some problems remaining, but a strong vibrant, healthy University can solve problems—indeed, it becomes stronger in doing so. I am reporting to you that in my best judgment, the University is secure, and the prospects for its becoming a stronger, more viable institution in the immediate future are good.

I have attempted to evaluate my own performance in several ways including asking people what they think of the job I have been doing. Last Tuesday, after my short speech to the faculty, I encountered a little old lady in tennis shoes outside the front gate and asked her what she thought of my remarks. Without hesitating a moment she told me it was without doubt the worst speech she had ever heard. I noticed a friendly face standing nearby. Its owner pulled me aside and urged me not to be disturbed by the lady's comments. "She is known all over town as a person of extremely low mental ability," he said, "and she is thoroughly incapable of forming a rational thought. All she does is repeat what she hears other people say."

In the main body of my remarks today I shall speak to three major points. First, I shall express my thoughts to you on what I think a University should be. These statements more often than not come out in general and exalted language, and this one probably will too, but I think I really must begin in this way to give you some feeling for my philosophical outlook on the institution which we all serve.

Then I shall give you my analysis of several major problem areas in the University along with my proposals for their solutions. Finally, I want to say some things about the day-today mechanics of operation of the University now and during the weeks ahead.

I. The University in America

A University in my view is mostly a climate in which people pursue ideas. It is a setting for experimentation in which reason and logic prevail over emotion and bias. In any University worthy of the name there must be freedom to teach and to speak and to engage in public dialogue without fear of what others will say or think. The key word throughout is freedom. It is this which really sets the University apart from other agencies of society—not freedom in the exercise of personal liberties to go beyond those of other citizens but freedom in the pursuit of knowledge and truth.

While Florida State University must be a citadel of freedom, it must also be a place where the sons and daughters of Floridians mostly, along with a few from outside the state, come to get a college education. As a public university we must give serious concern to quality education in the most direct, fundamental sense. This goal, and the one described above, are not mutually exclusive. There is no substitute for good teaching and none for a faculty who care about their students. The young people who come to this University, oftentimes at great sacrifice to themselves and their families, deserve the best instruction we can give them. They are looking for education that is relevant to the problems of the day, and they expect to acquire their education with as little time and concern devoted to extraneous and non-relevant matters as possible. I am satisfied that part of the discontent in American universities today stems from a dissatisfaction with both the quality of teaching and the relevance of what is being taught.

My point is simply that a great university cannot be great in research and development to the exclusion of high quality learning experiences for its students. Nor the other way round.

II. The Problems We Face

In the next section of my remarks I should like to address myself to nine different topics, each of which I believe to be a matter of interest to the faculty and students in an immediate sense. I shall in each case present my own analysis of the problem and then tell you what I expect to try to do about it. The SDS matter is probably the one of greatest interest, and I am going to treat it last in the hope that the other eight will have a better chance of getting their fair share of attention.

1.The problem of communication among individuals and groups in the University community.

It is widely believed throughout the University that our communications have not been all they should be. On the basis of my ten days as Acting President, I must acknowledge this to be true, for many of our problems have been revealed as little more than the failure of one side to hear what the other is saying. In my opinion, this is a greater problem than any fundamental disagreement among individuals and groups. It may also be a difficult problem to solve because we are a large, complex organization, and there is no simple way to establish effective dialogue among all elements. But there are some things we can at least try, and this we shall do. Beginning at once the following steps will be taken:

A. As Acting President I will set aside a block of two hours one day each week for conferences with students in my office. These will be widely advertised on the campus, and students will be invited to call in advance for appointments to run between ten and fifteen minutes each. Admittedly, that is not much time, and in two hours I cannot see a large number of people, but the procedure nevertheless seems to have some merit. I assume that the students who come will represent the views of others, and I will therefore be getting indirect input from a much larger group. In addition, my own views will be expressed in still another context from those now employed and as a consequence those views will surely be diffused throughout sorority and fraternity houses and dormitories and classrooms and student organizations and in other ways. And then I confess I felt a twinge of sharp pain the other day when a student said that in three years at Florida State University he had never once seen the President. I suspect the same would be true at other large universities. Ways must be found for students to see the President and for him to see them and one of these ways ought to be sitting down in the President's Office and talking with him on a one-to-one basis if only for a few minutes. Even if some waiting is required to work one's way up the list, I feel certain that students who really want to see him will be able to do so.

B. I have given considerable thought to conducting an open forum periodically in which I would meet in one of the smaller auditoriums with perhaps a couple of hundred students and would listen to their comments and questions and try to respond to them. This will continue to be examined and if other methods do not appear to meet the need, I will be pleased to try such a plan. I shall continue meeting frequently with student organizations which have a communications function, especially the *Flambeau* and Student Government. Mr. Sam Miller, the editor of the *Flambeau*, and I have discussed a format for periodic interviews—I would prefer to call them exchanges—and this plan will go into effect at once.

The exchange with students in various informal settings will continue as a regular feature of my responsibilities. I have sought out students on the sidewalks, in the cafeterias, and in numerous other places and have found these encounters to be among the most profitable methods for gathering information and ideas.

C. I am not proposing any new vehicles of communication with the faculty, for none seem to be indicated. The faculty and administration of the University are engaged in a common enterprise, which is the education of our students. There is no shortage of opportunities for me to meet with the faculty in academic and other settings. I hope to avail myself of opportunities to meet with faculty by departments and by schools and colleges, especially the smaller ones. In addition, there are countless ways to confer with faculty informally, and I expect to employ many of these. If they prove to be inadequate, I shall look for new vehicles.

III. Freedom of Speech

One of the questions asked of me repeatedly during the

past several days relates to concern by faculty and students for the kind of articulation we have with the larger community outside the University. I am asked what I think the Acting President's role should be.

Clearly, the President of any university must serve as an effective two-way agent of communication between the two groups. As the most visible person on the campus and the one in most frequent contact with other institutions and agencies, especially agencies of government, the President must take special pains to reflect the views of the faculty. But, it is more than transmitting information from the campus; it includes conveying to those outside the academic community something of the value system of the University. He must help people to understand what University people care about and what kind of setting creative, scholarly work must have. While the President and other administrative officials have a crucial role to play, it is essential that others engage in this enterprise, too. The job is simply too big in this kind of institution to be done entirely by the administration and the public relations office.

There is one role for the President of a university which is unique in this regard. It is he who must protect and defend the faculty from attack by those who, for one reason or another, would try to weaken it. At the same time there will be occasions when the opposite will be true, when the President must carry out action in the University which is not well understood by the faculty. I have no doubt that there are in the operating manual of the Board of Regents regulations with which I disagree. Nevertheless, I am pledged to enforce these regulations, and I shall do so to the best of my ability while at the same time protesting those I believe are not in the University's best interests and seeking to have them changed as quickly as possible.

I cannot move on without a special word about the need for temperance in expressing one's views, especially on sensitive matters. Members of the academic community should have all the freedoms that other citizens have, and no one should attempt to deny them these freedoms. But there is nothing in this which prevents a faculty member from expressing himself in tactful language, if it conveys his thoughts adequately, or selecting a time and place for his remarks which will reduce the trauma among the audience. The issues we deal with are by definition often times explosive, and it behooves us, therefore, to handle them with care. Freedom is not strengthened by flaunting it, and while it is useful to test our freedoms, I doubt that it is necessary to push them to the limit every few days. It seems to me that we can accept historical precedence as some evidence of the viability and strength of our constitution and its guarantees of freedom.

Living as we do in the capital city, we have a history of interesting relations with the Legislature, and it seems that there are sometimes people from both groups who operate on a policy of intemperance. Just as some faculty people see an oppressive reactionary under every seat in the Legislature, so some legislators see a Marxist under every desk in the University. Temperance practiced by one side might be returned in kind by the other.

IV. Student and faculty participation in maintaining the University's integrity

This was treated at some length in the section above when I spoke of the need for the Acting President to play a role between the University community and the larger community beyond the campus.

As I indicated, I believe that students and faculty and administration of the University must try to understand and be understood by the community beyond the campus and especially by those who make the laws and regulations which govern higher education in Florida. This job is important enough and challenging enough to command the best efforts of all of us.

Two facts stand out in this analysis: The first is that we derive our support from the taxpayers of Florida through decisions made by the members of the Legislature, the Board of Regents, and other agencies and individuals in government. The second is that the integrity and independence of the University cannot be compromised if we are to be worthy of the name. I do not believe these are in conflict with one another, and my responsibilities as Acting President will be discharged with this as an operating principle.

V. Professional Performance at Florida State University

When one engages in earnest dialogue with other people, especially students, he must be prepared for what he hears. I am satisfied that there is widespread concern on the campus over the quality of the classroom interaction between faculty and students, and in a few cases worry and embarrassment over the interaction outside the classroom. Our students and faculty have told me things that please, worry, concern, amuse, and sometimes confuse me. All of the things I have been told have been taken seriously. Some must, of course, be viewed as exaggerations or strongly biased views, but most strike me as valid.

What faculty sometimes forget—and I think the number is small—is that they are obliged to be as objective as they can in presenting their views to students; and that their authority in the classroom is a function of their expertise in their areas of specialization. Thus, a professor of French literature, for example, or of chemistry or business management has no more authority to speak on matters outside of his field regardless of the degree of his interest or that of his students than anybody else. He may have more knowledge, but he does not have the right to use his classroom as a platform from which to inform or persuade his students in any area save that of his own expertise.

VI. Concerns of our black students

I have talked with only a few of our black students, and I am not as well informed about their concerns as I will be in a week or so. I do know that there has been some interest expressed in a Black Studies Program. You will be interested to know that on Tuesday afternoon of this week I met with Chancellor Mautz and his staff and President Ben Perry of Florida A & M University and several members of his staff to discuss positive steps that our two universities might take at once to enrich and extend the educational opportunities of both groups of students. You will be hearing more on this from Vice President Chalmers shortly, but let me tell you now that we are moving immediately to an active phase in the development of inter-institutional affiliations. Three separate thrusts have been agreed upon: We hope to arrange for the exchange of faculty between the universities on a regular basis along the lines of the pattern already in operation between the two Schools of Education. In this we will trade faculty services. This arrangement is neat and simple and does not require extensive paperwork either in the universities or the Chancellor's office since the whole thing is arranged at the level of the department and approved by the academic dean. It simply means that Professor X from Florida State University is assigned part-time— perhaps full-time for a quarter—at Florida A & M. We are compensated by receiving roughly equivalent time from Professor Y of the Florida A & M faculty who is assigned here. The second provision of the new agreement encourages students at both universities to take courses at the other. This arrangement is not greatly different from provisions which now exist in our regulations, but we now hope to make it possible for students to satisfy major and degree requirements in this way—that is, to include in their academic programs course work taken at the other university.

The third element is in the area of special projects. There are any number of projects of an R & D nature; there are

special institutes, and an almost infinite variety of special programs relating to the integration of the schools and the im-
provement of educational opportunity for black people which
the two universities can and should engage in cooperatively.
The net effect of this will certainly be the strengthening of
both universities.

VII. The Appointments of the Vice President for Academic Affairs and the Vice President for Administration

I have received this morning from the Faculty Senate the
nominations for Advisory Committees for the two Vice Presidencies to be vacated this summer, and I expect to name those
committees next week. They will be asked to proceed promptly
in their search for worthy candidates.

VIII. The Special Presidential Committee on Student Affairs

Though this committee may consider most of its work to
be done, I should like to ask those subcommittees which now
have work in progress to complete their missions and to submit their reports as soon as they can. I shall examine their
reports with care and implement their recommendations where
it appears in the best interest of the University to do so. I am
not closely familiar with the work of the committee, but my
inclination is to consider how the structure which that committee represents might be utilized in the future.

IX. Now to the SDS issue

During the past several days I have studied at length the
question of what the University's position should be on SDS.
I have had the benefit of the best thinking of dozens of students and faculty. I have talked with some of the most respected citizens of Florida including some distinguished lawyers. And, I have studied carefully the files covering every sig-

nificant aspect of the matter for the past several months.

On the basis of my investigation, I should like to present for your considerations a short summary of my analyses, giving the reasons for and against official recognition of SDS.

In Favor of Recognition:
1. There appears to be nothing legally objectionable in the national or local constitutions of SDS. We have no legally tested precedent for denying recognition.
2. As far as I have been able to determine, Florida is one of the few—perhaps the only—states in which a public university has arbitrarily denied recognition to SDS. Our stance could result in a loss of respect in the national academic community and perhaps in the community at large.
3. It appears that the SDS group on the campus is small and if recognized would probably not be a major factor in campus political action. There is evidence to indicate that few members of the University community actively support SDS. At the same time, there is sufficient evidence to lead me to conclude that a sizeable segment of the University community believes SDS should be recognized.
4. Even though those students on campus who claim an affiliation with SDS have the same freedom of expression as all other students, failure to give the organization official recognition gives the SDS students a convenient cause for the headlines they seek.
5. Recognition would, at least for a time, eliminate the only issue which provides any substantial support to SDS from the University community and to some degree the larger community beyond

the University.

6. Whether we take official cognizance of it or not, SDS, in fact exists on the campus. Non-recognition does not lessen the presence of SDS, and recognition will not advance its course.

7. Florida State University is a strong viable democratic institution which has no need to fear dissent in whatever form it occurs. The orderly kind it welcomes; the disorderly kind it can control.

In Opposition to Recognition of SDS:

1. Despite the fact that the national and local SDS constitutions reflect no unlawful purposes, statements of national officers who, under terms of the SDS constitution, are the spokesmen of SDS, have advocated violence and destruction.

2. The national organization, and its leaders who have been shown to be destructive, will be strengthened by the establishment of a chapter at Florida State University.

3. Those purporting to be members of SDS have failed to follow reasonable and clearly established procedures on the campus in recent weeks. Their behavior on at least two occasions has been such that had I been the University's chief executive at the time and, had the organization been officially recognized, I probably would have revoked its charter.

4. A good deal has been said by the administration about the failure of those who applied for recognition to appeal Vice President Arnold's rejection. It seems not to be well understood that Mr. Arnold turned down the application for good and acceptable reasons as he would have had to do for any other organization applying for recognition. The normal

course would be to appeal this decision, and the sponsors were encouraged to do this. Their failure to follow established and reasonable University procedures honestly stated by the University raises serious question about their desire to participate constructively in the academic community—in other words, to contribute to the orderly processes of education at Florida State University.

In addition, SDS students have made threats in my presence to disobey the rules of the University with the strong implication if not a promise that there would be violence.

5. There are existing University regulations applicable to all student organizations (as opposed to those of the Board of Regents) with which the SDS application appears to conflict. To the best of my knowledge, the sponsors have not made it clear that they would conform to these regulations.

Before telling you of my decision on this matter I want to share with you some of the deepest thoughts I have had in the past several days about my responsibilities as Acting President.

Not many days ago, when I was first confronted by the SDS problem, my first act was to turn to the Operating Manual of the Board of Regents and see what it told me to do. I looked for answers there that were not to be found, and it was not until earlier this week that the realization came to me in the fullest sense that those regulations were never intended as the only guidelines for administering the University. Maybe I am a slow learner, but in any case it is very clear to me now that I must go beyond the four corners of the Regents' regulations in the decisions I must make.

It follows then that subjective judgments are required. I am fully aware of the boundaries that must be imposed on the place of personal values in the academic or any other community, and I intend to observe careful limits. But in the end there is no substitute for the exercise of human judgment by the man who must accept the final responsibility for the welfare of the University.

Some of you have found the Board of Regents' regulations unclear. I confess that I, too, believe there are various interpretations of that portion of the Operating Manual, and I have written Chancellor Mautz asking the Board to clarify this. In my opinion their action cannot help but improve the situation on this campus and others in the State University System. Leaving aside the matter of my own judgment on issues beyond the realm of the regulations, I would still find it difficult to make a decision in which I would have confidence based on the regulations as presently stated. I look forward to the Board's review if they elect to do so and I believe they will.

At this time, however, my decision based on the evidence before me is that I cannot approve recognition of SDS.

This has been an anguished decision, and I am not sure it is the right one. I will be frank to state that I dislike the idea of seeing restrictions placed on any individuals or groups whether it be in my own family or in the University. There will surely be many who disagree with my decision in this, and I welcome their opinions. It may be that in time SDS will be recognized in Florida.

Some additional comments on this decision may be helpful.

The SDS students have the same freedom in actual practice as all other university students. To the best of my knowledge, their freedom of expression is unrestricted. To those who believe that the University's regulations which prevent their sponsoring outside speakers is repressive, my reply is that this does not restrict the freedom of the individual in any way. In any event, it seems to have worked out in practice that there has been no real restriction on outside speakers.

Some consideration has been given to asking the local SDS people to dissociate themselves from the national organization and the violent actions of its leaders. Some say that this is not a reasonable request to make. My answer is that those people and those actions are well recognized symbols which might well serve to encourage violence on this campus. Of course, I can't prove that they would, but it is my judgment that it would not be wise to increase the strength voluntarily of any organization which threatens to damage the University.

What must be avoided at all costs is the closing of the University, and I confess that this weighs heavily in my thinking. In my view, the closing of this University and many others over such issues as the one which we face in this is a real possibility. Sometimes I feel that there are those among us who do not fully comprehend the implications of the closing of a university. To me it is a tragedy of such enormous proportions that I am unable to express my feelings on it. It is an act that strikes at the heart of the American democracy and of nearly everything that you and I stand for. It must never happen here. But it could happen by extreme action from either side. It has happened in some cases because of acts of violence by students, and in other cases it has happened as a response by government officials to such acts. From where I stand, it is not sufficient to say that the closing of this University is not likely. Any threat to orderly education on this campus must be viewed seriously as the first step toward closing the University.

The public interest in the SDS question is intense, and the opinions generally not very moderate. The plain truth is that we live in a democratic society in which elected officials along with others appointed by them must be responsive to the public will.

Earlier I said that part of my two-way position between the academic community and the public is to represent them to you. I am telling you now that the public mood seems to be something less than fully supportive of violence on our campus or anything that smacks of it, and that there is considerable sentiment all across the country for taking a harsh line against violence on the campuses. This is one University which, as long as I am its Acting President, is going to remain open. Open and free.

In view of the concern within the University and without over the possibility of violent action on the campus, I should like to make clear precisely what the University's policy will be.

The University's position with respect to any who attempt to interfere with the orderly processes of education will be to take whatever action is required to restore order immediately. The campus security offices are prepared to meet any emergency that we can foresee, and plans exist for enlisting the aid of other law enforcement agencies in the area if they are needed.

It must be understood by all members of the University community that stern action will be taken promptly against any who attempt to take over University facilities. On other campuses where such threats have been made, a period of deliberation has been allowed before an effort has been made by university officials to dislodge the occupation forces. At Florida State University the period of deliberation must come before occupancy, not after. In other words, students should think carefully in advance of their action about the consequences, and if they decide to occupy buildings or other facilities, they should be fully prepared for whatever counter action is taken against them. With all due respect and with malice toward none, I urge all members of the University community not to take any buildings with the expectations of holding them.

III. As the last part of my address, I should like to comment briefly on a number of operational matters of interest.

    1. The Council of Deans will function as it has in

the past, as essentially an advisory body to the Acting President. As a former member of that group I refer to it as an advisory body with some reluctance, for the Council makes decisions and takes action on important administrative questions regularly. Its place in the University organizational plan nevertheless is advisory in character. Vice President Chalmers and I intend to continue to depend heavily on the Council of Deans on decision making in the academic area.

2. The Faculty Senate has been helpful in the selection of screening committees for the two new vice presidents to be named, and I look forward to their help and support in other ways. My relations with the Steering Committee in particular have been close and cordial. The Senate can be a strong influence for progress and stability in the University, and I have no doubt that the Senate and I can help each other in various ways.

3. The same set of remarks apply to the Student Government. I have not yet become well acquainted with most of its officers nor with its method of operation, but I hope to do so.

There is the temptation to describe still other matters of interest to various people among the students and faculty but at this late hour I am a bit like the wealthy Italian who bought the Leaning Tower of Pisa, installed a clock at the top, and then saw the whole thing come crashing down—I have neither the time nor the inclination. But there is a certain temptation to tell you that I think a program in Journalism in the University might be a good thing, if only because our students will become better writers, thus freeing those faculty for other things who have found it necessary to ghost write some of the students' material.

I have touched on many things, some of them a bit super-ficially, but I have felt that is was necessary to come before you at the earliest possible time to give you some idea of the kind of leadership I expect to provide to the University in the next few weeks. There is no doubt that other steps will be taken to alleviate the problems I have described and others. I have done nothing more than make a start on the problems, but a start is a start is a start is a start. The next ten days will no doubt bring problems that demand still different solutions, but I for one am ready to meet them. And I believe the great majority of the students and faculty are, too.

That brings me to a remark that I made last Tuesday and which has been brought to my attention several times since. I said I expected the job to be great fun. Some people took this to mean that I had a somewhat cavalier attitude about it, and it may be that my expression was not well chosen. Let me try again. I expect the acting presidency to be fun like mountain-climbing is fun or a trip in space must be great fun for the astronauts; it is arduous work with some danger and a good many demands on one's physical and nervous energies, and I have found this job to be that way so far. I did not mean it would be fun like fun and games. Administering the Univer-sity is serious business, a fact which all of us will keep in mind, but man was made for joyous combat with his existence, and I invite you to join our common effort over the weeks ahead to bring Florida State University a step closer to greatness.

Finally my friends, I invite you to ponder that magnificent message that is attributed to Epicurus:

"Only one principle will give you courage; that is the prin-ciple that no evil lasts forever; nor indeed for very long."

EXCERPTS FROM REMARKS BY ACTING PRESIDENT STANLEY MARSHALL TO THE FLORIDA STATE UNIVERSITY FACULTY SENATE
March 5, 1969

I should like first to address myself to the events of yesterday.

The confrontation between the SDS students and the law officers of the University and Leon County was one which I earnestly sought to avoid. Let me describe briefly the steps which led up to it.

The rally scheduled for Landis Green in the afternoon seemed to have been an attempt to bring about a confrontation in the sense that it violated several University regulations—but in my opinion not very important ones. For example, the group had not registered in advance, as is customary and as they could easily have done. In Monday's *Flambeau* it was stated that SDS would operate as usual and that SDS would continue to insist that it has the right to function in the same fashion as a recognized student organization. Yesterday's *Flambeau* made it clear that the rally scheduled for Landis Green and the meeting scheduled for the University Union last night were to be "sponsored by" SDS and that the room for this meeting would not be checked out by any other organization for SDS use as in the past. The Young Liberals, which had reserved the room, cancelled their reservation about noon

In the hours between 11:00 p.m. on March 4—the Night of the Bayonets—and 4:00 p.m. the next day, this speech was written. My purpose was to try to reduce the tension that gripped the campus by describing what had taken place the day before and why.

yesterday.

Let me try to make clear what the University's position was in all of this. It was to go as far as possible, even to the point of being open to a charge of hypocrisy to avoid denying any student the freedom of speech which is the guaranteed right of all citizens. Please bear in mind that I announced last Thursday that I had asked for a clarification of Regents' policy on student organizations. As I have said since then several times, I did not consider it proper for me to establish a new policy for the University pending clarification by the Regents that I had asked for. The rationale for my decision on SDS last Thursday was given at that time and has been elaborated upon numerous times since then, although I regret that my statements have not received as wide distribution as I hoped they would.

Thus, I was saying that for the time being the University would follow a policy which was not very comfortable either for me or for the students and that it would be clarified shortly, if not by the Board of Regents then by a review and restatement of the University's policy, the background for which I have been considering and evaluating through frequent conferences with many people. The course that the University was following seemed to me to be a rational one, and I hoped the others, including members of the SDS, would see it that way too.

About mid-afternoon yesterday it became clear that the SDS students had decided they would not take any of the several alternatives open to them to conduct last night's meeting under circumstances which the University could accept. Thus, after counseling with the Attorney General and his staff, I made the decision to seek a court injunction preventing the SDS students from holding their meeting last night in a University building. I want to emphasize that this seemed to me to be the most orderly and restrained way to proceed. Moreover, it brought into the controversy the laws of Florida and the

United States, a step which I had hoped would have been taken by the SDS some time ago.

It is worth noting that restraining orders are not simply issued upon request. In this instance, the Attorney General weighed the merits of my request carefully, and the judge of the circuit court listened with great care to my testimony before issuing the injunction.

It was my great hope that the SDS students would recognize this as a helpful rather than a coercive step. The reaction I expected was counteraction in the courts. My action gave SDS an appropriate and easy legal basis to challenge my decision of Thursday in the courts. And they would have had a cause and a great deal of visibility to go with it and if they had taken this path. They would have shown respect for due process in the same sense that the University did. In addition, we would all have avoided the painful confrontation of last night.

That they did not choose to follow this course leads me to believe that what they really sought was a dramatic confrontation, and indeed the evidence that this was a carefully planned strategy on their part is convincing. My office let it be known during the late afternoon that we had obtained an injunction, and this was apparently widely discussed by the students that had assembled in the Union. Thus, they had every opportunity to consider what they would do. The best information I have is that they considered the matter and decided to violate deliberately the order of the Court. The issue of freedom of expression apparently did not enter into their deliberations, nor were they willing to accept other means by which they could have conducted their meeting and heard the speaker—means which they have used on numerous occasions during the past several weeks.

In view of the above, I believe my observation that it was a confrontation the SDS wanted—not freedom of speech—stands up.

I doubt that anybody in the University regrets the display

of weapons in the confrontation last night more than I. The spectre of bayonets in a citadel of freedom is repugnant to me as it is to academicians everywhere and to many citizens. It is a matter of some regret to me that the sheriff's deputies found it necessary to display their weapons so prominently. But let me point out that it is not my prerogative to dictate the means by which they carry out their responsibilities. The operating manual for law enforcement officers apparently calls for the prominent display of weapons in crowd control, and the police apparently believe that it is an effective deterrent. But I want the academic community to know that I wish desperately that there had been another way. At the same time the entire community must feel a sense of relief and gratitude at the professional performance of Sheriff Hamlin and his men. To the best of my knowledge there was no injury to people and no property damage. As I said in this morning's *Flambeau*, this is a great tribute to all who were involved in any way, and I hope you will agree this must include law enforcement officers. On the basis of observations on other campuses, those who believe that the appearance of outside law enforcement agencies means that violence must follow, to those it must now be clear that there are restrained and responsible police officers, and we have some in Tallahassee.

Now some further comments about SDS.

I believe that most of the people in the University who are sympathetic to SDS are just that—they support the students' right to speak freely, and they are uncomfortable about controls placed on them that are not placed on other citizens. I agree. But I do not evaluate all of the SDS students on the campus in this way. It is apparently not widely understood that some of the SDS students presumably acting in the name of that organization have come close to serious disruptive and illegal acts on this campus. In the light of recent events, I believe you should know the following: A few weeks ago a small group entered the Love Building and occupied a portion of it for about four hours late one night. And they entered illegally. The action taken at that time, since it was at night and they did not interrupt classes, was to permit them to remain until 7 a.m. if they chose to, at which time other steps would have been considered. They left voluntarily in the early morning hours.

Several weeks ago a group of about 30 SDS students entered Dr. Champion's office in response to his agreement to speak to four of their number. They refused to leave when requested to do so several times. Vice President Arnold was asked to come to the Office by Dr. Champion and request the students to leave. They left voluntarily after the second recitation of a warning to leave or be subject to disciplinary action.

But before going they reportedly made strong threats to Dr. Champion against the University.

On at least two occasions SDS students have made strong verbal threats to me either to take over University facilities or to commandeer University equipment.

My purpose then is to describe as completely and candidly as I can the basis on which my judgment was made. I expected considerable disagreement with my decision because I knew that some would see greater strength in the arguments for than those against. But the important point is that these factors had to be weighed and a decision made. In my view, the points against outweighed those in favor—it is as simple as that. I am the person who had to make the judgment, and I did so knowing it would not be well received by some people. I said on Thursday that it was an anguished decision—and it was. I asked many people for their advice, and it was given freely, but much of it was conflicting. I suppose it is hard for people to accept, when asked for their advice, that it is being pooled with the advice of others and the ultimate decision cannot please everybody or even always the majority.

It was pointed out to me this morning that the press has recently carried an article about a public figure in Florida referring to the SDS students as bums or words to that effect. In line with my intention to represent the University community to the community at large, I will say now for all to hear that I do not believe they are anything like that. Their dress and some of their actions seem to vary from that of most students, but I will defend their behavior and other personal manifestations vigorously. The University must never become a conformist agency of society in that sense.

In closing, I should like to ask the members of the University community to be temperate at a time when temperance does not come very easy. The problems before us now need "cerebration" more than anything else, and I urge all of us to deal with them at that level. In the interest of creating the harmony we all seek, I ask you to consider seriously what you can do for Florida State University. I promise you that I will continue to execute the responsibilities of my office consistent with my own concepts of integrity, democracy, and justice, and I ask you to execute yours in the same way. None of us can do more and all of us should do no less.

STATEMENT TO THE
COMMITTEE ON UNIVERSITIES
& COMMUNITY COLLEGES
January 19, 1971

Chairman Haverfield and Gentleman:

In his Inaugural Address, Governor Askew wisely observed that we must, "continue to strive for excellence in our state university system." "Moreover," he stated, "as we seek that goal, we must encourage needed change—but without making education a scapegoat for political gain." In the spirit of his call for a continuing and fair review of our educational system, I am pleased to join President O'Connell today in a discussion with you of pertinent issues affecting our State University System.

Preview

Generally speaking, we will discuss the problem of rules and regulations affecting student conduct on campus; in particular, we will deal with one of the eight questions Senator Pat Thomas posed at the November 18, 1970, meeting of your Committee. That three-part question, you will recall, directed inquiry as to whether students over-control the universities, whether the universities have abdicated authority to the students, and whether the universities' moral posture was determined by the students. A firm "No" could be given as answer

---

*The president of the University of Florida during this period was Steve O'Connell, a former justice of the Florida Supreme Court and a deeply respected son of Florida. The two of us felt a strong kinship, based largely on common views of the role of Florida's public universities, and our testimony before the powerful Haverfield Committee, we felt, was the right opportunity to try to win over some key legislators to more reasoned views. I regret that I have not been able to locate President O'Connell's statement.

to each question. However, such a response, while categorical, would be superficial. For that reason, we want to respond to the questions in greater depth to give you more complete answers.

My remarks will concern parietal rules and the general role of the university in the area of student conduct. President O'Connell will address the related issues of student publications and student participation in university governance. At the conclusion of our comments, we would welcome any questions directed to us, members of our staffs, or to the students we have invited to accompany us.

Regulating Student Conduct—The Complexity of the Problem

An examination on student conduct on our campuses necessarily begins with a look at the times in which we live. For, events occurring on our campuses are not isolated from those in the larger society. The entering freshmen we admit are products of that society. Therefore, it is obvious that if problems exist with young people in the larger society, such problems are likely to accompany them when they "go off to college."

The Times Provide Perspective. When we examine American Society in 1971, what do we see? First we see *change*, the one social constant of our times. We see changing attitudes toward the use of drugs, premarital sex, respect for authority, and adherence to traditional values. We see dissatisfaction with many of our major institutions, and we see efforts to change them.

Second, we see a *lessening of traditional restraints*. In dress, language, personal lifestyles, we witness daily the effects of a decline in influence of such bulwarks of American life as the family and the church. Two national magazines recently reported in-depth on the declining influence of the family and an increase in occurrence of what was called the "nuclear family," a small family unit created by the increasingly mobile nature of our society and separated from the traditional circle of relatives.

Third, we see an *increased emphasis on the value of individual freedom*. From the ranks of opinion leaders on both the right and the left as well as the center, we daily hear appeals for less institutional control over the lives of individual Americans and more participation by individuals in decisions that affect them. Both political "conservatives" and "liberals" agree that the nature of modern "big government," depersonalized and sprawling, clearly threatens to deny many Americans the options required to live meaningful lives. All the effects of this new emphasis are clearly not desirable. However, its existence can hardly be denied.

Finally, we see *the growing influence* of what some writers have labeled a *"new youth culture."* The young men and women in our society have become a major social force to be reckoned with in the political arena, marketplace, church, and yes, even in our homes. The children who grew up in the age of Sputnik are now young adults who vote in some elections at eighteen and who affect our society in ways unprecedented in history. So, we find it increasingly difficult to understand some of them. One writer articulated the frustrations of many of us over thirty when he asked, "What is happening to our young people? They disrespect their elders, they ignore the laws, and they riot in the streets, inflamed with wild notions. Their morals are decaying, what is to become of them?" Diogenes, a Fourth Century B.C. philosopher, posed these questions. In doing so, he doubtless was not the first man to note the fact that every generation has its own form of youthful rebellion. Our task today is not to wring our hands in despair and pose difficult questions, but to respond appropriately to the young people of our own time.

The larger question which underlies this discussion—and one which is placed before university administrators repeatedly today—is, what can be done about all the trouble on the

American college campus?

The facts that bear on this question, as I see them, lead to the conclusion that the college campus in Florida is one of the most orderly places in the state. It has been the scene of less disruption, in my considered opinion, than most other agencies that serve young people.

We are often asked pointed questions about drugs on campus. Information in the news media suggests that universities are probably in third place as the locus of drug problems, behind the armed services and the high schools.

With respect to general disruption and disorder, surely there can be no doubt that Florida's universities have been more tranquil than our high schools. In saying this, let me emphasize that it is not my wish to focus the spotlight of blame on others—but I do want to call attention to a simple truth some overlook and to offer the services and facilities of the Florida State University to try to help as the state addresses itself to this difficult problem and attempts to understand it—and eventually to solve it.

My contention is that Florida's state universities are governed well, if student behavior on campus is any measure—and to the extent that students participate in university governance they deserve more praise than censure.

Many speakers, inside and outside the universities, have observed that the young people who come to the universities at age 18 or 19—or 20 or 21—come from the homes of the people of Florida, and their personal values and behavior patterns have been pretty well established by their parents and churches and schools—agencies over which we at the universities have little control. When they arrive on the campus, they have had training—basic training we might call it—and some have had combat experience as well.

Let me speak as clearly as I can on this subject: The great majority of the students on our campuses are fine young people of whom we should all be proud. A few are not—but the problems created by those few should not be laid at the feet of the universities in the same proportion as the credit for the constructive efforts and good behavior of the majority.

Universities Are Not Immune. You gentlemen are well aware that our universities are neither immune to nor separated from these problems of the larger society. Universities are part of our society and thus necessarily reflect the same problems. In fact, our universities represent a microcosm of the tensions in our society. For this reason alone, we must take care not to accuse the university of failing to solve problems which no other institution in our society has been able to solve. If we single out our universities for criticism because of instances of drug use, sexual laxness, and disrespect for the traditional symbols—all problems of society at large—then we run the risk of doing what Governor Askew has specifically warned us against: "Making education a scapegoat."

Now, these observations should not be taken to indicate that I condone or even like some of the changes I've described. No parent today can be pleased with all of the things he views on the evening news programs. Nor do they indicate that universities are powerless to influence the lives of students who live and study within them. However, these observations do suggest that it is no longer possible to treat students as we once did, nor even as some people today would like for us to.

The Doctrine of "In Loco Parentis." For many years the university observed "in loco paretnis," that is, "in place of the parent." This concept placed the student within the jurisdiction of the university in such a way that the institution was thought actually to replace the family, and thereby, to regulate the life of the student to the extent normally exercised by the parent. This doctrine was almost universally accepted in the 19th Century and, until recent years, had many adherents in the 20th. But today, in a period of history when both parents and societal institutions are exercising less influence on young people and citizens, the influence of the university has also changed. In a society where adolescents are frequently allowed freedom at home to come and go as they please, is it appropriate for the university to regulate their freedom stringently and to establish rigid curfews?

Many of the students at institutions of higher education are legal adults. A large number are married. At Florida State University for example, some 52% of the students are 21 years of age or over, and one in five is married. Moreover, since we can only house 5,000 students on campus out of a student population of 17,252, we require only freshmen to live on campus. In addition, we cannot control the lives of those students living off campus, and the actual physical task of supervising students housed in our facilities on campus becomes more demanding each year. Thus, we find ourselves unable to exercise the traditional role of "in loco parentis."

Apparently, though perhaps for different reasons, the courts are reaching the same conclusion, for they have further limited the doctrine of "in loco parentis." In fact, the federal court in Moore v. Student Affairs Committee of Troy State University specifically noted that a college does not serve "in loco parentis." The California Court of Appeals in Goldberg v. Regents of University of California also held that, for constitutional purposes, colleges and universities should no longer stand "in loco parentis" to their students.

There are now almost 25 million Americans of college age, that is, roughly 18-24 years old. Of that number, about 8.5 million go to college, and thus, over 16 million do not. Those who do not go to college usually leave home to work, join the Armed Services, and/or marry. They then no longer are subject to direct parental control. The question naturally follows as to why the university should be expected to parent only to those persons who are in fact in college. In other words, should we treat one 18-24 year old person differently from another merely because he happens to be a student?

Specific Regulations Exist. To state that the University no

longer stands in place of the parents as it once did is not however, to suggest that the University exercises no control over its students or that university students arc immune from the restraints that affect the rest of us. In the first place, students of the University are governed by the same state, federal, county, and municipal laws that affect all members of society. In addition, Board of Regents' policies and university codes of conduct further define expected student behavior. We will provide each of you with a copy of the Florida State University Pow Wow, our official student handbook. It contains a statement of the Florida State code of conduct and Board of Regents' policies. Our disciplinary system operates within this framework. That system assumes that the student can conform to the rules and regulations and expects him to do so. It is designed to encourage responsible action within accepted standards of society and promotes the welfare of the individual and the institution. It also encourages mature and moral student behavior and complements the aims and goals of the institution.

Student Participation. In fact, we seek and encourage student participation in the governance of the University. Perceptive college administrators realize that government without input from the governed is as difficult on campus as it is anywhere else in society. For that reason, President O'Connell will talk specifically about the role of students in governing the modern university. However, I would like to point out that we have student participation in a wide variety of Florida State University committees. For example, students serve on the Budget Committee, the University Advisory Committee, the Athletic Committee, a newly-created President's Advisory Council of Student Leaders, as well as others.

The Learning Environment. This philosophy of student participation is consistent with our practices for providing an environment for self-directed, individual growth. Neither learning nor morality can be legislated, although we can develop an environment that encourages learning and moral growth with minimum disruption. We cannot, however, control the rate of absorption—it is always ultimately the choice of the individual to accept or reject ideas. A system of morality is generated from within an individual, as is motivation to learn.

At Florida State University, we have attempted to provide both a comfortable living environment and a non-academic educational program in our residence halls designed to develop the individual into a mature, rational, intelligent and moral person. We do not require our freshmen to live in a residence hall simply to meet our mortgage obligations. The law does not permit it. (Mollere v. Southeastern Louisiana State College), nor can we expect forced control to develop the individual. But as the student handbook makes clear, rules do exist, and students are expected to conform to them, just as members of any organized "society" must do if it is to exist for long.

Nevertheless, because of student unrest and protest, some people have mistakenly assumed a lack of university control. I believe that a clear response to such a misunderstanding was made last quarter, when several students were suspended for disruptive activities on our campus. That action was taken through our disciplinary system and clearly indicates that we are willing to take firm and responsible action to maintain a free and open, but orderly, campus.

What is Required to Meet the Challenge? To deal effectively with the complex problem of regulating student conduct requires many things of us all. First, we university officials must be willing to enforce—fairly, but firmly—the Constitution and the statutes. And we are. Second, we must also be willing to review continually the appropriateness of any existing regulation. Third, we must work to preserve and maintain public confidence in our institutions of higher learning. Fourth, we must seek and maintain the constant understanding and support of you members of the Legislature. Fifth, we must stop accusing the universities of failure because they have not been able to solve all of the major ills of our society. Sixth, we must ensure that the major myths of our times are properly identified and that they do not unduly influence the hard decisions we must make. These myths are (1) that college students are somehow not our children, (2) that universities have no rules that are enforced, (3) that college administrators are somehow "soft", and (4) that students are not full-fledged citizens. Each of these views reflects a basic misunderstanding—due in part perhaps, to the failure of those of us in the colleges to communicate effectively with those who hold those views. With meetings like this one, we hope to inform better the public whose support we must have and thereby to replace those myths with facts.

The university cannot realistically hope to solve all the problems which ultimately cause campus tensions. Most discussions of the factors that produce campus unrest assign some responsibility to the family and the social environment from which the students come, some to the university environment they enter, and some to the larger, societal environment which encompasses them in school. While we willingly assume responsibility for whatever shortcomings are pointed out to us—and we recognize the right, indeed the obligation, of the people to help us identify those shortcomings—it must be remembered that the university cannot stop the war, eliminate poverty, rebuild cities, expunge racism, or even solve the drug problem by ourselves. Through developmental education, research, and the diffusion of knowledge, the university can however, influence the decisions that affect the nation's quality of life. If it is to do this, we must work with the community at large to prevent the political exploitation of campus problems.

Only in this way can the beneficial effects of education permeate our society. Public officials and other citizens who have positions of public trust, should gauge their response to campus disruption by recognizing that provocative pronouncements by those in authority have an inflammatory effect which can be damaging to the constructive nature of the educational process and to institutional management. I am pleased to commend your Committee, Senator Haverfield, for the constructive nature of your inquiry into higher education in Florida. For, only with friends such as you, can we hope to build a better future.

Conclusion

In conclusion, let me say explicitly what I have only implied to this point: A university today simply cannot regulate the conduct of its students in ways some members of our society apparently desire. Why? Because, (1) the changing nature of the relationship of the individual to the institutions of society militates against it, (2) the theoretical base for it—the doctrine of "in loco parentis"—won't support it, and (3) the practical problems of selective enforcement against the on-campus resident student are just too great. However, again I say—we do have rules. These rules are enforced. Thus, the answer to the question of whether students control the universities of our state is clearly negative.

Thank you, Mr. Chairman.

1970s Campus Map of FSU

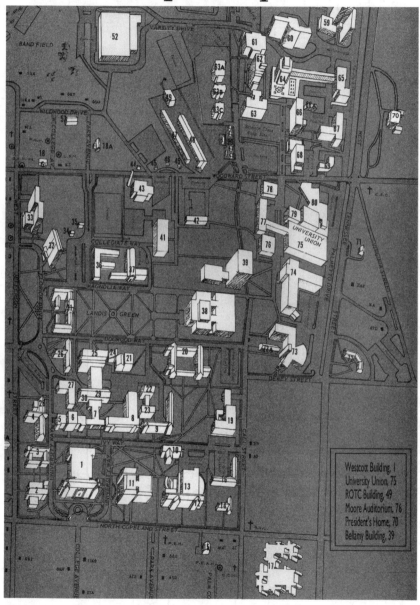

To
Florida
A&M
University

←

To Downtown ↓
Tallahassee

Westcott Building, 1
University Union, 75
ROTC Building, 49
Moore Auditorium, 76
President's Home, 70
Bellamy Building, 39

Year	Executive Vice President	Vice President for Academic Affairs	Vice President for Administration	Vice President for Student Affairs	Vice President for Educational Services	Vice President for University Relations	Executive Assistant for Human Rights	Executive Assistant to the President	Special Assistant to the President	Director of University Relations	University General Counsel
1968-69	----	Chalmers	Waldby	Carey	----	----	----	----	Gibson	Hogan	----
1969-70	----	Chalmers	Waldby	Arnold (Acting)	----	----	----	Gibson	----	Hogan	----
1970-71	Mackey	Craig	Peirce	----	----	----	----	Slepin	----	Hogan	Clark
1971-72	----	Craig	Peirce	Kimmel (Acting)	----	----	----	Hogan	----	----	Bickel
1972-73	Sliger	----	Peirce	McClellan	----	----	----	Hogan	Hiett	----	Bickel
1973-74	Sliger	----	Peirce	McClellan	----	----	Groomes	Hiett	Hiett	Hogan	Bickel
1974-75	Sliger	Sliger	Fisher	McClellan	Hiett	McClellan	Groomes	Wester	----	----	Bickel
1975-76	Sliger	Sliger	Fisher	Bass (Acting)	Hiett	McClellan	Groomes	Wester	----	----	Bickel
1976-77	Sliger	Sliger	Fisher	Bass (Acting)	Hiett	McClellan Hogan, Associate	Groomes	Wester	----	----	Bickel

Officers of the University, 1968-1977 (in alphabetical order)

John Arnold	John Carey	Paul Craig	Freddie Groomes	Robert Peirce	Odell Waldby
Edwin Bass	Lawrence Chalmers	Homer Fisher	Joseph Hiett	Robert Kimmel	Stephen Slepin	Ruth Wester
Robert Bickel	James Clark	Juanita Gibson	Patrick Hogan	Cecil Mackey	Bernard Sliger
				Stephen McClellan	

Index